# Contents

# TESTS-ANSWERS FOR FCC GENERAL RADIOTELEPHONE OPERATOR LICENSE

by
Warren Weagant

Radio Engineering Division
P.O. Box 2223
San Francisco, CA 94126

FOURTEENTH EDITION - FIRST PRINTING



Library of Congress Cataloging in Publication Data Main Entry Under Title:

TESTS-ANSWERS FOR FCC GENERAL RADIOTELEPHONE OPERATIOR LICENSE



Printed in the United States of America

INTERNATIONAL STANDARD BOOK NUMBER: 0-933132-11-5

# Introduction

The purpose of this testing manual is to prepare you to pass the Federal Communication Commission's General Radiotelephone Operator License examinations. The questions and answers are based on those suggested by the FCC in their study guide, and provide an added means of preparation for the federal exams.

The holder of a General Radiotelephone License can operate, maintain and repair transmitters in the Maritime, Aviation and International fixed Public Radio Services. This includes:

* Ship radio and radar atations on all types of vessels from small motor boats to large cargo ships.

* Marine coast stations of all classes.

* Portable transceivers used to communicate with ships and coast stations on marine and aviation frequencies.

* Radios on all types of aircraft from small planes to large commercial airlines.

* Aeronautical ground stations (including hand carried portable units) used to communicate with aircraft.

* All ships weighing more than 500 tons must have a one or more FCC licensed operators on duty at a radiotelephone installation.

* All aeronautical transmitters with more than 1,000 watts of peak envelope power must be operated by persons holding an FCC General Radiotelephone License.

The FCC examination for the General Radiotelephone License (FCC Element #3) currently consists of 100 multiple-choice questions. Seventy-five (75) questions answered correctly is the passing mark for the exam.

The holder of a General Radiotelephone License must obtain a special FCC endorsement to legally install, maintain and service ship radar equipment. To obtain the radar license endorsement for your General Radiotelephone license, you must pass the FCC exam (FCC Element #8), consisting of 50 multiple-choice questions. Thirty-eight (38) answered correctly is the passing grade. This endorsement is not necessary for most license applicants, only for those people entering the ship-radar installation and maintenance radio services.

Examinations are given at FCC Field Offices on specified dates and times. Examination schedules and application forms can be obtained by writing to the Federal Communications Commission, 1919 "M" Street, Washington, DC 20036, or to the District Field Office nearest to you, listed in the "FCC Examination Offices" section.

Before studying toward the FCC exam, take time to work the SELF-STUDY ABILITY TEST. The results of this test will help you to determine your ability to successfully study and understand the FCC material. After analyzing your test score, plan your hours of study as close together as possible. Three hours of study per day for a concentrated period is far more beneficial than only a few minutes per day for several months. Don't allow yourself to forget material by delaying too long before taking the FCC examination.

The copyrighted testing manual has been prepared to enable the student to concentrate on FCC exam questions and answers. While the majority of the material is newly revised, several tests were printed in previous editions. The previously published tests were selected for re-printing in this manual because the material is currently being used successfully to pass the FCC exams.

There is no shortage of text books on electronic theory on the market. Many license applicants attempt to learn all facets of electronics while preparing for the federal exam. However, since the FCC exam covers only certain specific areas of electronic knowledge, you will save hours of study time by using this manual as your learning outline. When you discover any question in this manual you cannot answer or understand then look up the material in any one of many excellent reference books and courses containing detailed discussion of essential electronic theory. Some highly effective learning aids are listed on the "References" page.

This testing manual concentrates on specific areas covered on the federal exam. An all-encompassing, general background is necessary for actual station operation and equipment maintenance, but specialized knowledge is required to successfully pass the FCC exam. If the material in this manual is completely learned and understood, you should easily answer questions on the FCC examination. It is important to note that the questions in this, or any other guide, are not the exact words of the questions on the actual FCC exam, although similar questions will appear.

Finally, you will notice that the format of this manual is concise and comprehensive. Everything contained is relevant to the actual FCC exam. Great effort has been made to eliminate all non-related material used by other publishers to "fatten-out" their study guides. This is to point out that is is important to learn all test material in this testing manual!

Studying on your own for the FCC examination is no éasy task! It requires dedication and great desire to operate and service sophisticated federally licensed transmitters. The additional money you will earn, the security and the attractive employment opportunities are certainly worth the effort.

Warren Weagant
San Francisco, California

# Operator Licenses

A General Radiotelephone Operator License is required for anyone responsible for internal repairs, maintenance, and adjustment of FCC Licensed radiotelephone transmitters in the Aviation, Marine and International Public Fixed radio services.

To be eligible for this license, you must:

1. Be a legal resident-eligible for employment in the United States.

2. Be able to receive and transmit spoken messages in the English language.

3. Pass a multiple-choice examination covering basic radio law, operating procedures and basic electronics.

There are no education, training or experience requirements to obtain an operator license. Knowledge of the telegraphic code is not necessary. Your age in not important - anyone, regardless of age, can apply for the license. The General Radiotelephone License is normally valid for the lifetime of the operator.

FCC EXAMINATIONS

Element 3 Examination - (General Radiotelephone) - Provisions of laws, treaties and regulations with which every radio operator should be familiar. Radio operating procedures and practices generally followed or required in communicating by radiotelephone. Technical matters including fundamentals of electronics technology and maintenance techniques as necessary for repair and maintenance of radio transmitters and receivers.

Element 8 Examination - (Ship Radar Endorsement) - Specialized theory and practice applicable to proper installation, servicing, and maintenance of ship radar equipment. This endorsement is not required for most license applicants - only for those persons working with Marine Radar equipment.

There is no limit to the number of times you may take the FCC exam. If you fail an exam, you must wait two months before reapplying for examination. Under conditions of unusual hardship, the FCC may waive the two-month waiting period. When such conditions warrant, you may apply for such waiver at the FCC Field Office which administered the failed exam.

The Federal Communications Commission holds Radiotelephone examinations only twice per calendar year - during specified one-week periods. Exams are given on the same calendar dales at all FCC Field Offices and are offered by appointment only.

Approintments will be scheduled by advance application only. No telephone requests will be accepted. All applications must be received by the deadline date in order to be scheduled for the exam.

Your should know that deadline dates are at least one month before the beginning of the month in which the examinations are given. For example, if you desire to be examined in February, your application must be received by the first of January. If you plan to take the exam in August, your application should be received by the first of July, etc.

How to apply for an FCC License: The FCC has recently changed the application procedure. Now, all appointment requests must be sent to the following special mailing address:

FEDERAL COMMUNICATIONS COMMISSION
P. O. Box 358105
Pittsburgh, PA. 15251-5105

You should request FCC Forms #155 and #756. When the forms arrive in the mail - fill them out completely and return them to the address above along with your application payment fee of $35. At the time of this writing the FCC Special Hotline telephone number is (202) 632-3337. This is a special phone number to obtain help in filling out forms, etc.

Additional information may be obtained from your local field office of the FCC listed on page 217. For additional information, you may ask for FCC Bulletin F0-28 and F0-4 for exam and operator license requirements.

The FCC has adopted a new style license certificate to replace the old diploma size certificate. Currently, the FCC issues a 2 by 3 inch size license card. This new smaller size license is designed to be kept on your person while operating and maintaining equipment in the field.

Special Broadcast Radio-TV station operation: Persons who operate Commercial Radio-TV transmitters may also want to obtain a "Restricted Radiotelephone Operator Permit" from the FCC. This permit is easy to obtain. You may apply for this special limited operating permit simply by requesting FCC Form #753. There is no examination required for this permit, but to be eligible for it you must be at least 14 years old; be a legal resident (eligible for employment) in the U.S. and be able to speak and hear - keep a written log and be familiar with provisions of applicable treaties, laws and FCC Regulations.

# Study Tips

1. Test yourself frequently with the tests in this manual. Use your reference books to clear up learning difficulties in the questions missed.

2. For best results, do not underline or mark the correct answers in this manual. Searching through the wrong answers for the correct answer provides realistic practice for the federal exam.

3. Entire books have been written on the subject of how to take multiple-choice exams. Careful study of the exams in this manual should give you ample experience with every trick and deception possible in making wrong answers look correct. Remember, often the exact answer to a question is not one of the possible choices. So, select the nearest correct answer. Also, you may discover the correct answer to be: None of the above, All of the above, or Both A and B above, etc. After studying the exams in this manual, you should be ready for every trick the FCC throws at you on their test.

4. When solving math problems, keep your formulas and figuring in a clear logical order. All problems solved should be saved for future reference.

5. For best results, learn and understand how to work math problems and electronic theory questions. Memorize: terminology, rules and regulations, diagrams, tolerances and definitions, etc.

6. PLEASE NOTE: Tests 3-I and 3-J are newly revised updated exams that concentrate and review new FCC exam questions for 1991. Although this material is very important - you will need to know virtually all information in this manual to pass current exams.

7. When reading this manual or any reference guide, keep thinking in termsof how the information could be transformed into a a multiple choice question. Also - many questions in this manual show "all of the above" as a correct answer. Don't expect to see this type of question as often on FCC exams. By giving you questions with four correct answers - you see the maximum number of possibilities for each question.

# Before The FCC Exam

1. Get a full nights sleep. The benefits to be gained by a few extra hours of study are more than offset by the detrimental effects of fatigue.

2. Don't review or study on the day of the test. You might lose confidence in your ability and not do as well.

3. Bring the following items to the FCC testing office with you:

   * Photo-identification is required (driver's license, etc.).

   * Several pencils and a ball point pen (blue or black ink).

   * For nervous types; chewing gum or mints to subdue tension. No smoking is allowed in most testing rooms.

   * Wear comfortable shoes and clothing. Most people spend several hours sitting on a hard "government" chair while taking the examination. And remember, the FCC tester will not allow you to leave the testing room to go to the restroom during the exam.

   * Electronic calculator.

   * Do not bring any test books, notes or scratch paper.

   * Have a good mental attitude. You may miss 25% of the questions of each test element and still pass the exam. Also, you should find the actual FCC examination no more difficult than the exams in this tests-answers training manual.

# Taking The FCC Exam

1. You will be required to fill out several information forms with your name, address and personal and family background material. (Example: your mother and father's birthday, maiden name, etc.) TAKE YOUR TIME! Any errors on these forms may cause you to flunk the exam! If you have any question on these forms do not hesitate to immediatley double check with the examiner.

2. Answer the exam questions in this order:

   A- Answer easy questions first (rules and regulations, terms, theory, etc.) Leave all math problems and all difficult questions for the last. The FCC usually places the most difficult questions at the beginning of the exam!

   B- Go back and solve the difficult questions you skipped.

3. Work all math problems on your scratch paper (supplied).

4. While reading each FCC question, cover the answers with your answer sheet. Attempt to answer the question, THEN read each answer carefully.

5. Some of the math questions may NOT be exact figures. So, you should select the NEAREST correct answer.

6. Answer EVERY question, even if you have to guess!

7. After completion of the FCC exam, double check to see if you have marked the answer sheet correctly. Since you will be skipping difficult questions in the first place, be sure to skip the appropriate spaces on the answer sheet.

# Self-Study Ability Test

To successfully pass the FCC General Radiotelephone Operator License, the student must fully understand the material covered on the federal examination. In order to read and comprehend the FCC material, a basic electronic and mathematical background is required! The results of this Self-Study Ability Test will reveal if you need to brush-up on electronic and mathematical basics before actual FCC license study. This test will also give you an educated guess as to the amount of study time you will need to set aside before you will learn enough information to successfully pass the government exam. A poor grade on this ability test would indicate the need for special school training, assistance from an electronic engineer or special home study training.

INSTRUCTIONS: Study all the questions and answers carefully. Select the answer you believe to be correct and indicate your choice with a "X" in the space provided (math answers; fill in solution).

| |  | |  |
|---|---|---|---|
| 1. | Add 327.2 and 66.31 | ANS-1 | 393.51 |
| 2. | Add 1/4 and 1/2 | ANS-2 | 3/4 |
| 3. | Subtract 1.3 from 300.02 | ANS-3 | 298.72 |
| 4. | Subtract 1/4 from 1/2 | ANS-4 | 1/4 |
| 5. | Multiply 68 by 197 | ANS-5 | 13396 |
| 6. | Multiply 1.8 by 3.36 | ANS-6 | 6.048 |
| 7. | Multiply 1/8 by 16 | ANS-7 | 2 |
| 8. | Multiply 1/4 by 32/50 | ANS-8 | 4/25 |
| 9. | Divide 237.6 by 32.87 | ANS-9 | 7.2284 |
| 10. | Divide 2 by 51 | ANS-10 | .03921 |
| 11. | Divide 1/4 by 1/2 | ANS-11 | 1/2 |
| 12. | Divide 4 by 0.001 | ANS-12 | 4000 |
| 13. | 0.8 squared= | ANS-13 | .64 |
| 14. | $\sqrt{324}=$ | ANS-14 | 18 |
| 15. | $\frac{(10 \times 500)}{(7 + 3.0)\times(25 \times 20.0)} = ?$ | ANS-15 | 1 |
| X 16. | 10 Log 100 = ? | ANS-16 | 1000 1 |
| 17. | $\sqrt{.5} = ?$ | ANS-17 | .707106 |
| X 18. | $P = I^2R \quad I = ?$ | ANS-18 | P/R |
| X 19. | $\sqrt{100^2 + 100^2} = ?$ | ANS-19 | 20,000 141.4 |
| 20. | The number of degrees in 2/5 of a circle = ? | ANS-20 | 144 |

— 21. Power is measured in:

___ a. amperes
X b. watts
X c. volts
___ d. farads
___ e. energy-hours

22. Current is measured in:
- X a. amperes
- ___ b. watts
- ___ c. volts
- ___ d. farads
- ___ e. ampere-hours

23. I = E divided by R is the mathematical formula for:
- ___ a. coupling coeffficient
- ___ b. resistance
- ___ c. reactance
- ___ d. capacitance
- X e. Ohm's Law

24. A device which steps up voltage is:
- ___ a. doubler stage
- ___ b. voltage divider
- ___ c. multivibrator
- ___ d. VTVM
- X e. transformer

25. Which of the following diameters of six mile lengths of copper wire offers the most resistance?
- X a. 1/32 of an inch
- ___ b. 1/16 of an inch
- ___ c. 1/2 of an inch
- X d. 3/4 of an inch
- ___ e. none of the above

26. A 12-volt automobile battery consists of:
- ___ a. 24 cells
- ___ b. 12 cells
- X c. 6 cells
- ___ d. mica
- ___ e. 1.5 cells

27. Which of the following materials is a good conductor of electricity?
- X a. zinc
- ___ b. glass
- ___ c. paper
- ___ d. mica
- X e. quartz

28. A blue haze is a normal operating condition in:
- ___ a. transformers
- ___ b. batteries
- ___ c. dummy antennas
- X d. mercury-vapor rectifier tubes
- ___ e. RF amplifiers

29. Which of following would be the best audio amplifier?
- ___ a. class 1
- X b. class A
- X c. class C
- ___ d. class A-1
- ___ e. class AF

30. A popular use for a PN Junction Diode is:
- X a. rectification
- ___ b. oscillation
- ___ c. modulation
- ___ d. RF amplification
- X e. regulation

31. VHF is:
- ___ a. repressed volume
- X b. very high frequency
- ___ c. 2 to 13 TV channels
- ___ d. very high fidelity
- ___ e. vertigial high frequency

32. The basic unit of measurement for capacitance is:
___ a. Ampere
___ b. Ohm
___ c. Dielectric
X d. Farad
___ e. Henry

33. Which of the following wire sizes has the largest diameter?
___ a. 24
___ b. 22HG
___ c. 16S
d. 12
X e. 8

34. Total voltage of two "D" size dry cell batteries in series:
___ a. 24 volts
___ b. 12 volts
___ c. 6 volts
X d. 3 volts
___ e. 1.5 volts

35. AGC is:
___ a. atmospheric GHz. carrier
___ b. audio generation chock
___ c. adequate grid control
d. actual ground connection
X e. automatic gain control

36. Which of the following has the lowest impedence?
X a. carbon microphone
X b. PM loudspeaker
___ c. telephone remote lines
___ d. broadcast audio lines
___ e. crystal phone cartridge

37. The best type of solder to use in electronic work is:
___ a. high temperature
b. aluminum core
X c. rosin core
___ d. acid core
___ e. stacked array

38. A modern advancement of the vacuum tube is:
___ a. printed circuit
___ b. transformer
___ c. micro wave
X d. transistor
___ e. stereo

39. The impedence of most loudspeakers is:
___ a. 33,000 ohms
X b. 8 ohms
___ c. 600 ohms
___ d. 100K ohms
___ e. 15 to 500 ohms

40. A capacitor connected in series between a DC battery and a light bulb causes:
a. AC current
X b. open circuit
___ c. closed circuit
d. increased voltage
X e. increased current

41. The schematic diagram shown is:
___ a. rheostat
___ b. potentiometer
X c. resistor
___ d. tube grid
___ e. voltage divider

42. The schematic symbol shown is:
___ a. "A" battery
b. one cell battery
X c. fixed capacitor
___ d. switch
___ e. electrolytic capacitor

43. The schematic symbol shown is:

- X a. ground
- ___ b. antenna
- ___ c. no connection
- ___ d. a terminal
- ___ e. capacitor

44. The schematic symbol shown is:

- ___ a. adjustable diode
- ___ b. AFC antenna
- ___ c. adjustable capacitor
- X d. rheostat
- X e. potentiometer

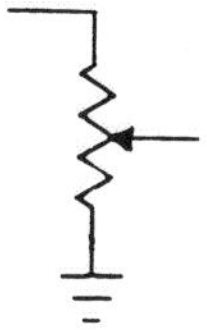

45. The schematic symbol shown is:

- ___ a. rheostat
- ___ b. switch
- ___ c. capacitor
- X d. one cell battery
- ___ e. electrolytic capacitor

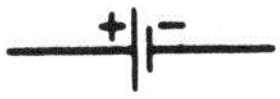

46. The schematic symbol shown is:

- ___ a. ground
- X b. antenna
- ___ c. terminal
- ___ d. crystal
- ___ e. lightning resistor

47. The schematic symbol shown is:

- ___ a. capacitor
- ___ b. rheostat
- ___ c. potentiometer
- ___ d. battery
- X e. adjustable capacitor

48. The schematic diagram shown is:

- A a. NPN transistor
- ___ b. PNP transistor
- X c. junction diode
- ___ d. triode amplifier
- ___ e. phase-shifter

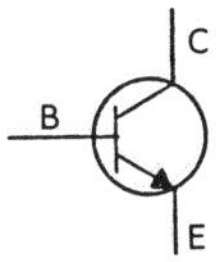

C
B
E

49. The schematic symbol shown is:

- ___ a. iron core choke
- ___ b. air core choke
- ___ c. IF transformer
- ___ d. bulk eraser
- X e. audio transformer

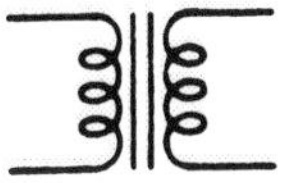

50. This diagram represents:

- X a. transmission path
- ___ b. rectifier-amp
- ___ c. reactance-stage
- ___ d. directional antenna
- X e. operational amplifier

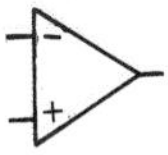

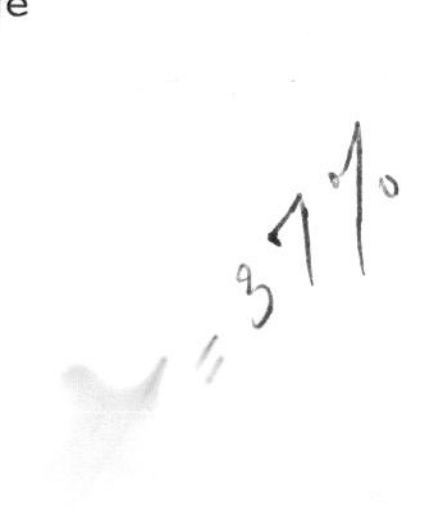

# Test 3-A Element Three

1. What is the distress carrier frequency in the 118-136 MHz. band?

   a> 121.5 KHz.
   b> 121.5 MHz.
   c> 131.5 MHz.
   d> 125.5 MHz.
   e> any of the above

2. When should you change the battery in an E.P.I.R.B. emergency transmitter?

   a> after an emergency
   b> before the date listed on the plate attached to the transmitter
   c> 35% of its useful life remains
   d> both a and b
   e> when charge lasts 24 hours or less

3. Who signs application requesting a shipboard station license?

   a> applicant
   b> Master of the ship
   c> president or owner of the ship
   d> Chief radio officer
   e> FCC Licensed Radiotelephone Operator

4. How does this circuit get the positive feedback needed for oscillation and what is the output frequency?

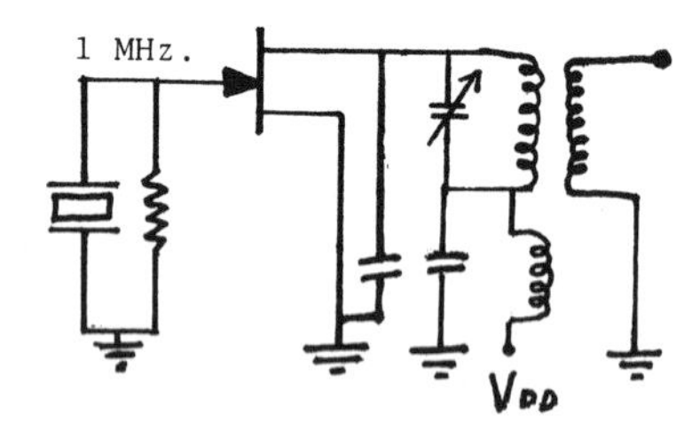


   a> coil inductive reactance, 2 MHz.
   b> crystal feedback capacitance, 1 MHz.
   c> drain to gate capacitance, 3 MHz.
   d> drain to gate capacitance, 2 KHz.
   e> crystal reverse feedback, 6 MHz.

5. On what element of a cathode-ray-tube (CRT) do you change the voltage in order to change the intensity of the trace?

   a> change loading values
   b> increase phosphorus DC potential
   c> increase voltage on horizontal deflection plates
   d> adjust anode voltage
   e> control grid to cathode voltage

6. What device do you use in order to control capacitance with a voltage?

a> silicon rectifier
b> zener diode
c> tunnel diode
d> varactor
e> triac

7. A 25 MHz. amplitude modulated transmitter's actual carrier frequency is 25.00025 MHz. without modulation and is 24.99950 MHz. when modulated. What statement is true?

a> if the allowed frequency tolerance is 0.001%, this is an illegal transmission
b> if the allowed frequency tolerance is 0.002%, this is an illegal transmission
c> modulation should not change carrier frequency
d> if the authorized frequency tolerance is 0.005% for the 25 MHz. band this transmitter is operating legally
e> none of the above

8. What is knife-edge defraction?

a> allows normally line-of-sight signals to bend around sharp edges, mountain ridges, buildings and other obstructions
b> arcing in sharp bends of conductors
c> phase angle image rejection
d> line-of-sight signals causing distortion to other signals
e> metal structures for control of microwave currents

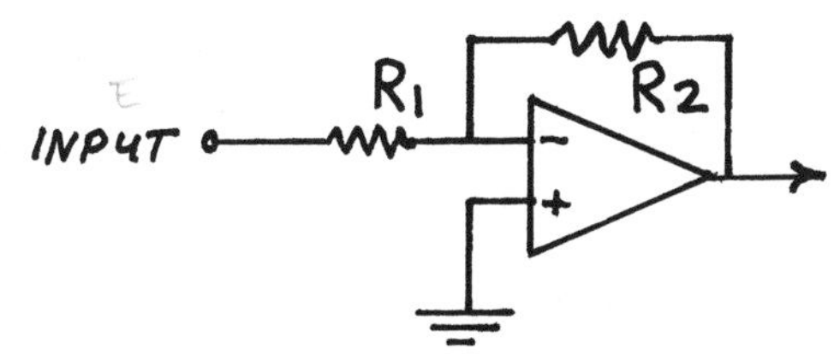


9. To determine the voltage output of the circuit above:

a> -R1 divided by -R2 multiplied by input
b> -R2 divided by -R1
c> R1 divided by R2 multiplied by input
d> -R2 divided by R1 multiplied by input
e> cannot be determined from information given

10. What is the gain of the circuit above?

a> -R2 divided by R1
b> R2 multiplied by R1 divided by input
c> -R1 divided by R2 multiplied by input
d> 100
e> 1000

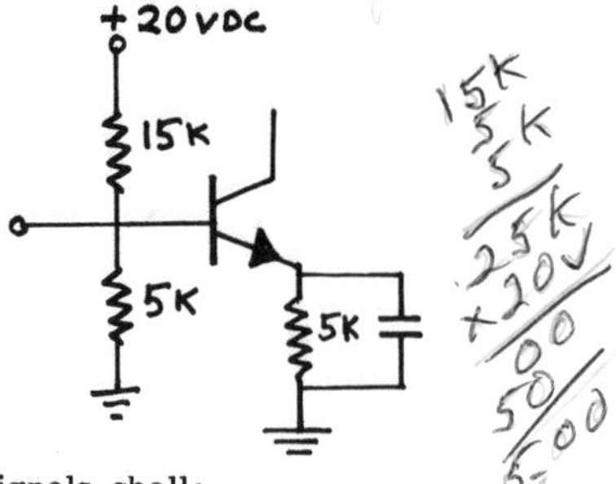


11. What is the voltage at the base of this silicon transistor?

    a> 15 volts
    b> 7.7 volts
    c> 6.7 volts
    d> 5 volts
    e> 2.1 volts

12. The Auto-Alarm device for generating signals shall:

    a> be tested monthly using an artificial antenna
    b> operate on the same frequency as the main VHF transmitter
    c) be tested every three months using an artificial antenna
    d> tested weekly using an artificial antenna
    e> receive all distress messages and relay them automatically to other ships on the open seas

13. How often should the emergency position indicating radio beacon be checked for proper operation?

    a> once per day
    b> once per week
    c> once per month
    d> once per year
    e> only after survival emergency usage

14. When should the battery be replaced in an emergency position indicating radio beacon?

    a> once per year
    b> after the transmitter has been used in an emergency situation or at the battery expiration date upon which 50% of its useful life has expired, whichever is earlier
    c> after the transmitter has lost 70% of its useful life has expired or within two years of its expiration date, whichever is earlier
    d> only when necessary to be fully operational during an emergency
    e> all of the above

15. What is the maximum power this circuit can handle without breakdown?

    a> 5 watts
    b> 10 watts
    c> 14.14 watts
    d> 20.4 watts
    e> none of the above

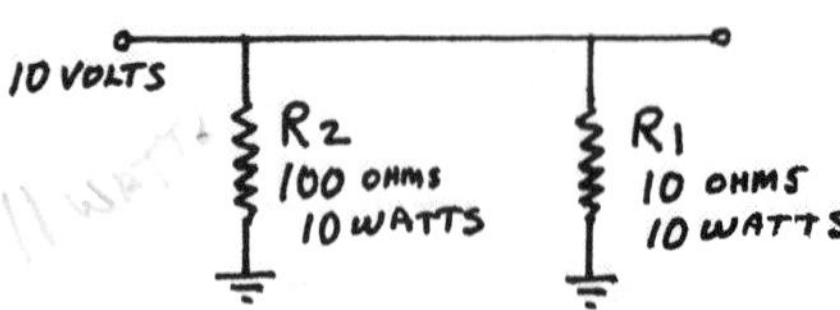

16. Residual magnetism in reference to magnetic materials means:

a> molecular alignment remaining in a material while not under the influence of an external magnetizing force
b> molecular alignment while in a magnetizing force
c> strong electromagnets are not influenced by an external force
d> lines of force in a solid coil
e> none of the above

17. On board a ship, the transmitter is found to be off frequency. What should the operator do?

a> make a notation in the log
b> reduce to low power
c> adjust the oscillator
d> shut down and repair the transmitter
e> both a and b above

18. A receiver must be tuned to the emergency frequency:

a> during an emergency
b> after receiving the auto-alarm signal
c> during normal watch hours
d> when ship is more than 100 miles from shore
e> at all times

19. In the marine radio service, from which of the following frequencies can a 250 kHz. square wave be obtained?

a> 250 kHz., 500 kHz., 1000 kHz.
b> 1 MHz., 2 MHz., 4 MHz.
c> 0.25 MHz., 0.5 MHz., 1 MHz.
d> 125 kHz., 62.5 kHz., 12.5 kHz.
e> an infinite number of odd harmonics of 250 kHz.

20. What frequency would you listen to if you are assigned the following receiving frequencies; 7400 KHz. 2800 KHz.?

a> 2182 KHz.
b> 2810 KHz.
c> 4800 KHz.
d> 4350 KHz.
e> 5100 KHz.

21. When if ever is it legal to transmit high power on channel 13?

a> during an emergency
b> failure to vessel being called to respond
c> in a blind situation such as rounding a bend in a river
d> ship is sinking
e> all of the above

22. What must be in operation when no operator is standing watch on a compulsory radio equipped vessel while out at sea?

a> an auto alarm
b> Indicating Radio Beacon signals
c> Distress-Alert signal device
d> Radiotelegraph transceiver set to 2182 Khz.
e> all of the above

23. What shall be announced by voice on a radio channel as a warning that test emissions are about to be made on the frequency?

a> call sign and nature of test to be performed
b> call sign, geographic location of testing station followed by the word "test"
c> call sign, name of vessel and details of test to be performed
d> the word "test" three times, followed by 1 kHz. tone
e> the auto-alarm tone for 1 minute followed by the word "test"

24. With whom are you allowed to communicate with a ship portable radio?

a> any station able to receive the signal
b> land stations if you are near the coast
c> other boats or stations affiliated with your ship
d> U.S. Coast Guard or government agency stations on shore
e> other ships at sea, provided they are within a 1 mile range

25. What is the voltage drop across R1?

a> 1.2 volts
b> 2.4 volts
c> 3.7 volts
d> 9 volts
e> 11 volts



26. If a ship radio transmitter signal becomes distorted:

a> notify the Master of the ship
b> operate at reduced power
c> hold the microphone farther away and speak softer
d> reduce modulation to avoid break-up of signal
e> cease operations

27. Tower lights not monitored by an automatic device should be checked:

a> once per week
b> once every 24 hours
c> prior to sunrise and just after sunset
d> when they are manually turned on and off; twice daily
e> as needed for proper operation

28. What do you do when you discover that your transmitter is producing spurious harmonics?

a> cease transmission
b> reduce transmitter power to one watt
c> perform frequency tests on 2182 KHz.
d> check antenna and transmitter output connections
e> all of the above

29. The expression "bandwidth occupied by an emission" means:

a> authorized bandwidth of a station
b> licensed band of emission of a station
c> 100% of the full carrier actually broadcast
d> the width of the frequency band containing those frequencies upon which a total of 99% of the radiated power and includes any frequency containing 0.25% of the total power
e> the width of the frequency band containing those frequencies upon which a total of 0.25% of the radiated power and includes all frequencies containing 99% of the total power

30. What is the purpose of a Buffer amplifier?

a> prevents overmodulation
b> makes the oscillator stable
c> varies the load of the oscillator
d> increases the bandwidth of the oscillator
e> prevents the oscillator from over-driving other circuits

31. What is the penalty for anyone willfully violating any rule, regulation, restriction, or condition of the FCC Communications act of 1934 or by international treaty?

a> $10,000 for each day the offense occurs
b> $1,000 for each day the offense occurs
c> $500 for each day the offense occurs
d> $250 for each day the offense occurs
e> imprisoned for not more than one year

32. Anyone who Willfully violates the Communications Act is subject to a fine of not more than:

a> $1,000 or imprisonment for not more than 6 months
b> $10,000 or imprisonment for not more than 1 year
c> $2,000 for each day the offense occurs
d> $500 for each offense
e> cancellation of operator licnese

33. Licensed radiotelephone operators are not required on board ships for:

a> the operation of a survival craft used only for survival purposes
b> voluntarily equipped ship stations on domestic voyages operating on VHF channels
c> ship radar, provided the equipment is non-tunable, pulse type magnetron and can be operated by means of exclusively external controls
d> installation of a VHF transmitter in a ship station where the work is performed by or under the immediate supervision of the licensee of the ship station
e> any of the above

34. When can a bridge to bridge transmission be more than 1 watt?

a> when broadcasting a distress message
b> when rounding a bend in a river or traveling in a blind spot
c> when calling the Coast Guard
d> both a and b above
e> none of the above

35. When applying for a transmitter check in the marine mobile service, application must be made _____ in advance by _____?

a> three days by vessel owner
b> five days by licensed marine radio operator
c> seven days by master, operator or vessel owner
d> two weeks by licensed marine radio operator
e> ten days by licensed radio operator or master of the ship

36. If a small boat, auxiliary ship or other unit is launched from a larger ship, who can this vessel transmit to?

a> boats in the area
b> the ship it was launched from
c> auxiliary boats launched by other ships
d> any station operating on the same frequency as the mother ship
e> both a and b above

37. What does an operator do if the compulsory equipped 2182 kHz. transmitter becomes inoperative when the ship is already out to sea?

a> the transmitter must be repaired immediately or the ship must return to port for transmitter repair
b> switch to another transmitter, such as emergency walkie-talkies
c> conduct all communication over the Bridge-to-Bridge transmitter
d> contact the Commission immediately via the back-up transmitter and request permission to use the Bridge-to-Bridge transmitter
e> no special action is necessary, continue journey and repair transmitter at next port of call

38. An FM receiver limiter circuit:

a> limits the amplitude to the carrier at a certain value
b> is a low gain IF amplifier
c> is connected in front of the discriminator
d> both a and b
X e> all of the above

39. To increase the bandwidth:

a> decrease the coefficient of coupling between amplifier stages
X b> increase the coupling between two tuned circuits up to the critical point
c> decrease the coupling between two tuned circuits up to saturation
d> decrease the power transfer between amplifier stages
e> increase the voltage on the buffer stage

40. The voltage drop from point Y to ground is equal to:

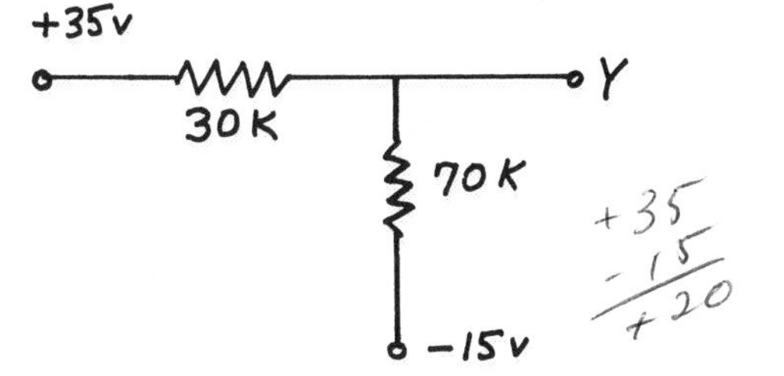


a> +10 volts
b> +14 volts
c> -7 volts
X d> +20 volts
e> 0 volts

41. What is the VHF international "Bridge-to-Bridge" frequency?

a> Channel 1A; 156.05 MHz.
b> Channel 6; 156.3 MHz.
X c> Channel 13; 156.65 MHz.
d> Channel 16; 156.8 MHz.
e> Channel 17; 156.85 MHz.

42. In a properly operating marine transmitter, if the power supply bleeder resistor opens:

e> short circuit of supply voltage due to overload
b> regulation would decrease
c> next stage would fail due to short circuit
X d> filter capacitors might short from voltage surge
e> no change in circuit response

43. What is the purpose of parasitic elements on an antenna?

a> makes the antenna uni-directional
b> increased antenna gain
c> reduced bandpass
d> reduced input impedance
X e> all of the above

44. If a radio station violates any provision of the Federal Communications Commission, how much time is allowed to submit a written statement?

a> 24 hours
b> 3 days
c> 10 days
d> 15 days
e> 30 days

45. What is the voltage drop across R1?

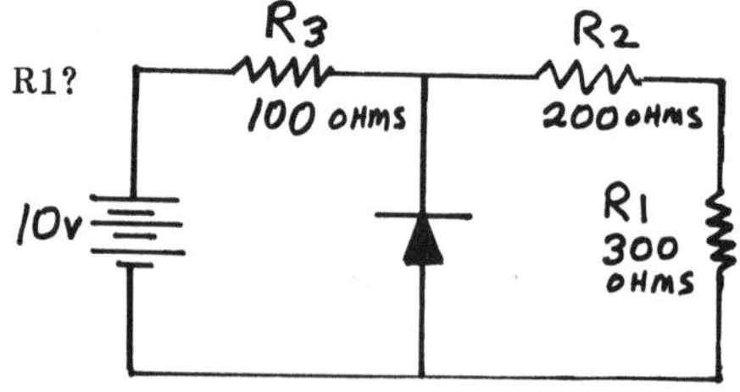


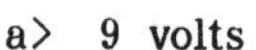

a> 9 volts
b> 7 volts
c> 5 volts
d> 3 volts
e> 0 volts

46. When and how long may an EPIRB transmitter be tested if authorized Coast Guard involvement is not practical?

a> within 24 hours of vessel departure
b> weekly while at sea
c> monthly while in port
d> yearly while at sea without FCC approval
e> during the first 5 minutes of an hour and limited to three audible sweeps or one second into a dummy load

47. What frequency must you listen to if you are assigned the following carrier frequencies: 2800 KHz. and 7200 KHz.?

a> 2182 KHz.
b> 2205 KHz.
c> 2805 KHz.
d> 7505 KHz
e> 2800 KHz. and 7200 KHz.

48. To prevent interference with other radio transmitters?

a> turn off when not in use
b> use lowest power necessary
c> use lowest percentage of modulation necessary
d> limit all calls to one minute or less
e> all of the above

49. What is Channel 16; 156.8 MHz. used for?

a> Bridge-to-Bridge calling and contact frequency
b> International Distress, Safety and Calling frequency
c> SSB long range communication
d> both and and b above
e> EPIRB emergency transmissions only

50. A fixed resistor and a variable resistor are connected in series with an applied voltage. If the variable resistor is decreased:

X a> current will increase
b> current will decrease
c> applied voltage will increase
d> applied voltage will decrease
e> fixed resistor will burn up

51. What qualifications must be met to be an authorized radio operator at an on-board ship station?

a> 21 years old
b> FCC licensed
X c> designated employee assigned to the control point
d> chief engineer of ship station
e> all of the above

52. Buffer stages are used in some transmitters to:

X a> keep a stable load on the oscillator
b> prevent parasitic oscillation
c> compensate for voltage fluctuation
d> protect the IF amplifier stage from front end overload
e> prevent overmodulation

53. 0.1 milliwatt equals:

a> +20 dBm
b> +10 dBm
c> 0 dBm
d> -10 dBm
e> -20 dBm

54. How often must you change EPIRB batteries?

a> after emergency use when battery life expires
X b> after emergency use and prior to battery expiration: month and year date of when 50% of its useful life has expired
c> after emergency use; every 12 months when not used
d> whenever voltage drops to 50% of full charge
e> when required by U.S. Coast Guard

55. In FM transmission, deviation is primarily related to:

a> modulating frequency
b> modulating amplitude
c> modulating phase
d> modulating phase angle
e> none of the above

56. When calling another ship on the open seas, if it is known that the other ship has a duel watch on both working and calling frequencies:

a> always use the calling frequency
b> make first calling attempt on the working frequency
c> call on 121.5 MHz.
d> listen of 5 minutes on the calling frequency before calling on the working frequency
e> call only at the top of the hour during the official 5 minute calling period

57. What is the purpose of this circuit?

a> detector
b> modulator
c> mixer
d> oscillator
e> all of the above

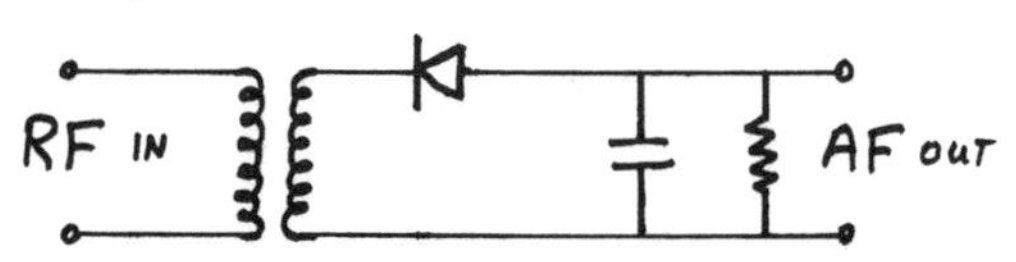


58. On board hand-held marine utility transceivers must be checked for proper operation how often?

a> daily
b> weekly
c> monthly
d> within 24 hours of departure from a port
e> not required

59. What to you do if you receive an URGENCY signal?

a> immediately transmit the distress message signal to alert other vessels to the coming urgency transmission
b> observe radio silence for 5 minutes
c> make a notation in the station log as to the time of day and the latitude and longitude in degrees of the received signal
d> continue to listen for at least 3 minutes and if no urgency message is heard, resume normal service
e> immediately transmit the words: roger your urgency message

60. A 300 ton ship operating with a VHF transmitter must:

a> be adjusted so that the transmission of speech produces peak modulation of 75 to 100 percent
b> have a carrier power of at least 8 watts and not more than 25 watts
c> be able to reduce carrier power to 0.1 and 1.0 watts
d> be capable of effective G3E (or F3E) emission on 156.3 MHz. and 156.8 MHz.
e> all of the above

61. What is the distress frequency and type of emission in the 1605-3500 kHz. medium frequency band?

a> 1700 kHz., A3N emission
b> 1880.2 kHz., R3E emission
c> 2500 MHz., A3N emission
d> 2182 KHz., J3E emission
e> 2182.5 MHz. G3E emission

62. Adding parasitic elements to an antenna will:

a> decrease its directional characteristics
b> decrease its sensitivity
c> increase its directional characteristics
d> decrease its sensitivity
e> reduce its electrical height

63. What does a distress message consist of?

a> Pan three times, this is (call sign)
b> Security three times, this is (call sign)
c> Mayday three times, this is (call sign)
d> this is (call sign), S.O.S. three times
e> this is (call sign and name of ship), Mayday three times

64. What is the audio heard on the auto-alarm?

a> 1 KHz.
b> 2182 KHz.
c> high pitched 2 KHz. tone for 30 seconds in 1/4 second bursts
d> two high pitched alternating tones, each segment 1/4 second in length for 30 or 60 seconds
e> 60 Hz. in 1/4 second bursts for 60 seconds followed by S.O.S.

65. What should an operator do when signals are weak?

a> turn off squelch circuit
b> open up the squelch control
c> turn on the squelch circuit
d> increase electrical length of antenna with an inductor
e> both a and b above

66. Marine transmitters in the 156-162 MHz. band shall be equipped with a low-pass filter installed between the modulation limiter and the RF stage and shall:

a> attenuate audio frequencies above 20 kHz. 50 dB more than 1 kHz.
b> attenuate audio frequencies above 5 kHz. 75 dB more than 100 Hz.
c> increase audio frequencies above 2 kHz. 20 dB more than 10 kHz.
d> increase audio frequencies above 5 kHz. 40 dB more than 10 kHz.
e> remove all audio frequencies above 3 kHz.

67. To increase the intensity (brightness) of the image on a cathode-ray-tube (CRT):

a> increase voltage to the anode
b> increase horizontal deflection plate voltage
c> change grid bias potential
d> decrease the voltage to the anode
e> both a and b

68. When does a suspension of an operator license become effective?

a> 7 days after the date listed on the official notification
b> upon official notification from the Commission
c> immediately upon receipt of the Notice of Suspension
d> 10 days after the date listed on the Notice of Violation
e> 15 days after the licensee receives the notice of suspension

69. If you hear profanity transmitted on your station:

a> make an official notation in operator log
b> stop the transmission immediately
c> make a report to the Master of the ship
d> file a report to the Commission of FCC Form 756
e> all of the above

70. On-board ship portable radios can be used to communicate to:

a> on-board units of other ship
b> any ship the mother ship can talk to
c> tug boats during docking maneuvers
d> the mother ship from the loading dock
e> none of the above

71. What are the FCC requirements for the identification of a ship radio station when calling another ship what should be transmitted?

a> station assigned call sign
b> station assigned call sign and name of ship
c> name of ship, country of origin and official call sign
d> name of ship only during Bridge-to-Bridge communication
e> any of the above

72. How long should an operator continue to listen after hearing the urgency signal?

a> 1 hour
b> 30 minutes
c> 10 minutes
d> 5 minutes
e> 3 minutes

73. The VHF receiver's ability to reject unwanted signals and accept only the desired signal is:

a> adjacent channel sensitivity
b> adjacent channel selection
c> adjacent channel rejection
d> required to be 20 dB below signal strength
e> 40 dB per 100 microvolts per meter minimum

74. If you measure the voltage from point A to ground, what will the volt meter read?

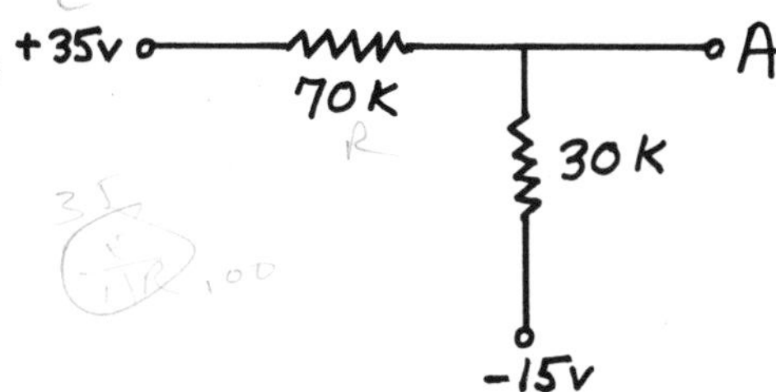


a> 4.4 volts
b> 14 volts
c> 24.5 volts
d> 35 volts
e> 0 volts

75. Which of the following receivers has the most ability to reject unwanted signals and accept only desired signals?

a> -40 dB adjacent channel rejection
b> -70 dB adjacent channel rejection
c> -20 dB adjacent channel sensitivity
d> -100 dB adjacent channel selection
e> 40 dB per 100 microvolts per meter

76. Before a SSB radiotelephone transmitter can be legally installed on a ship the FCC must recognize that the equipment meets their specifications. How do you know if the transmitter you install is "type accepted or certified as appropriate" for shipboard use?

a> furnish the FCC Field Office with station license, manufacture's model number
b> approval date and official FCC notification will be printed on the station license
c> furnish the FCC Field Office with the manufacture's name and the FCC ID number on the plate attached to the transmitter
d> check model number and type acceptance number with station license
e> all transmitters manufactured or imported into the U.S. are type accepted

77. When installing single-sideband transmission equipment, considerable care must be taken to:

a> connect the proper antenna tower
b> connect a good ground system
c> provide good regulated voltage to the output buffer amplifier
d> install a VHF receiver with SSB capability
e> all of the above

78. Under what license are portable hand-held transceivers covered when used on-board a ship at sea?

a> special FCC hand-held communications license
b> under the main ship station transmitter license
c> under the authority of the licensed operator
d> walkie-talkie radios are illegal to use at sea
e> each hand held unit operates under a separate license

79. If a technician services more than one location:

a> an operator license is carried on the person
b> if an operator license is posted at a transmitter a photocopy may be carried on the person
c> a photocopy must be posted at each transmitter location
d> a license verification must be obtained from the FCC
e> both a and b above

80. The radiotelephone distress message consists of:

a> MAYDAY spoken three times
b> name of vessel, aircraft or vehicle in distress
c> particulars of its position latitude and longitude, and other information which might facilitate rescue, such as length, color and type of vessel, number of persons on board
d> nature of distress and kind of assistance desired
e> all of the above

81. In the marine mobile service, what should an operator do to prevent interference?

a> turn off transmitter when not in use
b> check ensure that no one is transmitting on the same frequency
c> transmissions should be as brief as possible
d> no unnecessary calls and transmission should be made
e> all of the above

82. In the band of frequencies of 1.6 MHz. to 23 MHz., what is the international distress frequency?

a> 2182 MHz.
b> 500 MHz.
c> 156 MHz.
d> 21.82 MHz.
e> 2.182 MHz.

83. What device is used as a tuning element in high-power frequency multipliers and for frequency control in VHF to microwave ranges?

a> triac
b> tunnel diode
c> zener diode
d> varactor diode
e> PIN diode

84. A voltmeter reads 120 volts full scale (12 units) in series with a 3750 ohm resistor. If the same meter reads 7.5 with an applied voltage of 135 volts, how much resistance has been added?

a> 750 ohms
b> 3000 ohms
c> 4500 ohms
d> 1500 ohms
e> 3500 ohms

85. What information does the plate on the side of a transmitter contain?

a> manufacturer
b> frequency
c> power output
d> FCC type approval ID number
e> all of the above

86. The maximum allowable transmitter frequency deviation on aircraft is:

a> 20 Hz.
b> 50 Hz.
c> 10 Hz.
d> 20 PPM
e> 50 PPM

87. What ferrite rod device prevents the formulation of reflected waves on a waveguide transmission line?

a> reflector
b> isolator
c> wave-trap
d> SWR refractor
e> SWR carbon resistor

88. All radiotelephone emissions of a ship station shall be clearly identified by:

a> station calling frequency
b> country of registration
c> official call sign assigned by the commission
d> name of the vessel
e> both c and d

89. When do you use 1 watt in Bridge-to-Bridge communication?

a> when transmitting within 1 mile from any shore
b> while in dry dock
c> when another ship is in sight
d> when transmitting off-frequency or overmodulating
e> at all times, except when going around the bend in a river

90. A capacitor will:

a> fail if operated at low frequencies
b> hold a charge indefinitely until bleed off
c> hold a charge equal to 63% of the charging voltage for 1 second
d> fail if polarity is changed
e> both a and b

91. The speed of a series DC motor will be affected by the:

a> line voltage frequency
b> number of windings
c> load
d> rotor coil windings
e> applied voltage

92. A common-base transistor circuit has:

a> low input impedance
b> high input impedance
c> input and output signals out of phase
d> high current gain
e> all of the above

93. Maritime emergency radios should be tested:

a> before each voyage
b> weekly while the ship is at sea
c> when the manufacturer recommends
d> every 24 hours
e> both a and b

94. A crystal oscillator frequency changes by .002%. The transmitter operates on 16 MHz. and the oscillator operates at 1/8th of the output frequency. Maximum transmitter frequency deviation will be:

a> 0.00032 Hertz
b> 40 Hertz
c> 320 Hertz
d> 0.3250 kHz.
e> 0.320 MHz

95. Type approval when applied to equipment indicates that:

a> FCC has tested transmitter and assigned an ID number to unit
b> it is authorized for marine or aircraft use
c> manufacturer is authorized to build radio equipment
d> only license operators may use the equipment
e> all of the above

96. Class B amplifiers may be used as single-ended linear amplifiers in RF applications because:

a> flywheel effect restores the complete wave form
b> the circuit is always operated less than cut-off
c> tank circuit is push-pull and allows full 360 degree cycle
d> both a and b
e> both b and c

97. What value of resistor would you select for most power dissipation?

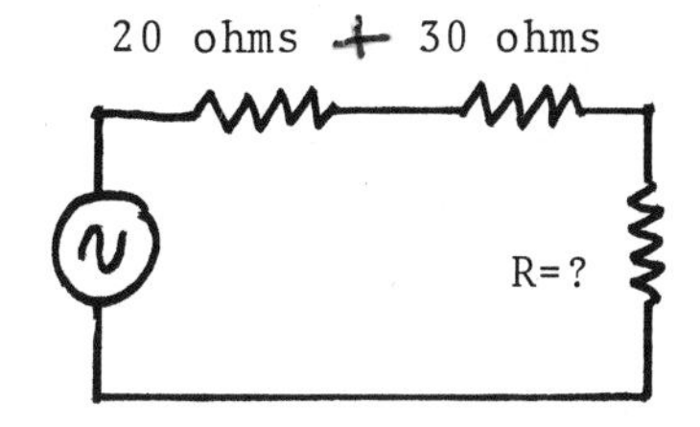


a> 1 ohm
b> 5 ohms
c> 20 ohms
d> 30 ohms
e> 50 ohms

98. The expression 'voltage regulation' as it applies to a shunt-wound DC generator operating at a constant frequency refers to:

a> voltage output efficiency
b> voltage in the secondary compared to the primary
c> voltage fluctuations from load to no-load
d> rotor winding voltage ratio
e> coil windings voltage efficiency

99. If a amplifier stage has an input of 1 milliwatt and it attenuates the signal -40 dB, watt is the output of the stage?

a> 0.0001 mw
b> 0.001 mw
c> 0.01 mw
d> 0.1 mw
e> 1 mw

100. The frequency bandwidth occupied by the carrier and both sidebands:

a> authorized bandwidth
b> emission bandwidth
c> full carrier emission
d> 100% bandwidth
e> full double-sideband emission

# Test 3-B Element Three

1. At 100 MHz. what has the least resistance?

   a> silver wire 6" long by 1 cm
   b> aluminum wire 6" long by 1 cm
   c> 0.1 mfd. capacitor
   d> small piece of copper sheet
   e> 24 gauge copper wire 6" long

2. When transmitting on the marine band:

   a> use minimum power necessary to contact other stations
   b> transmit call sign and name of ship on every station contact
   c> always use 2.182 MHz. calling frequency within 5 miles of shore
   d> listen on channel before transmitting to avoid interfering with other stations
   e> all of the above

3. A limiter circuit is a:

   a> buffer stage to protect the oscillator
   b> amplifier with neutralization
   c> low gain amplifier with relatively constant output
   d> high gain amplifier with a relatively constant output
   e> unity gain amplifier with variable output

4. A series circuit has an XL = 200 ohms, XC = 140 ohms and a R = 60 ohms. What is the phase angle?

   a> 30 degrees
   b> 45 degrees
   c> 90 degrees
   d> 180 degrees
   e> 270 degrees

5. When a Beat-Frequency Oscillator is turned to the same frequency of an incoming carrier:

   a> duplication of incoming signal is produced in BFO and is heard in the speaker
   b> zero beat is produced; no sound is heard
   c> 1 Khz. tone is heard in BFO speaker
   d> rapid pulse-tone is zero-beat in BFO speaker
   e> 450 Khz. tone is produced in BFO

6. What is the proper method for using flux when soldering?

a> use adequate quantity of flux to hold wires
b> use enough flux to oxidize the solder connection
c> apply ample flux to assure wetting of the leads
d> always use acid core solder with acid flux
e> rosin core solder is prefered in electronics

7. What type of emission is J3E (previously A3J)?

a> double-sideband, full carrier telephony
b> single-sideband, suppressed carrier telephony
c> single-sideband, reduced carrier
d> phase modulated, keyed carrier telegraphy
e> facsimile

8. What is the authorized bandwidth of J3E (previously A3J) emission?

a> 0.4 KHz.
b> 2.8 KHz
c> 3.0 KHz.
d> 8.0 KHz.
e> 20.0 KHz.

9. Frequencies most affected by knife-edge refraction:

a> low and medium frequencies
b> high frequencies
c> very high and ultra high frequencies
d> 100 kHz. to 3.0 MHz.
e> ultrasonic frequencies

10. What is the maximum frequency tolerance of aircraft stations in the 100 to 137 MHz. band?

a> 20 parts per million
b> 50 parts per million
c> 20 Hertz
d> 50 Hertz
e> plus or minus one percent

11. What is the maximum frequency tolerance of survival craft and emergency locator stations transmitting in the aeronautical services in the 100 MHz. to 137 MHz. band?

a> 20 parts per million
b> 50 parts per million
c> 20 Hertz
d> 50 Hertz
e> no tolerance for survival craft emergency transmitters

12. If power remains constant when the voltage is doubled, the resistance must:

a> double
b> remain the same
c> reduce by 1/4
d> quadruple
e> reduce 1/2

13. If you are listening to an FM radio station at 100.6 MHz. on a car radio when an airplane in the vacinity is transmitting at 121.2 MHz. and your car radio receives interference the possilbe problem could be:

a> improper shielding in receiver
b> poor "Q" receiver
c> image frequency
d> high standing wave ratio
e> intermodulation or coupling

14. Determine the frequency of an oscillator if it operates at 1/8th of the 2182 kHz. frequency?

a> 174.56 kHz.
b> 272.75 kHz.
c> 2182 kHz.
d> 21.8 MHz.
e> 1091 kHz.

15. Why is the grid sometimes grounded in circuit?

a> when used as a Class A amplifier
b> to obtain maximum voltage output
c> no neutralization is required if used as a class C RF power amp
d> neutralization is required if used as a class B RF power amp
e> all of the above

16. In a parallel LC circuit, as the capacitor is adjusted from below resonance through resonance and above resonance, the voltage will:

a> increase from minimum to maximum and back to minimum
b> decrease from maximum to minimum and back to maximum
c> stay the same through resonance and then increase
d> not change voltage
e> none of the above

17. What is the purpose of neutralization?

a> decrease degeneration
b> increase output voltage
c> prevent oscillation
d> excite oscillator stage
e> reduce changes in current

18. What is the penalty for anyone who willfully does anything prohibited by the Communications Act of 1934 or knowingly omits to do anything required by the act?

a> a fine of not more than $10000 or imprisonment for one year
b> a fine of not more than $1000 or imprisonment for not more than two years
c> a fine of $500 and imprisonment for not more than one year
d> cancellation of operator license
e> imprisonment for not more than two years and cancellation of operator license

19. When is it legal to carry a photocopy of an FCC Radiotelephone License on your person?

a> when working for more than two stations
b> when the original license is posted at the primary transmitter location
c> when the original license is posted at the operating point
d> at any time when work is performed and must be immediately available for inspection by Commission representatives
e> any of the above

20. When an emergency transmitter uses 325 watts and a receiver uses 50 watts, how many hours can a 12.6 volt, 55 ampere-hour battery supply full power to both units?

a> 6 hours
b> 3 hours
c> 1.8 hours
d> 1.2 hours
e> 0.5 hours

21. How many nautical miles should the emission radiate in a ship that is equipped with only a temporary Marine Radiotelephone installation?

a> 100
b> 150
c> 200
d> 250
e> 300

22. A crystal oscillator frequency changes by 0.002%. The transmitter operates on 16 MHz. and the oscillator operates at 1/8th of the output frequency. What is the maximum transmitter deviation?

a> 400 Hz.
b> 320 Hz.
c> 8 kHz.
d> 16 kHz.
e> 400 kHz.

23. At 130 MHz., and all things constant, if the input frequency is increased, the output frequency will:

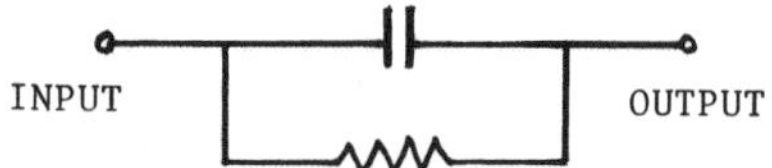


a> remains the same
b> decrease steadily
c> increase steadily
d> go up, then down
e> go down, then up

24. The expression "voltage regulation" as it applies to a generator operating at a constant frequency refers to:

a> full load to no load
b> limited load to peak load
c> source input supply frequency
d> field frequency
e> output frequency "Q"

25. When measuring I and V along a 1/2 wave hertz antenna where would you find the points where I and V are maximum and minimum?

a> V and I are high at the ends
b> V and I are high in the middle
c> V and I are uniform throughout the antenna
d> V is maximum in the middle, I is maximum at the ends
e> V is maximum at both ends, I is maximum in the middle

26. What is the total capacitance between points A and B of this circuit if each capacitor is 2 mfd.?

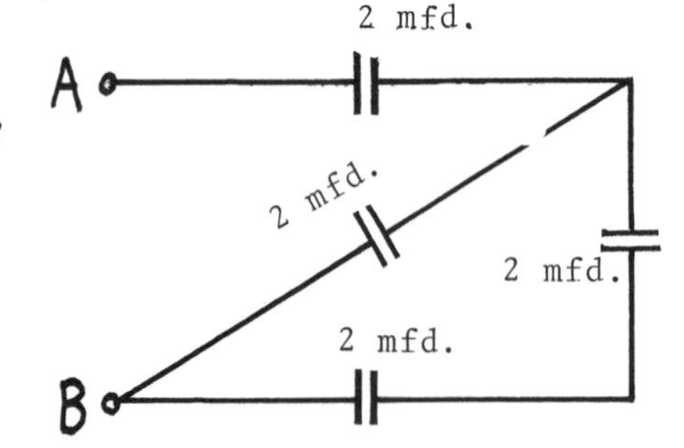


a> 8 micro farads
b> 5.43 micro farads
c> 3.2 micro farads
d> 1.2 micro farads
e> 0.67 micro farads

27. Compared to a duo-diode full-wave rectifier, a Bridge rectifier:

a> requires minimum filtering
b> operates at higher voltage filtering levels
c> requires transformer with a center tap on the secondary
d> does not require a transformer with a center tap on the secondary
e> requires a transformer with a center tap on both primary and secondary

28. Survival craft emergency position indicating radiobeacons, Class S, required to comply with the Title 46 of the Code of Federal Regulations must have batteries replaced:

a> when 50% of its useful life will have expired; expiration date marked on battery and outside of transmitter
b> after the transmitter has been used in an emergency situation
c> once per year for cargo ships of 300 or more tons
d> both a and b above
e> all of the above

29. Who may operate Bridge-to-Bridge radio equipment?

a> FCC Radiotelephone or Radiotelegraph licensed operators only
b> the master or person in charge of navigating the vessel
c> the operator in charge of the ship transmitter room
d> anyone in control of the transmitter
e> persons hold a Marine Operator Permit or higher grade license

30. Hand-held portable transmitters are authorized at what carrier frequency and power when used from shore in Dry Dock or other land or mobile facility at shore?

a> 2182 KHz., 1 watt
b> 156.8 Mhz., 1 watt
c> 467.775 MHz., 50 watts
d> 121.5 MHz., 5 watts
e> shore transmissions are not authorized

31. What is the meaning of CLEAR?

a> your message is received
b> transmission complete; await your reply
c> communication is completed and do not expect to transmit any further traffic
d> wait for another call or further instructions
e> expression used to request receiving operator to indicate if all messages transmitted thus far received clearly

32. How often must the red avoidance lights on a tower at an airport be checked?

a> at least once per hour between sunset and sunrise
b> at least once per 8 hour shift between sunset and sunrise
c> at least once each 24 hours
d> hourly; between 3pm and 9am local time
e> avoidance lights are not required to be checked

33. Which of the following can occur that would least affect this circuit?

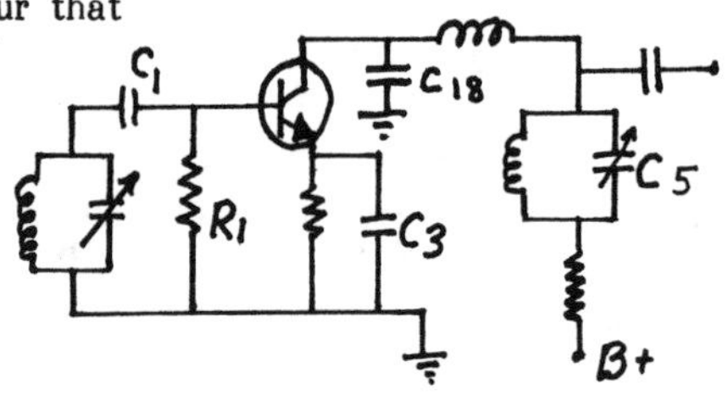


a> C1 shorts
b> C1 opens
c> C3 shorts
d> C18 opens
e> C5 shorts

34. - 20 dBm is equal to:

a> 0.001 mw
b> 0.01 mw
c> 0.1 watt
d> 1 watt
e> 2 watts

35. Eddy currents are formed:

a> within the electrostatic shield of a transformer
b> when cutting lines of force
c> within transformers
d> when connecting a transformer to an improper load
e> and filtered out in the buffer amplifier

36. The average range for VHF communications is:

a> 5 miles
b> 15 miles
c> 30 miles
d> 100 miles
e> 150 - 1500 miles

37. In a VHF-FM receiver, the sensitivity is usually given as:

a> microvolts per dB
b> rejection ratio
c> number of microvolts required to produce 20 dB of quieting
d> number of millivolts required to produce 50 dB of quieting
e> percent of adjacent channel rejection

38. To increase the resonant frequency of a 1/4 wavelength antenna:

a> add a capacitor
b> lower capacitor value
c> cut antenna
d> add an inductor
e> not possible

39. 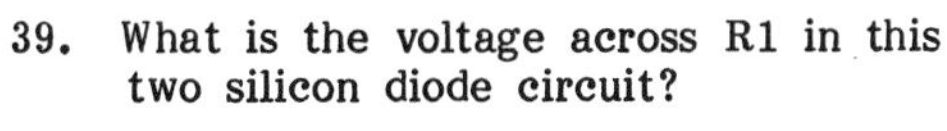
What is the voltage across R1 in this two silicon diode circuit?

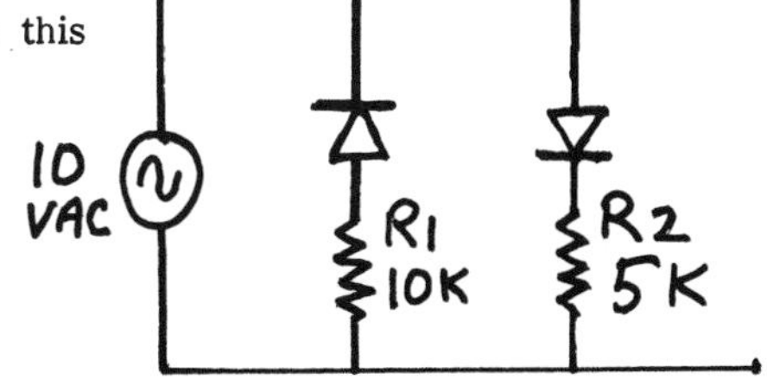


a> 9.4 volts
b> 7.3 volts
c> 6.2 volts
d> 3.1 volts
e> 2.3 volts

40. If a ship sinks, what device is designed to float free of the mother ship, is turned on automatically with a mercury switch and activates a a 700 Hz. tone signal on what transmission frequency?

a> E.P.I.R.B. on 121.5 MHz. and 243 MHz.
b> E.P.I.R.B. on 2182 KHz.
c> Bridge-to-Bridge transmitter on 2182 KHz.
d> Auto-Alarm keyer on any frequency
e> SOS Emergency Alarm Remote Transmitter

41. The carrier power is suppressed on J3E emission at a power level of how many decibels below peak envelope power?

a> 2 db
b> 20 db
c> 30 db
d> 40 db
e> 50 db

42. A ship over 300 or more gross tons is required to have radiotelephone equipment capable of transmitting a minimum of:

a> 25 miles
b> 50 miles
c> 150 miles
d> 250 miles
e> 500 miles

43. Hand-held portable marine utility radios used on-borad vessels:

a> can be used in any manner provided they do not cause interference
b> can be used in Bridge-to-Bridge communications only
c> do not have to be licensed if power is under 1 watt
d> can be used either on ship or shore, provided it transmits on the ships licensed transmitter frequency
e> none of the above

44. What are Eddy currents?

a> I2 losses
b> losses in the core
c> electromagnetic flux losses
d> hysteresis losses
e> both a and b above

45. The purpose of a limiter in an FM receiver:

a> to provide medium gain and high output
b> to provide high gain and constant output
c> to provide low gain and constant output
d> reduces the amplitude of the output wave
e> increases the frequency modulation detection

46. Inductance directly varies with:

a> increased capacitance
b> square of the turns of a coil
c> square of the resistance of a coil
d> inverse of the number of winds of a coil
e> proportion of capacitance to inductance ratio

47. Why are concentric transmission lines sometimes filled with nitrogen?

a> reduce resistance at high frequencies
b> prevent water damage underground
c> keep moisture out and prevent oxidation
d> reduce microwave line losses
e> all of the above

48. How often should the frequency be checked on an airport aviation transmitter?

a> upon notification by FCC
b> when you beleive transmitter is not within tolerance
c> once per year
d> all of the above
e> daily or prior to every transmission

49. The output of a separately excited AC generator running at a constant speed can be controlled by:

a> armature
b> brushes
c> field current
d> exciter
e> driver

50. When are you required to change the batteries in an EPIRB transmitter?

a> every six months
b> once a year
c> during required maintenance testing
d> after every emergency use
e> none of the above

51. What offers the lowest impedance to 1 MHz.?

a> 1 Meg ohm resistor
b> 10 mil aluminum wire, 6 inches long
c> 10 mil silver wire, 6 inches long
d> 1 micro-farad capacitor
e> thin piece of copper, 2 inches by 6 inches

52. When may bridge-to-bridge transmissions be identified by the name of the ship only in lieu of the official call sign?

a> never
b> while in dry dock
c> when directed by government agency or foreign authority in a congested vessel traffic service system
d> during low power transmissions to portable boats
e> during equipment tests

53. The URGENCY signal concerning the safety of a ship, aircraft or person shall be sent only on the authority of:

a> Master of ship
b> person responsible for mobile station
c> either a or b above
d> an FCC licensed operator
e> anyone during an emergency

54. Survival craft emergency transmitter tests may NOT be made:

a> for more than 10 seconds
b> within range of automatic alarm receivers which may actuate
c> without using station call sign, followed by the word: test
d> within 5 minutes of a pervious test
e> all of the above

55. In what kind of diode does the capacitance vary?

a> varicap
b> varactor
c> diac
d> triac
e> a and b

56. A vertical 1/4 wave antenna receives signals:

a> in the microwave band
b> in one vertical direction
c> in one horizontal direction
d> equally from all horizontal directions
e> equally from all vertical directions

57. RMS value of a sine wave is:

a> peak value divided by the square root of 2
b> average value divided by the square root of 2
c> peak value divided by the square of 2
d> average value multiplied by the square of 2
e> none of the above

58. In a parallel LC circuit at resonance:

a> impedance increases if a resistance is added
b> impedance is infinite if circuit has low resistance
c> impedance increases first and then drops to zero
d> impedance decreases if a resistance is added
e> both a and b above

59. What emission do tone pagers use?

a> J3E
b> A3A or A3B
c> 15F2, 16F3 or 16F9Y
d> R3E or R4E
e> all of the above

60. What is the voltage across R1?

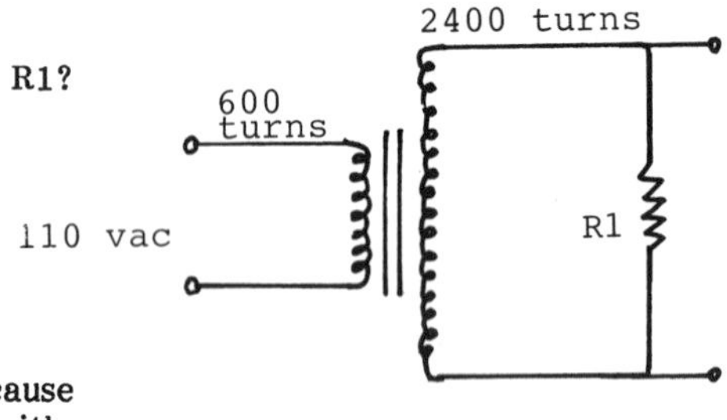

a> 440 volts
b> 220 volts
c> 110 volts
d> 27.5 volts
e> 18.33 volts

2400 turns
600 turns
110 vac
R1

61. What would be a possible cause of a CB radio interfering with TV channels 2 through 6?

a> intermodulation
b> front end overload
c> second harmonic interference
d> image distortion
e> poor shielding

62. Who may sign an application form to apply for a ship station license?

a> the applicant; owner or operator of the vessel
b> the Chief Engineer in charge of the vessel radio station
c> an FCC Licensed General Radiotelephone Operator
d> FCC Field Office engineers
e> the authorized FCC licensed chief of vessel radio operations

63. How do you test your distress signal?

a> use a dummy load
b> on any non-distress frequency
c> with less than 5 watts
d> when ship is docked in any U.S. port
e> all of the above

64. Portable hand-held transmitters on-board a ship are not authorized:

a> to transmit more than one watt
b> for communication with another vessel
c> beyond the immediate vicinity of the mother ship
d> to be used from shore
e> all of the above

65. Which of the following frequencies would NOT be used by aircraft when communicating with the tower during landing procedures?

a> 121.225 MHz.
b> 121.5 MHz.
c> 124.7 MHz.
d> 127.750 MHz.
e> 135.7 MHz.

66. Transmitters using F3E (or G3E) emission in the 156-162 MHz band shall be capable of proper operation with a frequency deviation of:

a> 50 KHz.
b> 5 KHz.
c> 5 MHz.
d> 15.6 to 16.2 Hz.
e> 20 Hz

67. International laws and regulations require a silent period on 2182 kHz.:

a> for three minutes immediately after the hour
b> for three minutes immediately after the half-hour
c> for the first minute of every quarter-hour
d> from 10 to 20 minutes past every hour
e> both a and b above

68. Which of the following represents the best standing wave ratio (SWR)?

a> 1:1
b> 1:1.5
c> 1:3
d> 1:4
e> 1:5

69. What occurs if the load is removed from an operating series DC motor?

a> it will stop running
b> speed will increase slightly
c> no change occurs
d> it will accelerate until it flies apart
e> speed will decrease slightly

70. What is the reactance of a 0.001 mfd. capacitor is 2 pi f = 1000?

a> 6.28 ohms
b> 37 ohms
c> 1 megohm
d> 0.006 ohms
e> 62 ohms

71. On towers without an automatic warning system, what should the lights be checked?

a> once every hour
b> once every three hours
c> once every 24 hours
d> hourly from sunset to sunrise
e> once per week

72. Class 'C' amplifiers:

a> have the ability to totally reconstruct the original wave form
b> have less power output than class A or B
c> are used only in vacuum tube circuits
d> provide good efficiency
e> poor quality and efficiency

73. If the modulated signal is ten times the level of the noise floor:

a> 10 dB quieting
b> 20 dB quieting
c> 3 dB quieting
d> 100 dB quieting
e> -20 dB quieting

74. Bridge-to-Bridge radiotelephone transmitters must be capable of at of transmitting:

a> SOS on 500 KHz. 50%+ modulated
b> at least 500 miles daytime; 750 miles nighttime
c> 1 and 8 to 25 watts of 5-KHz. deviation F3E on 156.3 MHz. and 156.8 MHz., plus other frequencies in the 156 to 162 MHz. band
d> 150 watts on 156.3 MHz. and 156.8 MHz. band
e> 300 watts A3E on 2182 KHz. and 50 watts J3E on 1605-2850 KHz

75. A compulsory equipped ship transmitter must be capable, with normal operating voltages applied, of delivering not less than:

a> 1 watt peak envelope power for H3E and J3E emission
b> 40 watts peak envelope power for H3E and J3E emission
c> 60 watts peak envelope power for H3E and J3E emission
d> 80 watts peak envelope power for all emissions
e> 450 watts peak envelope power for H3E emission on 2182 KHz.

76. Hand-held portable transceivers on board a ship are authorized to communicate:

a> with other mobile units of the same station
b> aboard the same vessel for operational communications
c> in the immediate area of the same vessel to communicate messages relating to docking or life boat drills
d> by designated members of the crew of the vessel
e> all of the above

77. How often must land based transmitters in the Aviation Services have operating frequencies measured?

a> daily
b> weekly
c> monthly
d> when a transmitter is originally installed and when any change or adjustment is made which may affect the operating frequency or if the operating frequency has shifted beyond tolerance
e> none of the above

78. For the FCC to inspect a ship radiotelephony station, _____ advance notice of the desired inspection date must be give by the _____.

a> three days, licensee
b> ten days, station's licensed operator
c> ten days, ship's Master
d> two weeks, station's maintenance person
e> twenty-four hours, licensee

79. This circuit has:

a> low gain
b> low frequency response
c> low input impedance
d> high input impedance
e> both a and b

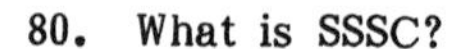

80. What is SSSC?

a> sideband single suppressed carrier
b> single-sideband suppressed carrier
c> super-suppressed sideband conversion
d> single-service sideband carrier
e> a direction finding radiotlelphone station

81. If 'P' does not change and 'V' doubles, what happens to 'R'?

a> remains the same
b> doubles
c> triples
d> quadruples
e> increases by a square of the original value

82. What band of frequencies are authorized for on-board UHF communications for ships at sea?

a> 626.882 MHz - 686.964 MHz
b> 525.000 MHz - 531.886 MHz
c> 457.525 MHz - 467.825 MHz
d> 121.500 MHz - 123.000 MHz
e> 2.180 MHz - 2.184 MHz

83. How much carrier suppression is required below peak-envelope power of a J3E single-sindband suppressed carrier transmission?

a> 50%
b> 85%
c> 10 dB
d> 20 dB
e> 40 dB

84. An acceptable method of insuring that the output frequency of a transmitter is being maintained within authorized limits:

a> oscilloscope
b> frequency counter
c> zero-beat the output frequency against WWV
d> zero-beat the output frequency against a suitable source
e> frequency deviation meter on the transmitter

85. Channel 13 Bridge-to-Bridge transmitter power on Channel 13 (156.65 MHz.) can not be increased beyond 1-watt unless:

a> emergency occurs, such as two ships colliding
b> failure of the vessel being called to respond to a second call at low power in an urgent situation
c> when going around the bend in a river and two ships can not see each other
d> all of the above
e> station authorization allows special high-power emission

86. A JFET is similar in operation to what other device?

a> triode
b> diode
c> modulator
d> triac
e> transformer

87. How is a distress call properly made on a radiotelephone transmitter?

a> three loud horn blasts
b> SOS transmitted in code three times
c> the word MAYDAY spoken three times
d> the URGENCY alarm tone transmitted, followed by the message
e> all of the above

88. All shipboard antennas operating in the medium frequency bands radiate what type of signals?

a> vertically polarized
b> horizontally polarized
c> pulse-code modulated
d> telegraphic via unmodulated carrier
e> SSSC

89. How should the value of a tank circuit capacitor be changed to change the frequency from 12 MHz to 24 MHz.?

a> 12 times original capacitance
b> 4 times original capacitance
c> 2 times original capacitiance
d> 1/2 of original capacitance
e> 1/4 of original caplacitance

90. What is correct about this amplifier stage?

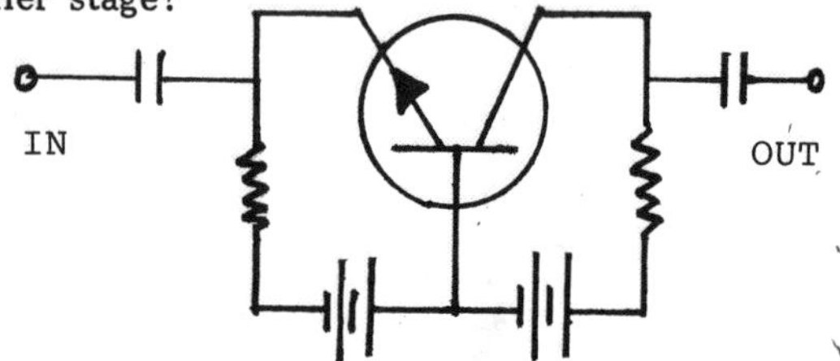


a> common base
b> common collector
c> common emitter
d> input and output
are out of phase
e> high input impedance

91. The purpose of a pre-emphasis circuit in an FM transmitter is to:

a> attenuate low audio frequencies to reduce noise
b> amplify low audio frequencies to reduce noise
c> attenuate high audio frequencies
d> amplify high audio frequencies more than low audio frequencies
e> attenuate high audio frequencies more than low audio frequencies

92. The batteries in an EPIRB transmitter on a ship should be checked:

a> after emergency use
b> when the manufacturer recommends
c> weekly
d> monthly
e> both a and b

93. When constructing radio circuits, leads should be kept as short as possible in order to:

a> reduce line losses
b> minimize stray inductive coupling
c> minimize stray capacitive coupling
d> prevent parasitic oscillations
e> prevent eddy current losses

94. What is the emission designator for a SSSC radiotelephone station with an authorized bandwidth of 3 kHz. and frequency tolerance of 20 Hz?

a> 2K80J3E (previously A3J)
b> 16K0F3E (previously F3)
c> 6K00A3E (previously A3)
d> 2K80R3E (previously A3A)
e> both c and d above

95. The power consumed in an AC circuit is equal to the product of the:

a> heating value and the total power factor of the circuit
b> efficiency of the circuit and the total power supplied
c> RMS values of the total voltage, current and power factor
d> power factor multiplied by the total current and voltage
e> actual reading of a wattmeter

96. Applications for a NEW ship station license must be filed how many days prior to the date license is required?

a> 120 days
b> 90 days
c> 60 days
d> 30 days
e> 3 days

97. What is a major source of parasitics?

a> oscillator
b> amplifier
c> receiver
d> transmitter
e> any of the above

98. If 480 Khz. is radiated from a 1/4 wavelength antenna, what is the 7th harmonic?

a> 3.360 MHz.
b> 840 Khz.
c> 3350 Khz.
d> 480 Khz.
e> 68.7 Khz.

99. Pre-emphasis is used in:

a> VHF receivers to improve the signal to noise of narrow bandwidth emissions
b> FM transmitters to increase the signal to noise ratio of the higher audio frequencies
c> AM transmitters to decrease the signal of low audio frequencies
d> SSB transmitters to increase the audio level of higher audio frequencies
e> FM receivers to increase the signal to noise ratio of the higher audio frequencies

100. To increase the bandwidth of a circuit, what would you do to the value of 'Q'?

a> increase
b> decrease
c> remains the same; increase input frequency to improve bandwidth
d> add an inductor in parallel
e> the Q of a circuit does not affect bandwidth

# Test 3-C Element Three

1. What is the maximum power this circuit can handle without breakdown?

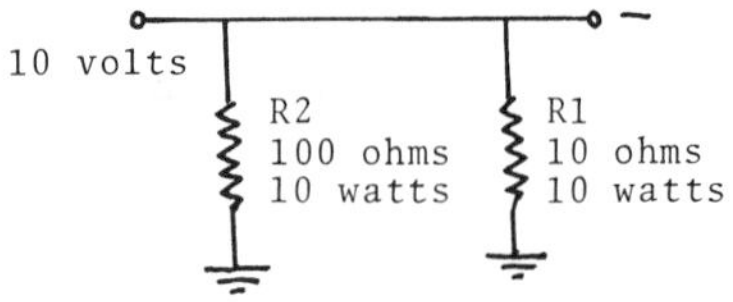

10 volts
R2
100 ohms
10 watts
R1
10 ohms
10 watts

a> 5 watts
b> 11 watts
c> 14.14 watts
d> 20.4 watts
e> none of the above

2. A continuous watch must be maintained on the bridge to bridge transceiver equipment:

a> when the transmitter power is more than 1 watt
b> by FCC licensed operators on 121.5 MHz. and 2182 KHz. when the vessel is 0-500 miles from any shore
c> by the official radio operator in charge of the transmitter when the vessel is 0-25 miles from shore on Channel 13
d> by the master or person in charge of navigating the vessel when traveling within 100 miles of U.S. shores on Channel 13
e> when the mother ship primary transmitter is off

3. Anyone willfully violating a law of the FCC by authority of the Communications Act or by international treaty, upon conviction, is subject to:

a> a fine of not more than $10000 for each day during which the offense occurs
b> a fine of not more than $500 for each day during which the offense occurs
c> cancellation of operator license for one year
d> imprisonment for a period of one year
e> $1000 fine and cancellation of operator license

4. The URGENCY signal indicates that the calling station:

a> is in extreme danger and seeks immediate help from another vessel
b> has a very urgent message to transmit concerning the safety of a ship, aircraft, or the safety of a person
c> is about to transmit a message concerning the safety of navigation or giving important meteorological warnings
d> is within 1 mile of shore and requires immediate instructions with regards to docking procedures
e> any of the above

5. To which input would you send a high level signal to obtain a high output?

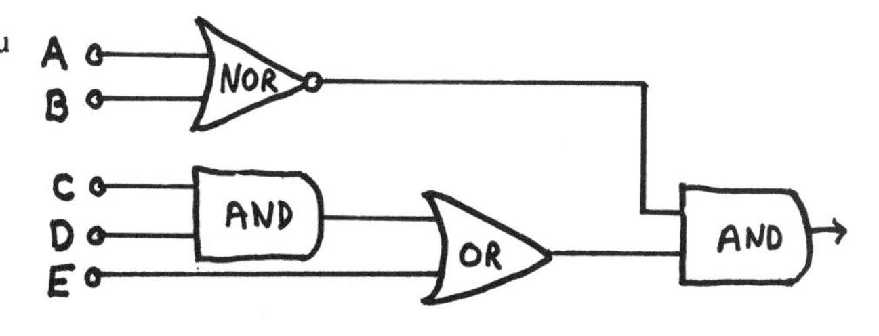


a> point A
b> point B
c> point C
d> point D
e> point E

6. How should the 2182 KHz. auto-alarm be tested?

a> on a different frequency into antenna
b> on a different frequency into dummy load
c> on 2182 KHz. into dummy load
d> on 2182 KHz. into antenna
e> under U.S. Coast Guard authorization

7. If a ship is required to have a transmitter, what distance in a radius should the transmitter be capable of sending a signal?

a> 500 miles
b> 300 miles
c> 150 miles
d> 50 miles
e> 25 miles

8. Carrier suppression for an aeronautical SSB transmitter is:

a> -80 dB
b> -60 dB
c> -40 dB
d> -20 dB
e> -10 dB

9. What do you do when you leave the radio unattended?

a> radio equipment must be secured so that it is not accessible to unauthorized persons who might board or be aboard your vessel
b> transmitter must be turned off and microphone removed
c> connection to the antenna must be removed
d> power source must be shut down until transmission is authorized
e> all of the above

10. Which of the following acts as a voltage-variable capacitor?

a> limiter stage circuit
b> diode
c> varactor
d> diac rectifier
e> zener control bias

11. "Bridge-to-Bridge" radiotelephone regulations cover:

a> inter-city communication for ship arrivals
b> communication with draw-bridge operators
c> both a and b above
d> in-ship personal communications
e> communications with other ships and coast stations for navigational purposes only

12. Each cargo ship of the United States which is equipped with a radiotelephone station for compliance with the Safety Convention shall, while at sea:

a> not transmit on 2182 Khz. during emergency conditions
b> keep the radiotelephone transmitter operating at full 100% carrier power for maximum reception on 2182 KHz.
c> reduce peak envelope power on 156.8 MHz. during emergencies
d> keep a continuous watch on 2182 KHz. using a watch receiver having a loudspeaker and auto alarm distress frequency watch receiver
e> keep a continuous watch on 156.8 MHz. from 9AM to 9PM using a watch receiver having a loudspeaker and auto alarm distress frequency watch receiver

13. What is the voltage drop across R3?

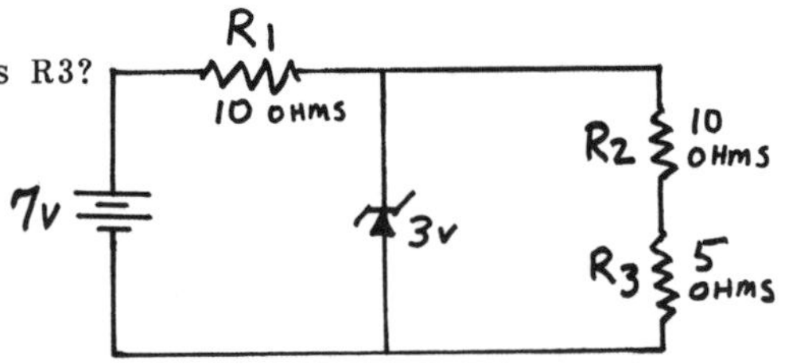

a> 1 volt
b> 2 volts
c> 3.17 volts
d> 4.8 volts
e> 6.7 volts

14. On ships weighing 300+ gross tons, as opposed to ships of 1600 gross tons, the 300+ gross ton ships are allowed to have radiotelephony instead of radiotelegraphy with a transmitted signal that reaches how many miles?

a> 25 miles
b> 50 miles
c> 150 miles
d> 300 miles
e> 500 miles

15. How long before the expiration of a ship station license should FCC application #405-B be submitted to the Commission for renewal?

a> 1 year
b> 6 months
c> 120 days
d> 90 days
e> 30 days

16. To avoid confusion with noisy or weak signals, what should an operator do?

a> increase transmitter power
b> use single-sideband
c> cup hands around speaker
d> spell out the message by using the standard phoenetic alphabet
e> all of the above

17. On towers without automatic warning systems, an observation is made:

a> at least once each 24 hours
b> at all times
c> hourly until warning system is fixed
d> from sunset to sunrise
e> every 30 minutes during nighttime hours

18. A ship station using VHF bridge to bridge Channel 13:

a> may be identified by call sign and country of origin
b> must be identified by call sign and name of vessel
c> may be identified by the name of the ship in lieu of call sign
d> must be identified by name of vessel and registry of call sign
e> does not need to identify itself within 100 miles from shore

19. When using a SSSC station on 2182 kHz. or VHF-FM on Channel 16:

a> preliminary call must not exceed 30 seconds
b> if contact is not made, you must wait at least 2 minutes before repeating the call
c> if no contact is made after three calling cycles, you must wait at least 15 minutes before calling again
d> once contact is established you must switch to an appropriate working frequency
e> all of the above

20. What is the wavelength of a 350 MHz. signal?

a> 1 meter
b> 85 cm
c> 60 cm
d> 1/5th meter
e> 1/3rd cm

21. The speed of a DC motor varies with the:

a> load
b> number of brushes
c> ripple frequency
d> RF field voltage
e> field frequency

22. Actual power of ship radiotelephony transmitters shall be no no more than necessary and in no even more than:

a> 1 kilowatt
b> 500 watts
c> 150 watts
d> no more than 20% above power specified in the license
e> no more than 10% above power specified in the license

23. A 30 watt transmitter is measured to have 10 watts of reflected power. What is the power entered in the transmitter log?

a> 35 watts
b> 30 watts
c> 25 watts
d> 20 watts
e> 10 watts

24. When portable hand-held marine utility stations are used near shore or other ships, what is the proper station identification:

a> the name of vessel followed by a number or name designating the respective mobile unit
b> example; "S.S. United States mobile one this is mobile two"
c> must be given at intervals not exceeding 15 minutes
d> all of the above
e> none of the above

25. How do you send an URGENCY signal?

a> transmit 1000 Hertz tone for 1 minute, followed by the spoken word URGENT three times
b> transmit the word SECURITY three times, followed by the call sign of your station
c> transmit the international distress signal: SOS, followed by your position in degrees latitude and longitude
d> transmit the word URGENT three times, followed by the call sign of your station and the DISTRESS message call
e> transmit the word PAN three times, followed by the call sign of your station and the URGENCY message call

26. When S1 is closed, lights L1 and L2 go on. What is the condition of both lamps when both S1 and S2 are closed?

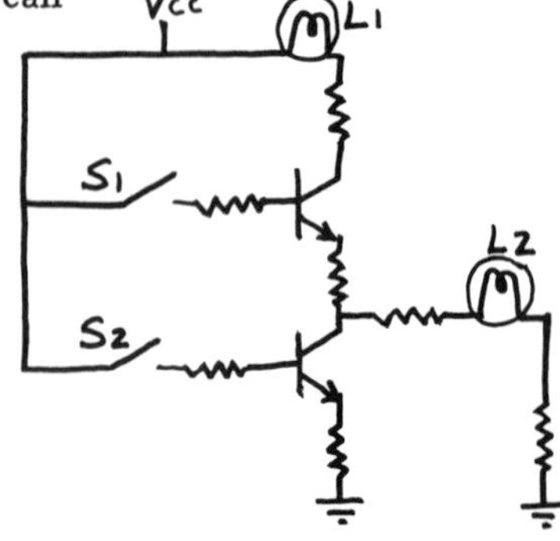


a> both lamps stay on
b> L1 turns off; L2 stays on
c> both lamps turn off
d> L1 stays on
e> L1 flashes; L2 stays on

27. What is the current through R1?

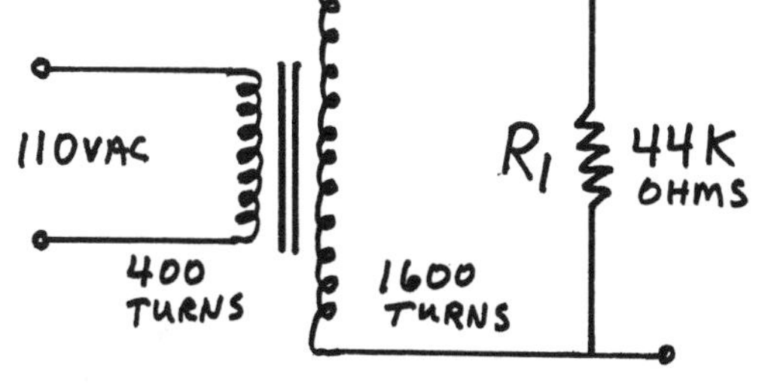


a> 10 ma
b> 20 ma
c> 30 ma
d> 40 ma
e> 50 ma

28. What is the Distress frequency and type of emission in the 156-162 MHz. frequency band?

a> 156.8 MHz., F3E (or G3E) emission
b> 156.8 MHz., J3E emission
c> 158.2 MHz., J3E emission
d> 160 MHz., F3E (or G3E) emission
e> 161.05 MHz., J3E emission

29. The inductance of a coil is proportional to:

a> number of turns on the coil
b> square root of the number of turns on the coil
c> square of the number of turns on the coil
d> inverse of the number of turns on the coil
e> inverse of the square of the number of turns on the coil

30. After adequate warm-up time, a 100 KHz. crystal frequency meter is calibrated. Which of the following calibration steps is improper?

a> tune the receiver to WWV
b> turn on calibrator
c> beat the crystal harmonic against WWV or a suitable standard
d> tune the meter 100 KHz. above and below the frequency
e> adjust the crystal trimmer for zero beat

31. When connecting electrolytic capacitors:

a> place bleeder resistors is parallel
b> polarity markings on the terminals should be observed
c> ground the negative terminal
d> check discharge time with direct short
e> all of the above

32. When properly operating a transistor in an amplifier:

a> base is usually reverse biased
b> emitter is neutralized
c> collector is forward biased
d> collector is usually reversed biased
e> emitter and collector are neutralized

33. By international agreement which ships must carry radio transmission and receiving equipment for the safety of life at sea?

a> cargo ships of more than 300 gross tons or vessels carrying more than 6 passengers for hire
b> all ships traveling more than 100 miles out to sea
c> ships of more than 500 gross tons or vessels carrying more than 12 passengers on international deep-sea voyages
d> cargo and passenger ships weighing more than 100 gross tons
e> all ships are required to have radios for safety at sea

34. All radiotelephone emissions of a ship station shall be clearly identified by:

a> transmitting call letters on 121.5 MHz. hourly
b> official call letters assigned by the Commission
c> call letters and location of ship
d> time of day, location and call sign
e> telegraphy every 30 minutes

35. When using a hand-held portable walkie-talkie, what gives you the authorization to use it on board a ship?

a> ship station license authorization
b> individual licenses
c> the chief radiotelephone operator
d> 2182 KHz. International Portable Unit Authority
e> international waters; no regulation apply

36. What is the procedure for testing a 2182 KHz. ship radiotelephone transmitter with full carrier power while out at sea?

a> transmit a 1 KHz. test tone
b> reduce to low power, then transmit 1 KHz. test tone
c> switch transmitter to another frequency before testing
d> simply say: "This is (call letters) testing." If all meters indicate normal values, it is assumed transmitter is operating properly
e> it is not permitted to test on the air

37. What is the purpose of the radiotelephone Auto Alarm signal generator?

a> warning to operator that transmitter is drifting off frequency
b> to transmit special audio tones on the transmitter carrier to get attention of other stations that a distress call or other important safety message is about to follow
c> to receive Auto Alarm messages; alert persons on watch duty
d> to signal the sinking of a vessel at sea
e> all of the above

38. Buffer amplifiers are used for:

a> reduction of parasitics
b> frequency multipliers
c> frequency stability
d> tight coupling of stages
e> loose coupling of stages

39. What happens to the output of the tripler circuit if C9 opens?

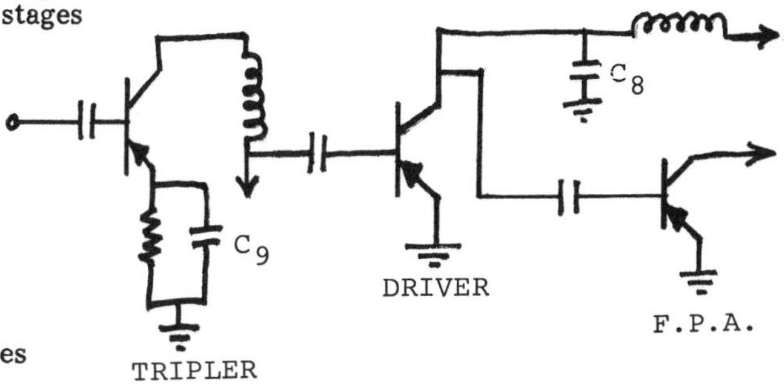

a> output increases
b> output decreases
c> circuit shuts off
d> voltage increases
e> frequency decreases

C8
C9
DRIVER
F.P.A.
TRIPLER

40. What is the most important practice that a radio operator must learn?

a> monitor the channel before transmitting
b> operate with lowest power necessary
c> test a radiotelephone transmitter daily
d> always listen to 121.5 MHz.
e> all of the above

41. A transformer with 100 volts applied to the primary reads 300 volts at the secondary center tap. What is the turns ratio of the transformer?

a> 1:1
b> 1:2
c> 1:6
d> 1:9
e> 1:1.5

42. What is the purpose of stacking elements on an antenna?

a> sharper directional pattern
b> increased gain
c> improved bandpass
d> discriminates against signals from back side
e> all of the above

43. Signal energy is coupled into a traveling-wave tube at:

a> collector end of helix
b> anode end of the helix
c> cathode end of the helix
d> focusing coils
e> either a or b

44. A 12.6 volt, 8 ampere-hour battery is supplying power to a receiver which uses 50 watts and a radar system that uses 300 watts. How long will the battery last?

a> 100.8 hours
b> 27.7 hours
c> 1 hour
d> 17 minutes or 0.3 hours
e> 38 minutes or 0.63 hours

45. What is the wavelength of a 500 MHz. signal?

a> 1 meter
b> 60 cm
c> 6 cm
d> 1/5th meter
e> 1/3rd cm

46. In a quarter-wave Marconi antenna, where is the voltage and current concentrated?

a> at the ends
b> voltage at the ends, current in the middle
c> current at the ends, voltage in the middle
d> evenly throughout
e> current at the top, voltage at the bottom

47. The phase angle and RMS value of voltage and current and the impedance of an AC circuit determines:

a> RMS voltage
b> heating voltage and current
c> actual power
d> RMS power
e> output frequency

48. Transmission of a fixed image which is stored permanently:

a> Radiotelephone
b> Facsimile
c> Television
d> Microwave
e> Loran direction finding

49. An approximate square wave of 25 MHz. can be obtained by combining:

a> 12.5 MHz., 6.25 MHz., 3.125 MHz., 1.56 MHz.
b> 125 MHz., 250 MHz., 200 MHz., 250 MHz.
c> 150 MHz., 200 MHz., 250 MHz., 200 MHz.
d> 25 MHz., 75 MHz., 125 MHz., 175 MHz.
e> 50 MHz., 100 MHz., 400 MHz.

50. The purpose of the resistors in this circuit:

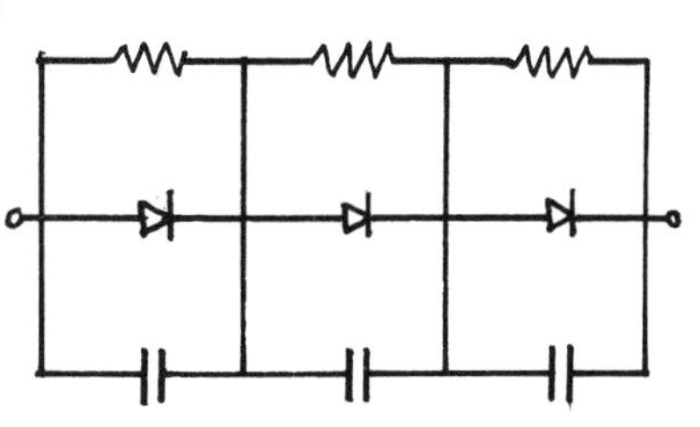

a> equalizing resistors; assures equal voltage across each diode
b> protect diodes from voltage surges; keeps constant voltage at each diode
c> improve ripple voltage frequency
d> to act as bleeder resistors, if one opens other resistors maintain voltage
e> either a or b

51. The frequency of a transmitter operating at 156.8 MHz. is off frequency by 1 millionth. How much is the frequency off by?

a> 0.156 Hz.
b> 15.6 Hz.
c> 156.8 Hz.
d> 1568 Hz.
e> 0.00156 Hz.

52. On a half-wave Hertz antenna:

a> voltage is maximum at both ends and current is maximum at the center of the antenna
b> current is maximum at both ends and voltage in the center
c> voltage and current are uniform throughout the antenna
d> voltage and current are high at the ends
e> voltage and current are high in the middle

53. What determines the time constant of a capacitive-resistive circuit:

a> is the product of the current times the resistance
b> is the product of the capacitive reactance times the current
c> is the product of the capacitance times the resistance
d> the temperature coefficient of the capacitor times the resistance
e> capacitance times the product of the current and voltage

54. What type of antenna is designed for minimum radiation?

a> dummy antenna
b> quarter-wave antenna
c> half-wave antenna
d> directional antenna
e> Marconi antenna

55. When modulating a transmitter 100%, meters will fluctuate in:

a> the master oscillator
b> modulating stage
c> modulator circuit
d> output power amplifier
e> none of the transmitter stages

56. All red obstruction tower lighting shall be exhibited:

a> from 6 PM to 6 AM
b> from sunrise to sunset
c> from sunset to sunrise
d> continuously 24 hours a day if tower is within ten miles of an airport
e> from 4:30 PM to 8:30 AM unless otherwise specified

57. If your transmitter is producing spurious harmonics or is operating at a deviation from the technical requirements of the station authorization:

a> continue operating until returning to port
b> repair problem within 24 hours
c> de-couple antenna
d> cease transmission
e> reduce power immediately

58. An alternative to keeping watch on a working frequency in the band 1600-4000 kHz., an operator must tune station receiver to monitor 2182 kHz:

a> at all times
b> during distress calls only
c> during daytime hours of service
d> during the silence periods each hour
e> all of the above

59. What should an operator do if the frequency of a transmitter on board a ship is found to deviate from licensed technical requirements?

a> the radiations of the transmitter involved shall be suspended immediately, except for necessary tests and adjustments
b> transmission shall not be resumed until deviation is corrected
c> transmitter shall cease radiation until approval by the FCC
d> both a and b above
e> all of the above

60. How many station licenses are required for a vessel having one radio-telephone fixed location transmitter and six hand-held portable transmitter/receiver units?

a> one
b> two
c> four
d> seven
e> none

61. What is the outcome when you stack antennas at various angles from each other?

a> a more omni-directional reception
b> a more uni-directional reception
c> an overall reception signal increase
d> both a and c
e> both b and c

62. Class C amplifiers have:

a> low driving signals
b> low efficiency
c> low distortion
d> high distortion
e> low power output

63. Power of an AC circuit is the product of:

a> RMS value of the current squared and the resistance
b> RMS value of the current and voltage
c> heating value of the load resistance and the current
d> actual current and the load resistance squared
e> actual reading of a voltmeter and the resistance

64. Medium frequency (MF) band is:

a> 30 KHz. to 300 KHz.
b> 30 MHz. to 300 MHz.
c> 300 KHz. to 3000 KHz.
d> 300 MHz. to 3000 MHz.
e> 3000 MHz. to 30000 MHz.

65. Class C amplifiers are used for:

a> audio amplifiers
b> amplitude modulators
c> frequency multipliers
d> discriminators
e> high power output sine-wave signals

66. What is the maximum frequency deviation of an F3E transmitter operating in the 156 MHz. to 162 MHz. band?

a> 20 Hz.
b> 20 PPM
c> 5 kHz.
d> 10 kHz.
e> 50 kHz.

67. After installing a new radio facility, you are not authorized to sign on the transmitter until:

a> approved for service by station Chief of Engineering
b> inspected and certified by the Commission
c> type-accepted approval granted
d> tested by an FCC licensed General Radiotelephone operator
e> all of the above

68. Where is a radio technician required to have his license if he services radio equipment at more than one location?

a> on his person
b> at the nearest Coast Guard station
c> at his main place of business
d> on file with the Coast Guard and a photocopy on his person
e> at his place of business

69. What is the maximum frequency deviation that a marine 2182 kHz. SSB transmitter is permitted to have in order to operate legally?

a> 10 Hertz
b> 20 Hertz
c> 30 Hertz
d> 40 Hertz
e> 50 Hertz

70. Under what conditions is it required that an operator or maintenance person hold a General Radiotelephone Operator License?

a> to adjust or repair FCC licensed transmitters in the aviation, maritime and international fixed public radio services
b> operate maritime land and compulsory ship radio transmitters with more than 1500 watts of peak envelope power
c> operate voluntarily equipped ship maritime mobile or aeronautical transmitters with more than 1,000 watts of peak envelope power
d> operate radiotelephone equipment on all ships of 500 or more gross tons, but not over 1600 gross tons
e> all of the above

71. Portable ship radio transceivers:

a> must be operated on the safety and calling frequency 156.8 (Channel 16) or VHF intership frequency
b> are not to be used from shore
c> must only communicate with the ship station with which it is associated or with associated portable ship units
d> portable UHF units may operate on Channels 1 - 4, 457.525 MHz. to 467.825 MHz.
e> all of the above

72. What is the current in the secondary of this circuit?

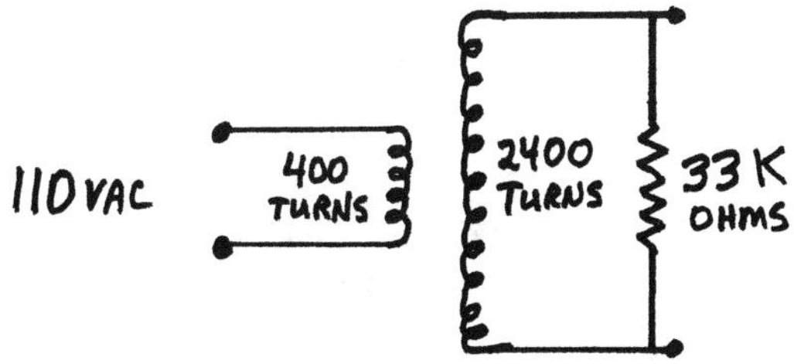

110 VAC — 400 TURNS — 2400 TURNS — 33 K OHMS

a> 2 ma
b> 20 ma
c> 3.33 ma
d> 0.33 ma
e> 0.2 amperes

73. An amplifier stage changing 1 mw to 100 mw has a gain of:

a> +40 dB
b> +20 dB
c> 0 dB
d> 10 dB
e> 100 dB

74. The batteries in an EPIRB transmitter on a ship should be replaced:

a> after every test
b> after emergency use and at six month
c> after emergency use and when manufacturer recommends
d> when 70% capacity remains
e> when 75% capacity remains

75. How far below peak envelope power is emission J3E carrier suppressed?

a> 20 dB
b> 30 dB
c> 40 dB
d> 50 dB
e> 70 dB

76. A radio receiver is tuned to 100.1 MHz. on the FM broadcast band, and cross talk interference is heard from a crystal controlled airport transmitter operating at 121.4 MHz. near by. What causes the interference?

a> poor grounding
b> IF stage not properly shielded
c> 121.5 MHz. entering IF stage
d> front end overload
e> bleed over transmission detected in audio amplifier

77. What is the authorized bandwidth of J3E stations in the Aviation Services below 50 MHz.?

a> 50 kHz.
b> 10 kHz.
c> 5 kHz.
d> 3 kHz.
e> 1.5 kHz.

78. Low input impedance and high output impedance is characteristic of:

a> common emitter amplifier
b> common base amplifier
c> MF transmission lines
d> half-wave transmission lines
e> all of the above

79. What is the total voltage when 12 Nickel-Cadmium batteries are connected in series?

a> 12 volts
b> 12.6 volts
c> 15 volts
d> 72 volts
e> 108 volts

80. What is the radiotelephony calling distress frequency?

a> 500 KHz.
b> 500RI22JA
c> 2182 KHz.
d> 2182R2647
e> 121R2182

81. What is the frequency bandwidth such that, below its lower and above its upper frequency limits, the mean powers radiated are each equal to 0.5 percent of the total mean power radiated by a given emission?

a> occupied bandwidth
b> authorized bandwidth
c> licensed bandwidth
d> carrier
e> any of the above

82. What is the maximum occupied bandwidth authorized to be used by a station?

a> occupied bandwidth
b> authorized bandwidth
c> licensed bandwidth
d> carrier
e> any of the above

83. How do you measure the percentage of modulation in an FM transmitter operating at 121.5 MHz.?

a> 0-10 MHz. bandwidth oscilloscope
b> FM receiver with 121.5 - 450 kHz. range
c> deviation meter
d> a and b
e> a and c

84. A wattmeter measures 20 watts direct power and 5 watts reflected power. What is the actual radiated transmitter power?

a> 15 watts
b> 20 watts
c> 25 watts
d> 5 watts
e> cannot be determined

85. What is the priority of communications in the mobile service?

a> distress, urgency, safety and radio direction finding
b> safety, distress, urgency and radio direction finding
c> distress, safety, radio direction finding, search and rescue
d> radio direction finding, distress and safety
e> distress, radio direction finding, urgency and safety

86. Which of the following classes of amplifiers is generally the most efficient?

a> Class A
b> Class B
c> Class C
d> Class AB
e> Class A-1

87. A ship radar unit uses 315 watts and a radio uses 50 watts. If the equipment is connected to a 50 ampere-hour battery rated at 12.6 volts, how long will the battery last?

a> 28.97 hours
b> 29 minutes
c> 1 hour 43 minutes
d> 10 hours 50 minutes
e> 50 hours

88. A ship with a gross weight of 300 tons to 1600 tons should be able to transmit a minimum range of:

a> 75 miles
b> 150 miles
c> 200 miles
d> 300 miles
e> 600 miles

89. The output voltage of a separately excited AC generator (running at a constant speed) is controlled by:

a> input voltage frequency
b> the load
c> primary voltage
d> field current
e> field frequency

90. If an automatic or mechanical control device, indicator or alarm associated with the tower lighting system is not functioning properly:

a> tower lighting shall be exhibited continuously
b> tower lighting shall be inspected hourly
c> tower lighting shall be controlled manually until automatic or mechanical device is repaired
d> the FAA flight service station must be notified within 30 minutes
e> all of the above

91. What frequencies are used by aircraft when landing at airports?

a> 118.000 to 121.400 MHz.
b> 121.600 to 121.925 MHz.
c> 123.600 to 128.800 MHz.
d> 132.025 to 135.975 Mhz.
e> all of the above

92. How often must the carrier frequency of a SSB transmitter on board a ship be checked to determine that it is properly transmitting signals within authorized specifications on 2182 kHz.?

a> once per week into dummy antenna
b> once per day into dummy antenna on another operating frequency
c> frequency tests are not required unless any change has been made that may affect stability of transmitter carrier frequency
d> once per day into dummy antenna with 1 watt of carrier power
e> once per day at sign on into dummy antenna at 2182 kHz.

93. Radiotelephone stations required to keep logs of their transmissions must include:

a> station, date and time
b> name of operator on duty
c> station call signs with which communication took place
d> what type of traffic handled
e> all of the above

94. Logs are usually required to be kept for:

a> 1 year
b> 2 years
c> 3 years
d> until authorized by the Commission to be destroyed
e> until renewal of station license; 5 years

95. If a ship radio transmitter signal becomes distorted:

a> cease operations
b> reduce transmitter power
c> use minimum modulation
d> reduce audio amplitude
e> test transmitter immediately

96. J3E communications using SSB are normally on what frequency band?

a> 500 Khz.
b> 20 MHz.
c> 40 MHz.
d> 60 MHz.
e> 8 GHz.

97. What causes the multiplication effect in a frequency multiplier?

a> stage efficiency factor
b> input frequency distortion
c> LC tank circuit
d> buffer amplifier stage
e> any of the above

98. The time constant of a resistance capacitance circuit is:

a> capacitance multiplied by resistance
b> capacitance multiplied by resistance squared
c> resistance divided by capacitance multiplied by 63%
d> capacitance squared multiplied by resistance
e> resistance squared divided by capacitance

99. If an airline transmitter has a frequency tolerance of 10 parts per million, what is the maximum allowable transmitter frequency deviation of a 156.4 MHz. signal?

a> 1.56 Hz.
b> 156 Hz.
c> 1564 kHz.
d> 1564 Hz.
e> 156.4 MHz.

100. Adding parasitic elements to a quarter-wavelength antenna will:

a> reduce its directional characteristics
b> increase its directional characteristics
c> increase its sensitivity
d> reduce its effectiveness
e> increase its bandwidth

# Test 3-D Element Three

1. How many degrees are there in three-quarters of a pure sine wave?

   a> 75
   b> 90
   c> 120
   d> 175
   e> 270

2. An FM transmitter pre-emphasis circuit:

   a> low audio frequencies are over amplified improving the signal to noise ratio in the receiver
   b> high audio frequencies are over amplified improving the signal to noise ratio in the receiver
   c> acts as a frequency multiplier
   d> increases the noise-to-signal ratio in the receiver
   e> decreases the noise-to-signal ratio in the oscillator

3. If a circuit has a 10 dB increase, what is the change in power?

   a> 10% power increase
   b> 100% power increase
   c> power is increased 10 times
   d> power is increased to 110% of circuit input voltage
   e> none

4. What is the voltage drop across R3?

   a> 1 volt
   b> 2 volts
   c> 3.4 volts
   d> 5.3 volts
   e> 7 volts

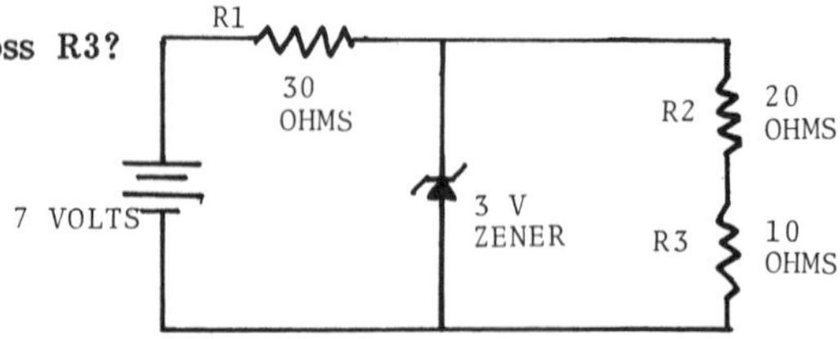

R1
30 OHMS
7 VOLTS
3 V ZENER
R2
20 OHMS
R3
10 OHMS

5. There is an improper impedance match between a 30 watt transmitter and the antenna and 5 watts is reflected. How much power is actually radiated?

   a> 35 watts
   b> 30 watts
   c> 25 watts
   d> 20 watts
   e> 10 watts

6. Tests of survival craft radio equipment, EXCEPT emergency position indicating radiobeacons and two-way radiotelephone equipment, must be conducted:

   a> at weekly intervals while the ship is at sea
   b> within 24 hours prior to departure when a test has not been conducted within a week of departure
   c> both a and b above
   d> when required by the Commission
   e> after emergency use only

7. What is A3E (previously A3) emission and authorized bandwidth?

   a> single-sideband, suppressed carrier telephony; 8 kHz.
   b> single-sideband, reduced full carrier telephony; 20 kHz.
   c> vestigial-sideband, analog telemetry data; 3 kHz.
   d> amplitude-modulation, keyed carrier; 20 kHz.
   e> double-sideband and carrier; telephony; 8 kHz.

8. Transmitters using F3E (or G3E) emission in the 156-162 MHz. band shall be capable of proper technical operation with a frequency deviation (defined as 100% modulation) of plus or minus:

   a> 100 kHz.
   b> 75 kHz.
   c> 25 kHz.
   d> 5 kHz.
   e> 1.5 kHz.

9. To change this amplifier to a frequency doubler (24 MHz.):

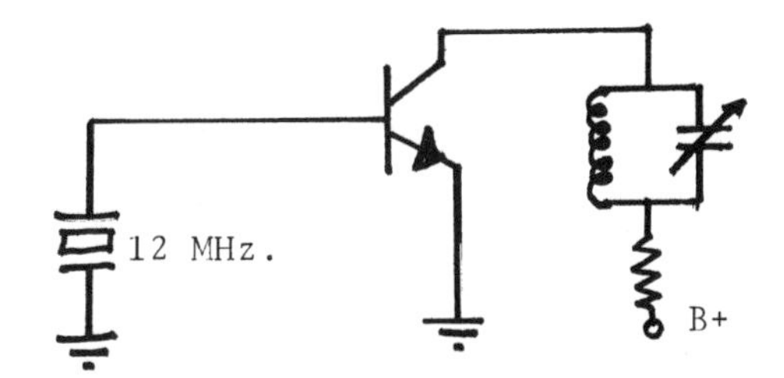


   a> increase C1 by four
   b> double C1
   c> decrease C1 by 1/2
   d> increase C1 by 1/4
   e> decrease C1 by 1/4

10. Each cargo ship of the United States which is equipped with a radiotelephone station for compliance with Part II of Title III of the Communications Act shall while being navigated outside of a harbor or port keep a continuous and efficient watch on:

   a> 2182 kHz.
   b> 156.8 MHz.
   c> both a and b
   d> scanner must monitor all frequencies within the 2000 kHz. to 3500 kHz. band
   e> cargo ships are exempt from radio watch regulations

11. Neutralization in an RF amplifier is not necessary usually when:

a> operated at high frequencies
b> operated at full power
c> tetrode is used
d> tank circuit has high Q
e> operated at low power

12. If any change is made to a marine or aircraft transmitter that could change the operating frequency:

a> apply for station modification
b> notify regional FCC office
c> test with dummy antenna prior to actual transmission
d> do not test on 2182 KHz.
e> all of the above

13. If the resistance is 30 ohms, inductance is 70 mfd., source is 100 volts and the current is 3.75 amperes, power is calculated:

a> product of V and A
b> product of V, A and power factor divided by resistance
c> product of power factor, resistance and voltage
d> product of V, A and R squared
e> cannot be calculated; wattmeter must be used

14. The limiter circuit of a receiver designed to receive F3E marine emissions:

a> has high gain and almost constant output
b> has low gain and almost constant output
c> follows the de-emphasis circuit
d> follows the pre-emphasis circuit
e> F3E receivers do not have limiter circuits

15. What one of the following would be a proper method of determining if the operating frequency of a ship board transmitter operating on 2182 KHz. is within authorized tolerance?

a> zero-beat the oscillator stage with a suitable reference
b> zero-beat the frequency multiplier with a suitable reference
c> zero-beat the transmitter output frequency with a suitable reference
d> zero-beat the oscillator stage with WWV receiver set 2000 KHz. testing standard
e> any of the above

16. This circuit was totally discharged before a test. If the switch is closed for 0.5 seconds and then opened, what is the voltage across the capacitor after the switch is opened?

$R_1$ 10M OHMS $C_1$ 0.1 mfd. 10v

a> 3.7 volts
b> 4.3 volts
c> 5.2 volts
d> 6.12 volts
e> 7 volts

17. All vessels, dredges, and floating plants subject to the Vessel Bridge-to-Bridge Radiotelephone Act must, while being navigated upon waters of the United States are required to:

a> have a 50 watt 2182 KHz. Bridge transmitter
b> keep a constant watch on the designated navigational frequency by the master, pilot or person designated by the master to pilot or direct the movement of the vessel
c> employ FCC licensed radiotelephone operators to Bridge transmitter
d> both and a and b above
e> all of the above

18. Where is the operator license posted if more than one transmitter is maintained?

a> in lieu of posting, operators may have a license on their person
b> posted on the wall or placed in a binder or folder which is maintained at the transmitter posting sight and a photocopy carried on their person
c> attach photocopy to maintenance log at each station
d> post photocopy at each transmitter
e> both a and b above

19. The bending of radio waves passing over the top or a mountain range that disperses a weak portion of the signal behind the mountain is:

a> Eddy-current phase effect
b> knife-edge diffraction
c> shadowing
d> mirror refraction effect
e> VHF phase-angle refraction

20. Knife-edge refraction:

a> is the bending of UHF frequency radio waves around a building, mountain or obstruction
b> causes the volocity of wave propagation to be different than original wave
c> both a and b above
d> attunuates UHF signals
e> is shadowing

21. An airport tower is transmitting ground-to-air communications on 121.4 MHz. nearby and is causing interference in an FM broadcast receiver tuned to 100 MHz. What is the problem?

a> improper shielding
b> intermodulation
c> 121.4 MHz. entering the IF stages
d> bleed-over transmission being detected in the audio circuit
e> image frequency being detected

22. Fly-wheel effect of a tank circuit restores a wave form in:

a> RF amplifiers
b> audio amplifiers
c> buffer amplifiers
d> phase shifting networks
e> Class A-2 amplifiers

23. What is the current through R1 if the turns ratio of the transformer is 1:6?

a> 50 ma
b> 20 ma
c> 30 ma
d> 40 ma
e> 1.3 ma

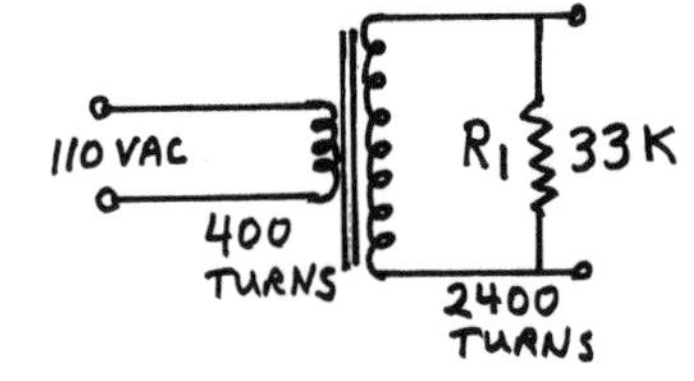


24. Frequency doublers:

a> must be neutralized
b> are not neutralized
c> operated Class A
d> operated Class AB
e> produce small harmonic output

25. What happens to a carbon resistor at 300 MHz. to 3 GHz. UHF frequencies?

a> appear to increase in value
b> appear to decrease in value
c> open circuit
d> heating followed by loss of resistor
e> both a and c

26. Kilowatt hour is a measurement of:

a> force
b> magnetic lines of current
c> product of current and voltage
d> energy
e> electron flow

27. When is the battery of an ELT (Emergency Locator transmitter) changed?

a> yearly
b> every six months
c> monthly
d> after the transmitter has been used in an emergency situation or after the battery voltage is 70% of authorized value
e> after the date specified by the manufacturer upon which 50% of the useful battery life has expired or after the transmitter has been used in an emergency situation

28. What is the maximum SSB radiotelephone transmitter carrier frequency tolerance in the Maritime band?

a> 10 KHz.
b> 20 KHz.
c> 50 Hz.
d> 20 Hz.
e> 3 Hz.

29. How do FM receivers normally indicate their sensitivity?

a> -20 dB per bandwidth
b> 0.5 micro-volts for 20 dB of quieting
c> -20 dB per 15 kHz. of quieting
d> micro-volts per 10 dB of signal strength
e> power input vs. power output

30. What call would you transmit if your ship was sinking in water?

a> SOS three times
b> MAYDAY three times
c> PAN three times
d> URGENCY three times
e> SAFETY three times

31. The operating frequencies of all non-airborne transmitters operating on the aviation bands shall be measured at the following times to assure compliance with tolerances rules:

a> when a transmitter is originally installed
b> when any change or adjustment is made which may affect the transmitter operating frequency
c> when a transmitter carrier frequency has shifted beyond tolerance
d> both a and b above
e> all of the above

32. When calling another ship:

a> you may interrupt other personal, non-emergency transmission
b> always use 121.5 MHz. as official calling frequency
c> use maximum carrier power to prevent poor reception
d> briefly monitor the working frequency before transmission
e> all of the above

33. When shall transmitter tower lights be exhibited?

a> from 4:30 PM to 8:30 AM daily
b> from 6:00 PM to 6:00 AM daily local time
c> from sunset to sunrise unless otherwise specified
d> continuously 24 hours a day
e> when requested by the Federal Aviation Administration

34. A characteristic of a tunnel diode that makes it useful in an oscillator circuit is:

a> varies capacitance with AC voltage changes
b> varies capacitance with DC voltage changes
c> negative resistance over part of its voltage vs. current curve
d> positive resistance over part of its voltage vs. current curve
e> none of the above

35. When may you test a radiotelephone transmitter on the air?

a> between midnight and 6:00 AM local time
b> only when authorized by the Commission
c> at any time as necessary to assure proper operation
d> after reducing transmitter power to 1 watt
e> after notification to U.S. Coast Guard; 3 days in advance

36. What is the required daytime range of a radiotelephone station aboard a 900 ton ocean going cargo vessel?

a> 5 miles
b> 25 miles
c> 50 miles
d> 150 miles
e> 500 miles

37. What is the purpose of an Auto Alarm receiver?

a> to attract the attention of the person on watch that a distress or other important safety message is about to follow
b> to actuate automatic devices giving the alarm
c> both a and b above
d> a life boat radio receiver used for emergency purposes
e> a receiver designed to alarm when S.O.S. in code is received

38. If this circuit is resonant at 12 MHz. and you wish to increase this to 24 MHz., how should the the value of C1 be changed?

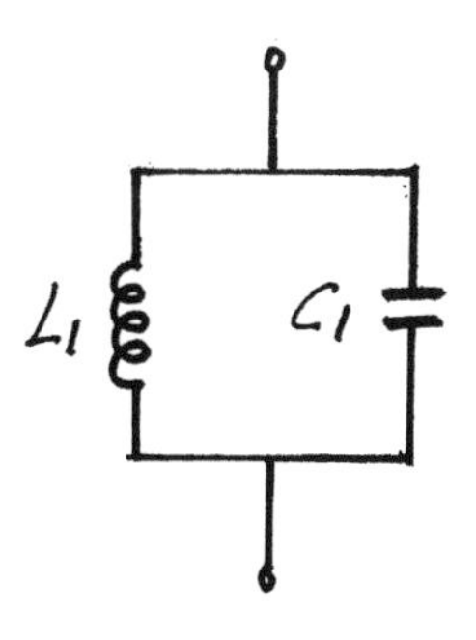


a> quarter it
b> half it
c> double it
d> triple it
e> quadruple it

39. Distress signal tests are conducted:

a> weekly into a dummy antenna
b> conduced within 24 hours prior to departure
c> daily on a different non-distress frequency
d> monthly into a dummy antenna
e> both a and b

40. What do you do if the transmitter aboard you ship is operating off-frequency, overmodulating or distorting?

a> reduce to low power
b> stop transmitting
c> reduce audio volume level
d> make a notation in station operating log
e> all of the above

41. What is the seventh harmonic of a 100 MHz. quarter wavelength antenna?

a> 14.28 MHz.
b> 107 MHz.
c> 149 MHz.
d> 700 MHz.
e> 707 MHz.

42. Inductance of a coil increases proportional to the:

a> cross sectional area of the wire
b> number of turn of the coil
c> number of turns of the coil squared
d> length and gauge of the wire
e> both a and b

43. What is the authorized frequency for an on-board ship repeater for use with a mobile transmitter operating at 467.750 MHz.?

a> 457.525 MHz.
b> 467.775 MHz.
c> 467.800 MHz.
d> 467.825 MHz.
e> 477.875 MHz.

44. When S1 is closed, both L1 and L2 will light. What happens when both switches are closed?

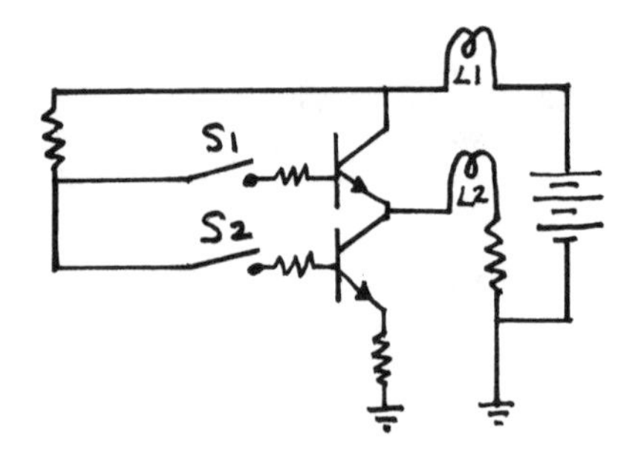


a> both lights will blink
b> both L1 and L2 light
c> neither will light
d> only L1 will light
e> only L2 will light

45. Antenna tower lights must be checked:

a> once per hour
b> once per 24 hours
c> once per week
d> once per month
e> continuously

46. What information must appear on the data plate attached to an FCC licensed marine or aviation services transmitter?

a> transmitter power
b> transmitter frequency
c> FCC Type Approval Number
d> bandwidth and emission designation
e> all of the above

47. What class of license is required to operate an aircraft station at which the installation is not used solely for telephony, or has more than 250 watts carrier power or 1 KW peak envelope power?

a> General Radiotelephone License
b> Marine Radiotelephone Operator Permit
c> Restricted Radiotelephone permit
d> General Radiotelegraph License
e> no license is required

48. What voltage will appear across the load resistor?

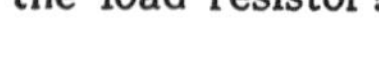

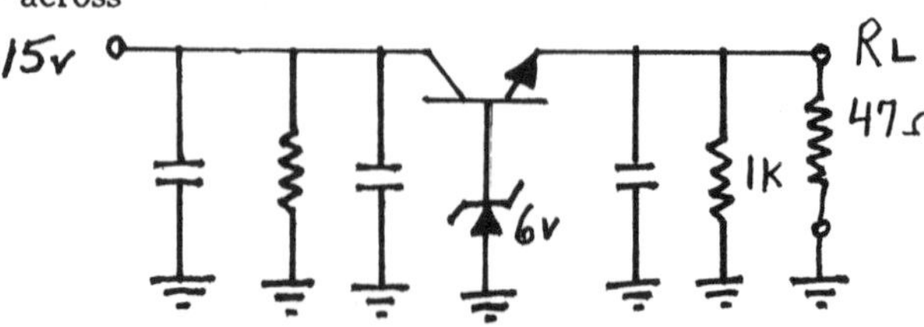


a> 15 volts
b> 9 volts
c> 7 volts
d> 6.2 volts
e> 5.3 volts

49. What is the maximum output power of aeronautical Multicom stations?

a> 1 KW
b> 500 watts
c> 150 watts
d> 25 watts
e> 10 watts

50. Survival craft emergency position indicating radiobeacons are tested:

a> with a manually activated test switch
b> with a dummy load having the equivalent impedance of the antenna affixed to the EPIRB
c> reduce radiation to a level not to exceed 25 microvolts per meter at a distance of 150 feet
d> both a and c above
e> all of the above

51. When can a Bridge-to-Bridge transmission be more than 1 watt?

a> when looking around a corner
b> only while in dry dock
c> during equipment tests transmitted on 2182 KHz.
d> when the ship is traveling 0-25 miles from shore
e> never

52. How long will a 12.6 volt, 50 ampere/hour battery last if it supplies power to an emergency transmitter with 531 watts of plate input power and an Emergency Locator Beacon with a power rating of 530 watts?

a> 6 hours
b> 4 hours
c> 1 hour
d> 35 minutes
e> 15 minutes

53. This receiver is set to receive 1000 kHz., but is interfered with by a transmitter which sends the image frequency of the desired frequency. The interfering transmitter is operating on what frequency?

a> 455 kHz.
b> 1000.1 kHz
c> 955 kHz.
d> 1455 kHz.
e> 1910 kHz.

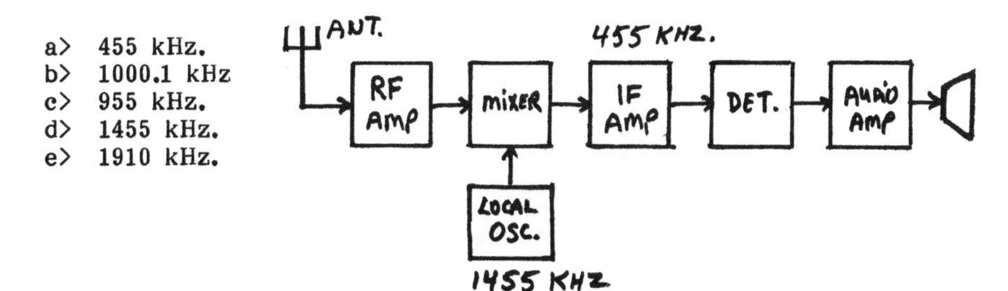


54. What is the safety signal call word spoken three times, followed by the station call letters spoken three times, announcing a storm warning, danger to navigation, or special aid to navigation?

a> PAN
b> MAYDAY
c> SOS
d> SECURITY
e> SAFETY

55. The main disadvantage of using a receiver squelch circuit is:

a> weak signals are distorted
b> weak signals are difficult to hear
c> strong signals are distorted
d> increased noise
e> all of the above

56. Class C amplifier plate current wave form is:

a> varying AC current with DC components
b> varying DC current with AC components
c> square wave with DC components
d> pure sine wave
e> varying sine wave with square wave components

57. Ignoring line losses, voltage at a point on a transmission line without standing waves is:

a> equal to the product of the line current and impedance
b> equal to the product of the line current and power factor
c> equal to the product of the line current and the surge impedance
d> zero at both ends
e> zero in the middle

58. If power remains constant, what change should be made to the resistance if the voltage is doubled?

a> halved
b> doubled
c> quadrupled
d> quartered
e> squared

59. Stacking antenna elements:

a> will suppress odd harmonics
b> decrease signal to noise ratio
c> increases sensitivity to weak signals
d> increases selectivity
e> all of the above

60. This circuit is:

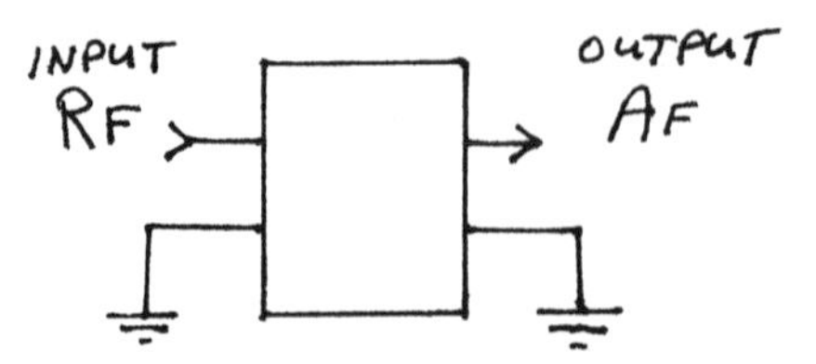


a> frequency multiplier
b> IF amplifier
c> detector
d> class AB amplifier
e> all of the above

61. How is an EPIRB emergency transmitter tested without the use of a dummy load aboard a ship?

a> with a maximum of one watt of transmitter power on any frequency not used for distress messages
b> it can only be tested with an artificial antenna or load
c> with prior approval of the U.S. Coast Guard
d> brief operational tests are authorized provided they are conducted within the first five minutes of any hour for a period not to exceed ten seconds
e> brief operational tests are authorized only on 2182 kHz. during the first ten minutes of any hour for a period not to exceed 5 seconds

62. You are not authorized to sign on a transmitter in a new radio facility:

a> without official notification by the nearest U.S. Coast Guard or port authority
b> without General Radiotelephone Licensed operators on duty
c> until application forms are submitted to the Commission
d> both a and b
e> until station authorization is granted by the Commission

63. At 100 MHz., what offers the least impedance?

a> circular mil of silver wire 6 inches long
b> circular mil of aluminum wire 6 inches long
c> sheet of copper 2 inches wide and 6 inches long
d> 1-ohm wire wound resistor
e> 10 micro-farad capacitor

64. A device containing a low pass filter, varactor, phase modulator and a linear amplifier:

a> Radar
b> AM transmitter
c> AM receiver
d> FM transmitter
e> FM receiver

65. What allows microwaves to pass in only one direction?

a> RF emitter
b> ferrite isolator
c> capacitor
d> varactor-triac
e> phase-shift reactor

66. The maintenance person performing service duties at more than one marine or aeronautical station may meet the requirements for the posting of an operator license by:

a> attaching a photocopy of the license to the radio log
b> carrying the license on person
c> sending a copy of the license to the U.S. Coast Guard
d> notification of duties and work performed submitted to the Commission prior to making any changes to transmitter
e> all of the above

67. Class C amplifiers:

a> have low efficiency
b> are audio amplifiers used in communications; 300 Hz to 2000 Hz
c> have high output distortion of the input wave shape
d> have low output distortion of the input wave shape
e> are high audio quality, medium distortion amplifiers

68. The urgency signal has less priority to:

a> direction finding
b> distress
c> safety
d> microwave relay
e> security

69. Buffer amplifiers:

a> prevent overmodulation in the oscillator
b> increases bandwidth in the receiver
c> provides cancellation of even harmonics
d> provides a stable load for the oscillator
e> are the same a frequency multipliers

70. What would be added to make a receiving antenna more directional?

a> inductor
b> capacitor
c> parasitic elements
d> height
e> directional shims

71. How the the frequency of a properly operating 700 KHz. crystal oscillator be changed?

a> connect a capacitor in parallel with the crystal
b> connect a capacitor in series with the crystal
c> connect a resistor in series with the crystal
d> connect a resistor in parallel with the crystal
e> crystal frequency cannot be changed

72. Tight coupling of an RF amplifier results in:

a> increased gain
b> increased selectivity
c> maximum frequency response
d> good efficiency
e> poor gain

73. Which of the following sets of frequency multipliers in cascade could be used to obtain 2.208 MHz. from an RF stage with a fundamental frequency of 184 Khz.?

a> four doublers
b> one tripler and one doubler
c> one tripler and two doublers
d> two triplers and two doublers
e> one phase shifter and one multiplier

74. What transistor circuit stage has an input impedance of usually less than 200 ohms, input and output signals in phase, no tendency to self-oscillate and can have voltage gain?

a> common-collector
b> common-base
c> Junction FET
d> Mosfet
e> Triac and Diac

75. Nitrogen is placed in transmission lines to:

a> improve the 'skin-effect' of microwaves
b> reduce arcing in the line
c> reduce the standing wave ratio of the line
d> reduce phase-shift and other losses
e> prevent moisture from entering the line

76. Neglecting line losses, the voltage at any point along a transmission line, having no standing waves, will be equal to the:

a> transmitter output
b> product of the line voltage and the surge impedance of the line
c> product of the line current and the surge impedance of the line
d> product of the resistance and surge impedance of the line
e> total inductive and capacitive reactance; zero

77. If a 100 mw signal is attenuated to 1 mw, this is a loss of:

a> 0 dB
b> 10 dB
c> 20 dB
d> 30 dB
e> 100 dB

78. The primary purpose of bridge-to-bridge communications:

a> search and rescue emergency calls only
b> all short range transmissions aboard ship
c> transmission of Captain's orders from the bridge
d> navigational
e> distress

79. What is the international calling and distress frequency in the 1605 kHz. to 3500 kHz. marine band?

a> 2080 kHz.
b> 2182 kHz.
c> 2340 kHz.
d> 3000 kHz.
e> any of the above

80. When should both the call sign and the name of the ship be mentioned during radiotelephone transmissions?

a> at all times
b> during an emergency
c> when transmitting on 2182 kHz.
d> within 100 miles of any shore
e> when using walkie-talkie transmitters on shore

81. How is an ELT emergency locator transmitter tested?

a> with a test switch; activating internal test circuit into dummy antenna
b> at any time, provided FCC authorization is obtained
c> at low power on non-emergency frequency
d> with FAA approval on non-emergency frequency
e> with U.S. Coast Guard approval

82. How often shall automatic control devices, indicators and alarm systems associated with tower lights be inspected to insure that such apparatus is functioning properly?

a> at intervals not to exceed one year
b> at intervals not to exceed three months
c> at intervals not to exceed one month
d> daily
e> continuously while on the air

83. When if ever is it legal to transmit high power on Channel 13?

a> during an emergency
b> failure of the vessel being called to respond to a second call at low power
c> when making a call in a blind situation
d> when rounding a bend in a river
e> all of the above

84. How often is the Auto-Alarm tested?

a> during the 5-minute silent period
b> monthly on 121.5 MHz. using a dummy load
c> after every emergency transmission
d> weekly on frequencies other than the 2182 kHz. distress frequency using a dummy antenna
e> each day on 2182 KHz. using a dummy antenna

85. What is the international radiotelephone alarm signal that when transmitted will attract the attention of operators and auto alarm receiving equipment?

a> a warbling 1.3 KHz./2.2 KHz. tone transmitted on 2182 KHz. or 156.8 MHz
b> two alternately transmitted audio tones of 1300 Hertz and 2200 Hertz with the duration of each being 250 milliseconds for a period of at least 30 seconds, but not exceeding one minute
c> either a or b above
d> S.O.S. in telegraphic code or the word Mayday
e> the word SECURITY spoken three times and transmitted before the important message call

86. What should an operator do before making a call to avoid interference with communications in progress?

a> transmit carrier without modulation to avoid interference, then when other transmissions have been concluded make the call with 100% modulation
b> reduce to 1 watt carrier power, then if your transmission is not received switch to higher levels of power until your signal is acknowledged
c> listen to the appropriate frequency or frequencies on the receiver and if interference is likely, wait until existing communications have been concluded
d> wait for a minimum of 10 seconds between received transmissions before switching to full carrier power
e> keep your transmission a short as possible, thus avoiding lengthy interruptions to other signals

87. Two equal capacitors are connected in parallel and charged to 120 volts. If they are disconnected from the power supply without discharge and a third capacitor is connected in parallel with the first two, what will be the voltage of the third capacitor?

a> 80 volts
b> 62.5 volts
c> 40 volts
d> 19.7 volts
e> cannot be determined

88. What is the seventh harmonic of 2182 kHz. when the transmitter is connected to a half-wave Hertz antenna?

a> 2182 kHz.
b> 15.27 MHz.
c> 311.7 kHz.
d> 7.64 MHz.
e> 15274 MHz.

89. When ship radiotelephone stations transmit, they must:

a> give call letters
b> give name of ship
c> both a and b
d> give call letters and country of origin
e> none of the above

90. A radiotelephone may be installed in lieu of a radiotelegraph transmitter on some vessels, provided:

a> its transmitter range is 25 miles
b> its transmitter range is 150 miles
c> its transmitter carrier power is 1500 watts SSB
d> its not traveling more than 20 miles from shore
e> a licensed General Radiotelephone operator is on board

91. Which of the following pertains to hand-held portable walkie-talkies?

a> must be licensed if power exceeds one watt
b> may be used in place of regular ship transmitter, provided other stations can receive signals clearly
c> may be used during docking procedures, tug boats and harbor officials
d> may be used in dry dock or on shore provided no interference with mobile transmitters occurs
e> none of the above

92. A 12.6 volt, 55 ampere-hour battery is connected to a radar unit rated at 325 watts and a receiver that uses 20 watts. How long will radar unit and receiver draw full power from the battery?

a> 6 hours
b> 4 hours
c> 2.3 hours
d> 2 hours
e> 1.2 hours

93. The licensee of any radio station which has an antenna structure requiring illumination pursuant to the provisions of the Communications Act of 1934, as amended:

a> shall make an observation of the tower lights at least once each 24 hours either visually or by observing an automatic properly maintained indicator designed to register any failure of such lights
b> shall provide and properly maintain an automatic alarm system to detect any light failure
c> shall inspect at intervals not to exceed 3 months all automatic or mechanical control devices, indicators and alarm systems to insure that such apparatus is functioning properly
d> all of the above
e> none of the above

94. The observed or otherwise known extinguishment or improper functioning of any TOP steady burning light or any FLASHING obstruction light, regardless of its position on the antenna structure:

a> shall be reported to the Commission immediately
b> shall be reported to the nearest Flight Service Station or office of the Federal Aviation Administration if not corrected within 30 minutes
c> shall be reported to the station licensee immediately
d> shall be telegraphed to the Army-Navy alert station and the FAA offices listed on station license
e> all of the above

95. An extinguished or improper functioning of a steady burning SIDE intermediate antenna tower light:

a> shall be corrected as soon as possible, but notification to the FAA is not required
b> shall be corrected within 30 minutes and notification to the FAA via telephone or telegraph is required
c> shall be corrected within 24 hours
d> shall be reported to the licensee and the date and time of malfunction noted in the transmitter log
e> both b and c above

96. What frequency is approved for testing the auto-alarm?

a> 121.5 MHz.
b> 500 KHz.
c> 2182 KHz.
d> any approved Distress frequency
e> frequencies other than distress frequency using an artificial antenna

97. How often is your ship inspected by the Commission?

a> before going out on open seas
b> annually
c> monthly
d> weekly
e> inspection is not required

98. What types of ships are required to maintain radios?

a> ships that carry 300+ tone operating at sea or on the Great Lakes
b> ships that carry 6+ people for hire
c> all cargo ships
d> both a and b above
e> all of the above

99. Maritime emergency radios should be tested:

a> before each voyage and weekly while the ship is at sea
b> one per day except while in dry dock
c> weekly on any frequency except 2182 KHz.
d> prior to usage and yearly under FCC supervision
e> all of the above

100. A radiotelelphone may be installed in lieu of a radiotelegraph on a vessel if its gross tonnage weight is less than:

a> 3000 tons
b> 2300 tons
c> 1600 tons
d> 500 tons
e> 300 tons

# Test 3-E Element Three

1. To correct split tuning:
   a. Employ a high L/C ratio
   b. Employ a low Q circuit
   c. Realign the detector stage
   d. Increase coupling between stages
   e. Decrease coupling between stages

2. Tetrode transistors are used:
   a. In lower frequency applications
   b. In higher frequency applications
   c. As power amplifiers only
   d. In push-pull circuits only
   e. In grounded collector circuits only

3. The speed of a series wound DC motor varies with:
   a. The number of commutator bars
   b. The number of slip rings
   c. The load applied to the motor
   d. The direction of rotation
   e. The strength of the interpoles

4. Which is a low pass-half-section M-derived filter?

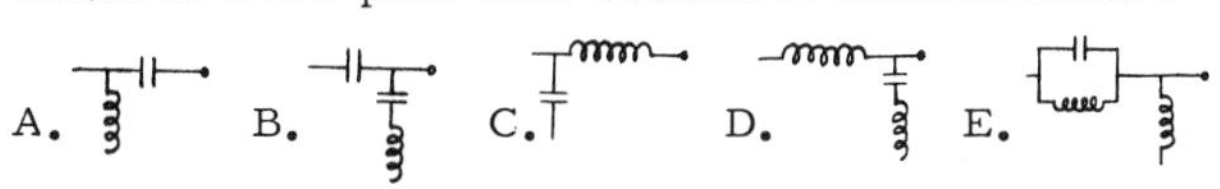


5. The frequency of the ripple voltage of a full wave, three phase, 60 cycle, power supply would be:
   a. 90 cycles
   b. 300 cycles
   c. 360 cycles
   d. 120 cycles
   e. 180 cycles

6. What is the voltage GAIN of this amplifier?
   a. 7
   b. -7
   c. 9.34
   d. 3.5
   e. unity

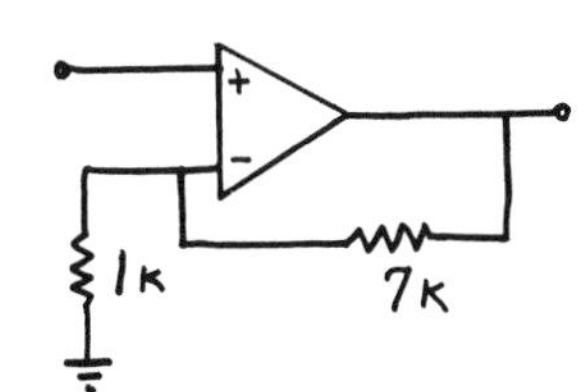


7. Adding a capacitor in series with a Marconi antenna:
   a. Increases the antenna circuit resonant frequency
   b. Decreases the antenna circuit resonant frequency
   c. Blocks the transmission of signals from the antenna
   d. Increases the power handling capacity of the antenna
   e. Decreases the power handling capacity of the antenna

8. Neutralization at high frequency is sometimes not necessary in an RF amplifier when:
   a. Tetrode is used
   b. Operating as a grounded grid
   c. Filaments are properly center-tapped
   d. Resistor is used
   e. AVC is used

9. To increase the output of a transmitter:
   a. Decouple antenna
   b. Increase direct-plate voltage in final stage
   c. Increase the grid bias
   d. Tune plate tank circuit to second harmonic
   e. Decrease signal output

10. RF amplifiers can be operated with minimum distortion because:
    a. the flywheel effect of the tank circuit restores the wave form
    b. phase shift effect of the input circuit
    c. of the low signal voltage level
    d. the high Q and bandwidth of the tank circuit
    e. all of the above

11. The bandwidth of an amplifier refers to the passage (at a certain level) of:
    a. All frequencies within 1000 Kc of the carrier
    b. Usually only the carrier frequencies
    c. The carrier, significant sidebands, and harmonic frequencies
    d. Usually only sideband frequencies
    e. The audio frequencies only if the carrier wave is modulated

12. At UHF and above, current has a tendency to travel on the surface of a conductor; this is known as:
    a. Miller effect
    b. Conductance effect
    c. Skin effect
    d. Output effect
    e. Center effect

13. If a non-resonant parallel circuit were composed of a pure inductance and capacitance (no resistance):
    a. Actual power consumed would be very high
    b. The power factor would be greater than 1.67
    c. The power factor would be .95
    d. There would be no current in the circuit
    e. The actual power consumed would be zero

14. Link coupling is often used to:
    a. transmit over long distances with rebroadcast transmission lines
    b. couple circuits having different impedances
    c. operate the main ship transmitter by remote control
    d. increase power transfer on Bridge to Bridge calling
    e. reduce harmonics by elimination of capacitive coupling

15. An antenna is carrying an unmodulated signal, when 100% modulation is impressed, the antenna current:
    a. Goes up 50%
    b. Goes down one half
    c. Stays the same
    d. Goes up 22.5%
    e. Goes down 2.25 %

16. J3E emission is:
    a. Facsimile
    b. Television
    c. Frequency modulation
    d. Telemetry
    e. SSSC telephony

17. A transmitter that operates on 16 MHz. is allowed a carrier frequency tolerance of 0.0002%. If the oscillator operates at 1/8th of the carrier frequency, what is the maximum allowable frequency deviation of the oscillator?
   a. 1.66 Hz.
   b. 2 Hz.
   c. 4 Hz.
   d. 32 Hz.
   e. 200 Hz.

18. Class C amplifiers:
   a. low quality audio amplifiers
   b. usually operated push-pull for maximum power
   c. operate with low efficiency
   d. cause great distortion of the input wave shape
   e. high power audio amplifiers; 1 KW to 10 KW

19. If $R_1$ = 20 ohms, L = o.1h, C = 60 mfd., V = 110 V and I = 3 A. Power is calculated:
   a. Power cannot be calculated but must be measured with a wattmeter
   b. Is a product of A squared turns
   c. As a product of V and A
   d. As a quotient of V divided by $R_1 + R_2$
   e. As a product of V, A and circuit power factor

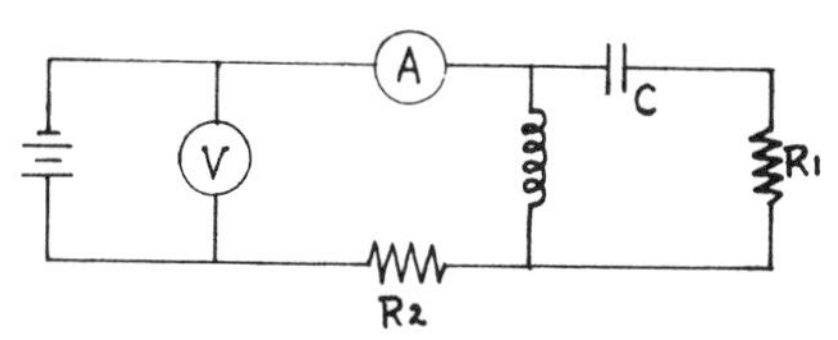


20. A reserve power source must be able to operate all radio equipment plus an emergency light system for how long?
   a. 72 hours
   b. 24 hours
   c. 12 hours
   d. 8 hours
   e. 6 hours

21. If the turns ratio of a transformer is stepped up 1 to 5:
   a. Current will be 20% higher in the secondary
   b. Current will be 125% higher in the primary
   c. Current in the secondary will be 20% of primary current
   d. There will be no difference
   e. Voltage will be 20% higher in the secondary

22. The collector-emitter in a PNP junction transistor, grounded-emitter, audio amplifier stage is forward biased with a voltage commonly used in that circuit. Which of the following statements is true?
   a. This is a normal situation
   b. Transistor would probably be ruined
   c. No current would flow in the emitter circuit
   d. No current would flow in the base circuit
   e. The collector would be more positive than the emitter

23. An electrical relay:
    a. Is a current limiting device
    b. Is a device used for supplying 3 or more voltages to a circuit
    c. Is concerned mainly with HF audio amplifiers
    d. Provides either an open or closed circuit to some portion of a device
    e. Is commonly used for tuning antennas

24. In the amplifier shown:
    a. Battery in emitter is reversed
    b. Emitter bias is too high
    c. Battery in collector is reversed
    d. Load register is too high
    e. Capacitor value is too high

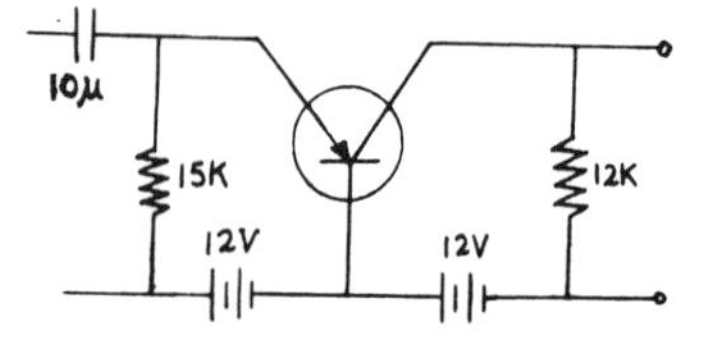


25. A high standing wave ratio on a transmission line can be caused by:
    a. Excessive modulation
    b. An increase in output power
    c. Detuned antenna coupling
    d. Poor B+ regulation
    e. Any of the above

26. The best insulation at UHF is:
    a. Black rubber
    b. Bakelite
    c. Paper
    d. Cotton
    e. Mica

27. Outer part of atom that is associated with electrical current usually is the:
    a. Outer or valence electrons
    b. Inner electrons
    c. Neutrons
    d. Nucleus
    e. Protons

28. The electrolyte in a lead storage battery is:
    a. Potassium Hydrate
    b. Pure spongy lead
    c. Sulphuric acid
    d. Iron oxide
    e. Nickel hydrate

29. The control grid of a triode vacuum tube is the equivalent of what in a PNP transistor?
    a. Emitter
    b. Collector
    c. Base
    d. Plate
    e. Bias

30. Under frequency modulation (FM) with a carrier of 5 Mc and a frequency deviation of 5 Kc, the highest frequency contained in the emission would be:
    a. It cannot be determined from this information
    b. 5 Kc
    c. 10 Kc
    d. 55 Mc
    e. 500.45 Kc

31. A dynamotor is used to:
    a. Step up AC voltage
    b. Step down AC voltage
    c. Change DC voltage
    d. Step down DC voltage
    e. Step up DC voltage

32. Why should unnecessary radiotelephone calling be avoided?
    a. it may cause interference with other stations
    b. to maintain safety of the operator
    c. the Coast Guard requires it
    d. it may cause overmodulation
    e. it may cause rectification

33. Overmodulation is often caused by:
    a. turning down audio gain control
    b. station frequency drift
    c. antenna decoupling
    d. weather conditions
    e. shouting into a microphone

34. What is the fifth harmonic frequency of a transmitter operating on 480 kHz. with a 1/4 wavelength antenna?
    a. 120 kHz.
    b. 240 MHz.
    c. 600 kHz.
    d. 1.2 MHz.
    e. 2.4 MHz.

35. Xc is 9900 ohms, L is 1.57 h, R is 12,500 ohms. What is Z at resonance?
    a. 24,100 ohms
    b. 12,500 ohms
    c. 22,400 ohms
    d. 3,100 ohms
    e. 850 ohms

36. A frequency doubler circuit:
    a. does not require neutralization
    b. doubles audio frequencies for equalization
    c. is operated Class A or Class AB-1
    d. has low efficiency
    e. all of the above

37. The frequency of an FM station has been measured:
    a. A grid dip meter was used
    b. A multivibrator was used
    c. Results are immediately mailed to the FCC
    d. Results are entered and recorded in the station log
    e. Only a first class license holder could take the measurements

38. Swinging chokes are used usually in power supplies which supply grid bias to:
    a. Class B amplifiers
    b. Class C amplifiers
    c. Class C-1 amplifiers
    d. Class A-1 amplifiers
    e. Master oscillators

39. The transfer of harmonics to a following stage from a radio frequency amplifier may be reduced by:
   a. Designing a tank circuit to have low values of circulating current
   b. Employing no electrostatic screen between the final amplifier tank and the antenna circuit
   c. Employing link coupling between stages
   d. Operating with very high grid bias and grid excitation values
   e. None of these

40. Frequency Tolerance means:
   a. Wavelength of a signal
   b. Frequency of emitted signal
   c. Maximum modulation of carrier wave
   d. Maximum difference of allowable frequency
   e. Maximum variation of amplitude

41. SHF means:
   a. 3000 to 30,000 Mc
   b. Above 300,000 Mc
   c. 300 to 3000 Mc
   d. 30,000 to 300,000 Mc
   e. 3000 to 30,000 Kc

42. Residual magnetism may be defined as:
   a. Polarized molecular alignment in a magnetized material while not under the influence of a magnetizing force
   b. Retentivity of lines of force in a coil
   c. The term applied to intense magnetic fields
   d. A strong permanent magnet
   e. All of the above

43. Minus 20 db represents a change of:
   a. 20 volts
   b. 1/100 of the voltage
   c. 10 watts
   d. 10 volts
   e. 1/100 of the wattage

44. What frequency is indicated on the vernier?
   a. 31.94
   b. 32.40
   c. 33.70
   d. 32.04
   e. 31.95

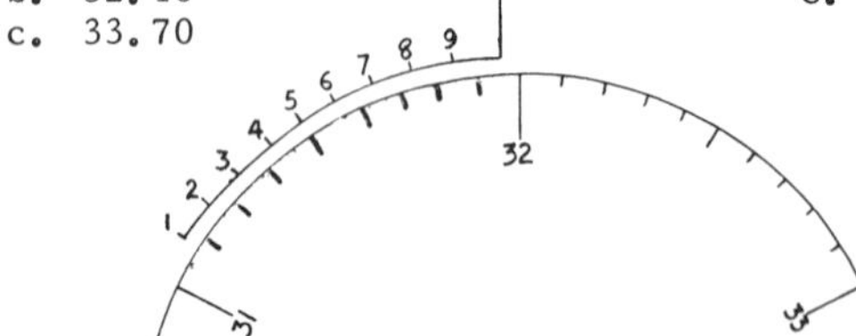


45. A grid-dip meter is useful in measuring:
   a. Tank circuit frequency
   b. Grid voltages
   c. Plate voltages
   d. Frequency requiring .001% (or better) tolerances
   e. Any of the above

46. Which of the following will operate with the greatest efficiency with a sine-wave input?
a. Class A power amplifier
b. Class B voltage amplifier
c. Class AB audio amplifier
d. Class C rf amplifier
e. Class CB audio amplifier

47. Which of the following will operate with the greatest efficiency with a sine-wave input?
a. class AB audio amplifier
b. class C radio frequency amplifier
c. class B audio/radio frequency amplifier
d. class D-3 radio frequency amplifier
e. class A-1 push-pull cascade amplifier

48. A 5 MHz. radio transmitter has a frequency tolerance of 0.002%. What is the upper and lower limits of the carrier frequency if it is measured with a secondary standard having a 0.002% accuracy tolerance?
a. 4.999 MHz. to 5.005 MHz.
b. 4.996 MHz. to 5.002 MHz.
c. 5.0 MHz.
d. 4.9994 MHz. to 5.0004 MHz.
e. 4.9999 MHz. to 5.0005 MHz.

49. When a high signal to noise is desired in FM where the signal is larger than noise:
a. Narrow band pass reduces noise when receiving weak signals
b. High percentage of modulation is used
c. Pre-emphasis and de-emphasis is used
d. Signals must be strong enough to produce sufficient limiting effect
e. All of the above

50. A Class A amplifier conducts plate current:
a. Only on the positive half cycle input
b. when grid bias is at cut off, and only on negative portions of inputs
c. Through the complete sinusoidal input
d. On only a small portion of the positive input
e. All of the above

51. When profanity is being used over the transmitter, what should the operator do?
a. use complete transmitter power rectification
b. begin overmodulation
c. change operating frequency
d. jam the frequency
e. end transmission

52. Input frequency is:
a. 4895
b. 2225
c. 450
d. 5800
e. 5350

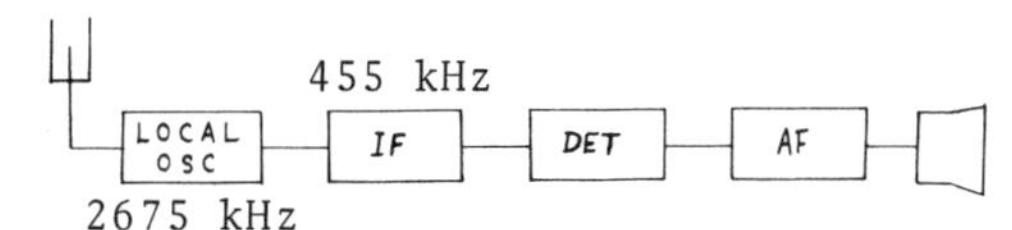

53. A transmitter buffer stage:
a. follows the AF amplifier
b. follows the frequency multiplier stage
c. usually has a gain of 5 to 10
d. is not utilized primarily as an amplifier
e. both a and b

54. The size of a wire with respect to amount of current flowing in it is important because:
a. The wire insulation would melt
b. Resistance increases as diameter decreases
c. Power loss in wire
d. Total voltage drop in wire would be excessive
e. All of the above

55. A 36 foot piece of copper wire having a resistance per foot length of 12 ohms is replaced by a piece of wire of the same material just 1/3 the cross sectional area of original. What is total resistance of new piece?
a. 39 ohms
b. 48 ohms
c. 644 ohms
d. 1296 ohms
e. 9770 ohms

56. A transmitter has a carrier frequency of 655 KHz. What is its highest harmonic radiation?
a. 1965 KHz.
b. 755 KHz.
c. 2570 KHz.
d. 4980 KHz.
e. 3750 KHz.

57. How much of a drop in power does 30 dB have?
a. 0.0001 watt
b. 0.001 watt
c. 0.01 watt
d. 0.1 watt
e. 1 watt

58. Time constant of a resistance-capacitance parallel circuit:
a. The time for the condenser to discharge thru the resistance
b. The time required for the condenser to completely charge
c. Sum of resistance and capacitance
d. The time required for the condenser to discharge thru the resistance to a specified % of the initial voltage charge
e. Capacitance divided by resistance

59. Single-Sideband plus reduced carrier telephony:
a. SS3A
b. FO2
c. R3E
d. J3E
e. F3E

60. The fundamental operating frequency of a crystal oscillator is determined by:
a. Size
b. Thickness
c. Angle of cut
d. Temperature
e. All of the above

61. When soldering electrical connections, care should be taken not to:
   a. Heat both connections
   b. Move the wire until solder has solidified
   c. Have solder on the connections
   d. Use Rosin Core solder
   e. Make physical connection before soldering

62. If an operator should leave his station unattended in a public place, he must:
   a. make it inaccessible to unauthorized persons
   b. broadcast the station call sign
   c. dismantle and remove all equipment
   d. report action to FCC field office
   e. decouple phonetic switch

63. A 6 volt battery with 1.2 ohms internal resistance is connected across two 3 watt bulbs. What is the current flow?
   a. .57 amps
   b. .83 amps
   c. 1.0 amps
   d. 6.0 amps
   e. 6.5 amps

64. Which of the following is most correct about wave form distortion in amplifiers?
   a. it should never be used for RF frequencies
   b. it reduces the amplifier output power
   c. high distortion limits its use at RF frequencies
   d. improves signal strength at audio frequencies
   e. it is utilized to generate harmonics

65. VHF means:
   a. 3000 - 30,000 kHz.
   b. 30,000 kHz. - 300 MHz.
   c. 300 - 3000 kHz.
   d. 300 - 3000 MHz.
   e. 3000 - 30,000 MHz.

66. The limiter of a frequency modulation receiver:
   a. Has a low gain and almost a constant output
   b. Follows the discriminator
   c. Has a high gain and almost a constant output
   d. Follows the de-emphasis circuit
   e. Used only in AM transmitters

67. Which of the following would, alone, be a proper method of determining if the operating mobile transmitter is being maintained within the specified tolerance:
   a. Check each stage with a grid-dip meter
   b. Zero-beat the oscillator frequency with a suitable reference
   c. Zero-beat any of the frequency multiplier output references with a suitable reference
   d. Zero-beat the transmitter output frequency with a suitable reference
   e. Any of the above would suffice

68. The signal completes 5 cycles in 1/50 of a second; its frequency is:
   a. 250 cps
   b. 0.1 cps
   c. 10 cps
   d. 5000 cps
   e. 0.5 cps

69. Inductance is proportional to:
a. Diameter of solenoid
b. The square root of the turns in the coil
c. The square of the turns in the coil
d. Type and make of wire
e. Direction of winding

70. What are the frequencies of the radiotelephone channel for aircraft?
a. 121.5 MHz and 156.8 MHz
b. 156.8 MHz and 2182 MHz
c. 2182 MHz and 121.5 kHz
d. 106.9 MHz
e. 2182 kHz and 156.4 MHz

71. What could cause parasitic osicllations in an RF amplifier?
a. excessive B+
b. improper grounding
c. lengthy wire leads causing unwanted tuned circuits
d. improper antenna impedance coupling
e. frequency modulation usually causes parasitics

72. The input to an active pi-filter, half-wave power supply is 120 volts, 60 c/s sinewave. A properly tuned oscilloscope placed between the cathode and ground would show which of the following traces?

A B C D E

73. Who has responsibility for station operation, when a non-licensed operator speaks into a microphone?
a. the person speaking
b. the owner of the station
c. the licensed operator in charge
d. the nearest FCC field office
e. the station chief engineer only

74. Neutralization of an RF amplifier:
a. is not required at high radio frequencies
b. usually results in loss of transmitter power
c. capacitance effect from ground to grid is zero
d. capacitance will vary grid current effect
e. capacitance effect from anode to grid is zero

75. The inductance of the coil arrangement below will be maximum if the following connections are made:
a. M to P
b. N to O
c. O to P
d. M to O
e. M to N

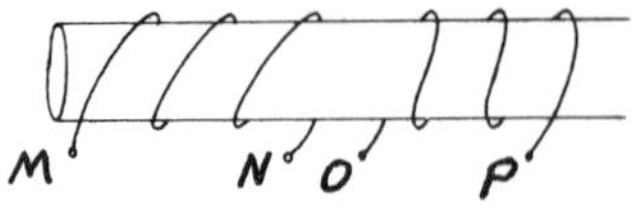

M N O P

76. A dynamotor is approximately:
a. 100% effieient
b. 85% effieient
c. 65% efficient
d. 40% efficient
e. 22.5% efficient

77. A buffer condenser is usually placed across a secondary of a vibrator power supply transformer to :
a. Reduce sparking at the vibrator terminals
b. Reduce secondary voltage
c. Load down the secondary
d. Increase the input power factor
e. Prevent DC from appearing across the secondary terminals

78. Why should all collector, base and ground leads be kept as short as possible in RF amplifier stages?
a. to eliminate possible interaction between stages
b. to decrease circuit resistance
c. to protect operator from possible shock
d. to increase capacitive coupling between transistors
e. to increase the Q of the circuit

79. A 50 MHz. radiotelephone station is transmitting on 50.010 MHz. By what percentage is the transmitter off frequency?
a. 0.01%
b. 0.02%
c. 0.001%
d. 0.002%
e. 0.003%

80. What is this circuit?
a. electron coupled oscillator
b. Colpits oscillator
c. shunt fed Hartley oscillator
d. series fed Hartley oscillator
e. Squelch circuit

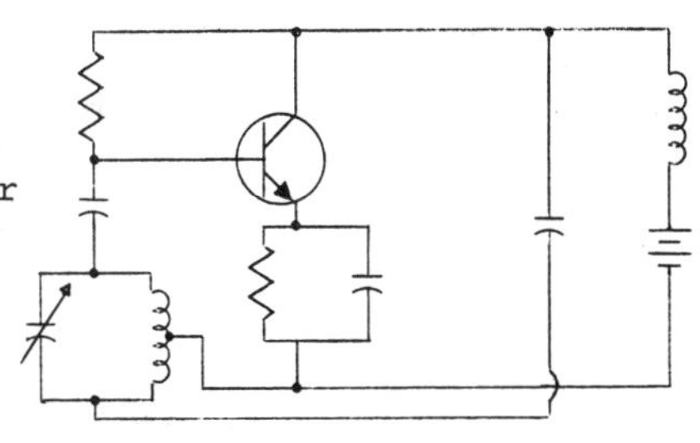

81. The word "clear" means:
a. safety of operator
b. last transmission received
c. my conversation has started
d. my conversation is ended and no response is expected
e. send message again

82. Permanent magnetic field that surrounds a traveling-wave tube is ( TWT ) intended to:
a. Provide a means of coupling
b. Prevent the electron beam from spreading
c. Prevent oscillations
d. Prevent spurious oscillations
e. Attenuate the signal

83. The sum of the readings of two ammeters connected in series in an electrical circuit indicates:
a. 1/4 the total current in the circuit
b. 1/2 the total current in the circuit
c. The total current in the circuit
d. Twice the total current in the circuit
e. The square root of the total current in the circuit

84. The diagram below is called what?
   a. Resistance coupling
   b. Impedance coupling
   c. Direct coupling
   d. Transformer or inductance coupling
   e. Capacitive coupling

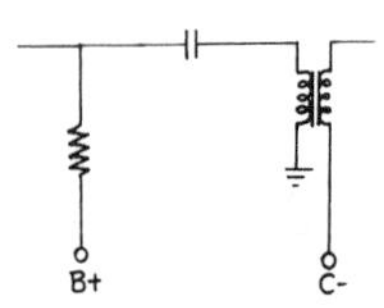


85. RF amplifiers can be used with little distortion because:
   a. Low signal drive
   b. RF coils are shielded
   c. All grid, plate, and ground leads are short
   d. High signal drive
   e. Fly-wheel effect of plate tank circuit restores wave form

86. When replacing components in RF circuits:
   a. Keep lead lengths as short as possible
   b. Make as many seperate ground connections as possible
   c. Always use electrolytic capacitors
   d. Always use iron core induction
   e. None of the above

87. What is this circuit?
   a. ratio dectector
   b. limiter stage
   c. voltage regulator
   d. frequency multiplier
   e. voltage doubler

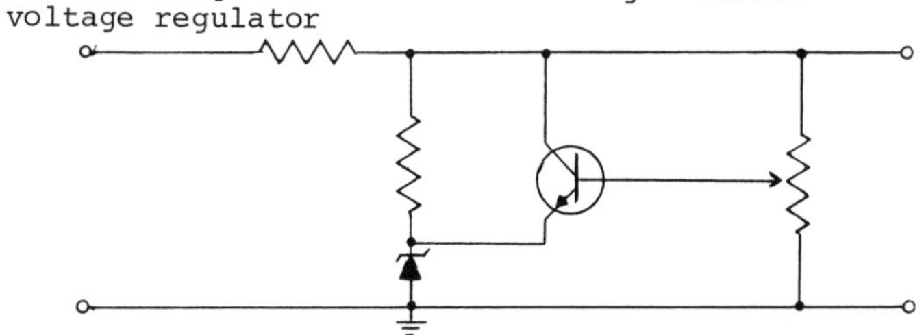

88. An excited 1/2 wavelength antenna produces:
   a. Residual fields
   b. An electro-magnetic field only
   c. Both electro-magnetic and electro-static fields
   d. An electro-flux field sometimes
   e. Both a and d above

89. Electromagnetic coils encase a traveling wave tube to:
a. Provide a means of coupling energy
b. Prevent the electron beam from spreading
c. Prevent oscillation
d. Prevent spurious oscillations
e. Attenuate the signal

90. "Packing" of the carbon granules in a carbon single button mike may be caused by:
a. Improperly connected polarity
b. Battery
c. Speech amplifier is overdriven
d. Excessive moisture
e. None of the above

91. The plate current in a thyratron tube can be cut off:
a. By making the plate more negative
b. By making the plate more positive
c. By connecting the grid to the plate
d. By grounding the grid
e. By giving high negative bias to the control grid

92. A dip in the antenna current when you speak into a mike may indicate:
a. Insufficient final stage plate voltage
b. Excessive grid bias on final RF amplifier
c. Too loose coupling between the antenna and transmitter
d. Insufficient excitation to the modulated stage
e. Any of the above

93. The transistor shown in this common-base amplifier:
a. is a PNP type
b. is a NPN type
c. has unity amplification
d. has improper bias
e. is improperly grounded

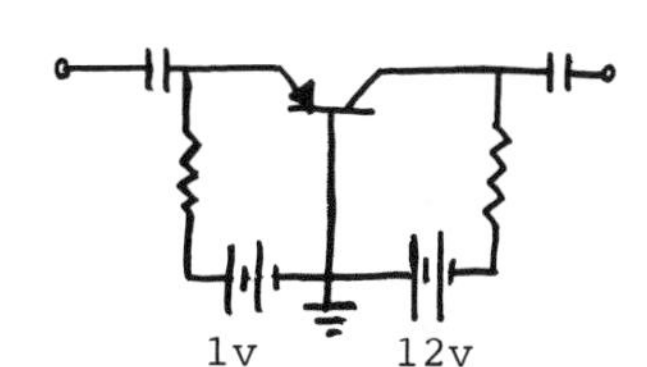


94. The frequency deviation produced by FM is controlled mainly by the:
a. Frequency of the carrier
b. Frequency of the modulating tone
c. Amplitude of the modulating frequency
d. Output power of the transmitter
e. Power in the carrier

95. Under conditions of 100% amplitude modulation of a radiotelephone transmitter, the ratio of power output of the modulator stage to the DC power input to the modulated stage is:
a. 1
b. 1/2
c. $\sqrt{2}$
d. $1/\sqrt{2}$
e. 1/3

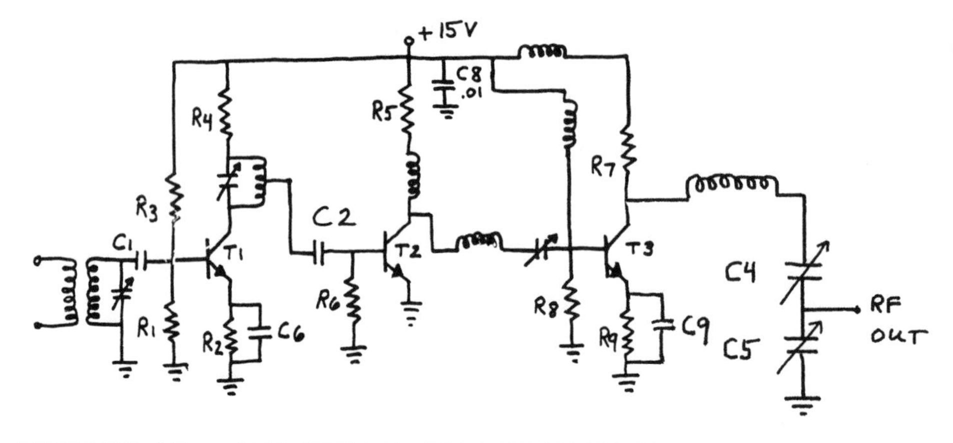


QUESTIONS #96 - #100 REFER TO THE DIAGRAM ABOVE

96. If C6 opens:
    a. the signal will increase through C2
    b. the signal output voltage will be higher
    c. stability increases and gain decreases
    d. tripler transistor will be saturated
    e. driver tranistor will cutoff completely

97. If C9 is shorted:
    a. reduced output
    b. degeneration
    c. more stable output
    d. output distortion
    e. no change

98. What design change would have the least effect on the circuit above?
    a. C8 opens
    b. C2 shorts
    c. C6 shorts
    d. R1 opens
    e. C1 opens

99. What is the purpose of C4?
    a. DC blocking
    b. AC coupling
    c. frequency adjustment
    d. loading
    e. tuning

100. What is the purpose of C5?
    a. DC blocking
    b. AC coupling
    c. matching
    d. loading
    e. tuning

# Test 3-F Element Three

1. What is the unit of energy measured in?
   a. Kilowatt hour
   b. Kilowatt
   c. Milliwatt
   d. Ampere
   e. Electron

2. If 100 volts at 60 cycles is connected to a solenoid of 4 ohms resistance and 0.2 amps flows thru the winding, the impedance of the solenoid is:
   a. .08 ohm
   b. 25 ohms
   c. 200 ohms
   d. 400 ohms
   e. 500 ohms

3. The inverse voltage on a rectifier tube is based on the:
   a. Peak voltage
   b. RMS voltage
   c. Average voltage
   d. DC output voltage
   e. Electrostatic voltage

4. Push-pull amplification rather than single ended amplification is frequently used in Class "A" audio stages because:
   a. Grid bias E is not necessary
   b. Neutralization will not be necessary
   c. Even harmonic frequencies will be suppressed
   d. All harmonics will be suppressed
   e. Less plate voltage is required

5. How can we correct the defect, if any, in this voltage doubler circuit?
   a. Omit C1
   b. Reverse polarity signs
   c. Ground X
   d. Reverse polarity on C1
   e. Reverse polarity on C2

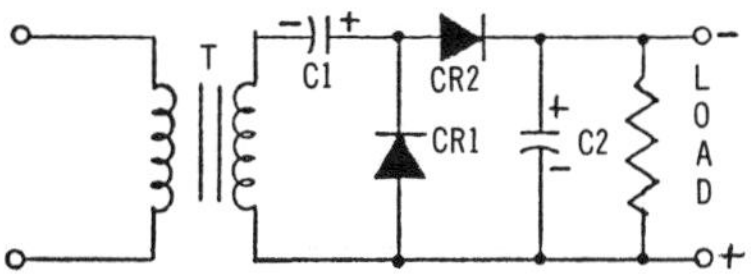

T C1 CR2 CR1 C2 LOAD

6. Distortion results if input signal level to the single-ended audio stage exceeds bias voltage or:
   a. Negative feedback is introduced
   b. The transconductance (GM) is high, which means high gain
   c. The bias voltage plate current curve is non-linear during any portion of the input swing
   d. The input signal level is reduced to under 1/2 it's designed (max) value
   e. The percent accuracy of the load resistor exceeds 10%

7. Wave form distortion in amplifiers is:
   a. useful in generating harmonics
   b. reduces parasitic oscillations
   c. undesirable in class B and C amplifiers
   d. desirable in class A amplifiers
   e. reduced by utilizing buffer amplifiers

8. 100 volts DC can be obtained from a 500 volt DC power supply by the use of:
   a. Frequency converter
   b. Polyphase transformer
   c. Selenium cell
   d. Voltage divider
   e. Voltage doubler

9. A resistor, RETMA type, has the following color code: Black, Red, Black, Gold. Which of the following statements is true?
   a. 100 ohm resistor
   b. Has a tolerance of 10% of nominal value
   c. 2 ohm resistor
   d. 20 ohm resistor
   e. 220 ohm resistor

10. An antenna which intercepts signals equally from all horizontal directions is:
   a. Parabolic
   b. Vertical loop
   c. Horizontal Marconi
   d. Vertical 1/4 wave
   e. Horizontal 1/2 wave

11. A 6000 Kc carrier is modulated by a 3 Kc tone that contains a high second harmonic content. What is the bandwidth?
   a. 3.2 Kc
   b. 12.0 Kc
   c. 6.4 Kc
   d. 21.2 Kc
   e. 60 Kc

12. If battery supply voltage is 100 volts and V1 reads a voltage drop across R4. R4 is 9 ohms. A1 reads 12.5 amps and A2 reads 2.5 amps, R2 is 4 ohms, V2 reads?
   a. 2 V
   b. 80 V
   c. 100 V
   d. 0 V
   e. 90 V

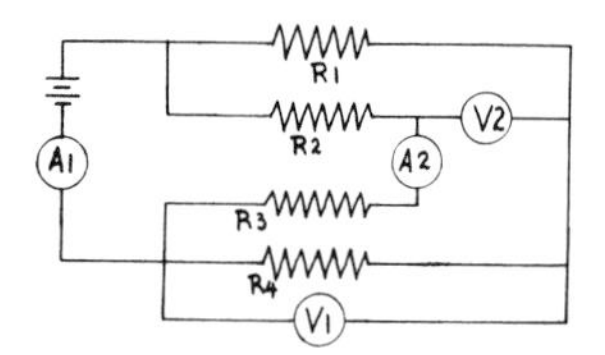


13. Amplifier stages in a transmitter are often neutralized to:
   a. prevent unwanted emissions
   b. eliminate harmonic radiation
   c. reduce odd harmonics
   d. amplify both odd and even harmonics
   e. both a and b

14. Too many harmonics from a transmitter, check the:
   a. Check biasing on final RF tube or stage
   b. Coupling
   c. Tuning of circuits
   d. Shielding
   e. Any of the above

15. A loop antenna:
   a. Is bi-directional
   b. Is usually vertical
   c. Is more often used as a receiving antenna
   d. If horizontal is omni-directional
   e. Any of the above

16. According to the Commission rules, the definition of "Bandwidth occupied by an emission" is the width of the band of frequencies:
   a. Which includes all frequencies emanating from the transmitting antenna, regardless of out power
   b. Whose component frequencies add up to 99%, and include any frequency containing 0.25% of the total power
   c. Which includes the carrier frequency and only those sideband frequencies containing 50% of the total radiated power
   d. Whose component frequencies are the sums and differences of the carrier frequency harmonics.
   e. Which the resonant circuit of the final power amplifier is capable of passing

17. Referred to the fundamental frequency a shorted stub line attached to the transmission line to absorb even harmonics could have a wavelength of:
   a. 1.41 wavelengths
   b. 1/2 wavelengths
   c. 1/4 wavelengths
   d. 1/6 wavelengths
   e. 1/8 wavelengths

18. A PNP junction transistor (common base) amplifier is conventionally biased. During the positive portion of input signal:
   a. The base to collector resistance increases in proportion
   b. The base to collector circuit becomes more negative
   c. The base to emitter current increases
   d. Power loss and current gain
   e. Majority of electrons are leaving the base

19. The source shown below has the following readings: What is the power factor?
   a. 1.2
   b. 1.0
   c. 0.8
   d. 0.2
   e. 0.5

20. The wavelength of a 500 MHz. wave is:
   a. 60 meters
   b. 6 meters
   c. 30 meters
   d. 60 cm
   e. 1 cm

21. What is prevented when you use decoupling circuits?
   a. phase reversal
   b. high-modulation
   c. cross-modulation
   d. parasitic coupling
   e. all of the above

22. The circuit shown:
   a. Has a $180^{o}$ phase reversal
   b. Has a $360^{o}$ phase reversal
   c. Battery polarities should be reversed
   d. Is a mixer
   e. None of the above

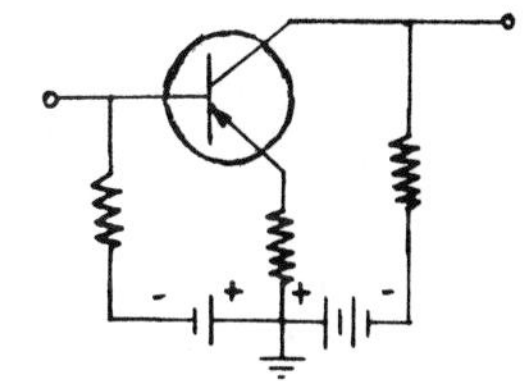

23. Nitrogen gas in concentric RF transmission lines is used to:
   a. Keep moisture out
   b. Prevent oxidation
   c. Act as insulator
   d. both a and b
   e. both b and c

24. A buffer amplifier stage:
   a. acts as a fuse circuit during over-load conditions
   b. prevents phase-shift of the crystal output
   c. provides a stable load for the oscillator
   d. changes impedance of the crystal to match load
   e. cancels all even harmonics

25. A frequency doubler:
   a. Requires only a small grid driving signal
   b. Is usually operated Class A
   c. Has very small harmonic output in the plate current pulse
   d. Does not have to be neutralized
   e. Has a sine-wave current

26. What kind of transistor is this?
   a. NPN junction
   b. PNP junction
   c. Tetrode point contact
   d. Collector
   e. None of the above

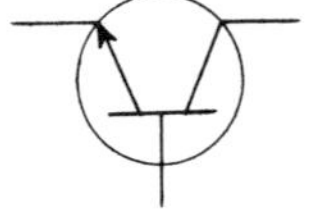

27. The difference between Bridge rectifiers and 2 diode full wave rectifiers is:
   a. Bridge output voltage is twice that of full-wave
   b. Bridge output current is half that of full wave
   c. Bridge cannot be used with power supply filtering
   d. a and b
   e. b and c

28. Frequency shift keying is often used in teletype and telegraphic circuits because:
   a. A continous carrier has a quieting effect on receivers
   b. A wide emission bandwidth is maintained
   c. Little power is required
   d. Its A3 emission has a low signal to noise ratio
   e. Its variations in amplitude are clearly defined

29. A test instrument that is most commonly used in locating open circuits in radio equiptment is:
   a. A milliammeter
   b. An ohmeter
   c. A voltmeter
   d. A cathode ray tube
   e. A wave trap

30. Shielding is used in multistage receivers to:
   a. Provide ample degree of regeneration
   b. Prevent undesired interstage coupling
   c. Induce interstage oscillation
   d. Provide high external fields
   e. Reduce skin effect

31. One piece of equipment to indicate neutralization is:
   a. A neon bulb
   b. A Tachometer
   c. Wave trap
   d. Filter
   e. Ohm meter

32. Where is signal energy coupled in a conventional transmitting wave tube?
   a. Plate circuit
   b. Suppressor circuit
   c. Screen grid
   d. Filament circuit
   e. Grid circuit

33. RF measurements shall be made by comparison with the primary standard of frequency Station WWV, Washington DC or:
   a. Temperature controlled crystal oscillator
   b. Pierce oscillator
   c. The frequency standard maintained at FCC monitoring stations
   d. The standard of frequency maintained by the National Bureau of Standards
   e. FCC approved frequency meter

34. The power in the carrier frequency of a transmitter as measured at the output is 10 watts; 2nd harmonic is 0.1 watts. The 2nd harmonic is:
   a. 1 db below center frequency
   b. 2 db below center frequency
   c. 10 db below center frequency
   d. 20 db below center frequency
   e. 100 db below center frequency

35. The circuit shown below is
   a. A vibrator power supply
   b. An FM receiver
   c. A superheterodyne AM receiver
   d. FM transmitter
   e. High level modulated AM transmitter

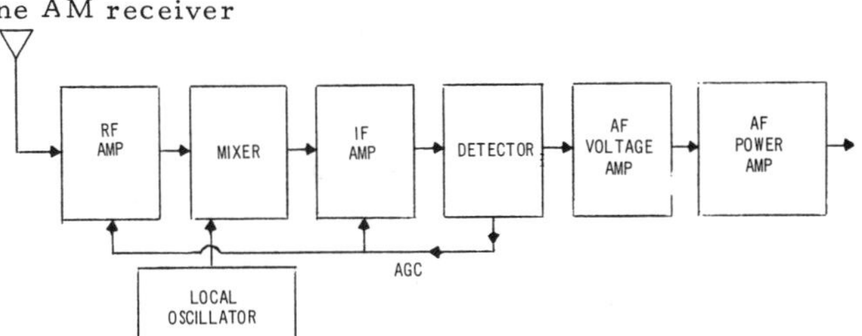


36. At UHF a fixed carbon resistor may:
   a. Appear to decrease in value
   b. Appear to have inductance and capacitance
   c. Open circuit as a result of high frequency
   d. Short circuit as a result of high frequency
   e. None of the above

37. The oscillator crystal in a transmitter has a positive temperature coefficient of 10 c/s per $1^{o}$ C/Mc. The oscillator frequency is 2 Mc. The carrier frequency of the transmitter is 24 Mc. If the temperature of the crystal should increase by $20^{o}$ C, the carrier frequency would drift to:
   a. 24,004,800 cycles
   b. 24,000,000 cycles
   c. 23,090,500 cycles
   d. 23,000,000 cycles
   e. 22,999,930 cycles

38. What emission is single sideband plus carrier telephony?
   a. R9E
   b. J7E
   c. H3E
   d. C3F
   e. K3B

39. The high frequency range is:
a. 30,000 c/s to 300Kc
b. 30 Mc to 300 Mc
c. 3000 Mc to 30,000 Mc
d. 3 Mc to 30 Mc
e. 3 Mc to 300 Kc

40. In an FM receiver, AM components of the received signal are removed by:
a. Limiter
b. Second detector
c. Discriminator
d. First detector
e. Tank type filter

41. A D'Arsonval type meter placed across the output terminals of a bridge rectifier circuit employing two 25 mfd filter capacitors and a 100,000 ohm bleeder resistor, gives a reading of 9 volts. What is the RMS value of the a-c input voltage?
a. 64 volts
b. 9.3 volts
c. 6.4 volts
d. 20.9 volts
e. 10.7 volts

42. A 250 watt transmitter operating at rated power shows the following meter readings in the final RF stage. The plate efficiency is approximately:
a. 69%
b. 73%
c. 64%
d. 66%
e. 59%

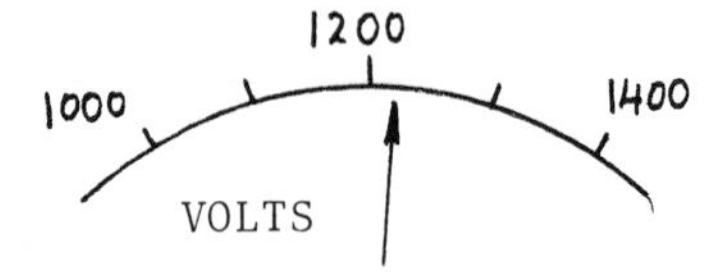


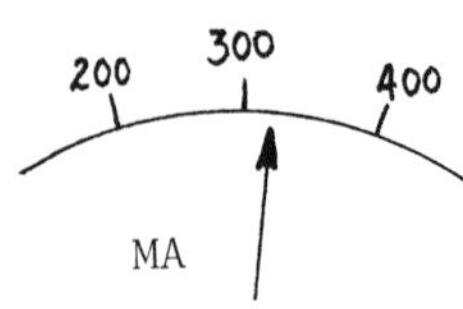


43. When may superfluous radio communications be broadcast?
a. when no response is expected
b. on non-distress channels
c. anytime by ships at sea
d. only during transmitter tests
e. never

44. In speaking of transistors, heat is:
a. Important because current increases as temperature increases
b. Important because current decreases as temperature increases
c. Unimportant as it pertains to majority current
d. Important only as it pertains to minority current
e. Not a factor to be considered

45. A 12 volt storage battery has internal resistance of 1.6 ohms connected to a 2 watt lamp. What is the current in the circuit?
a. 0.167 amps
b. 0.75 amps
c. 0.163 amps
d. 3.6 amps
e. 6.0 amps

46. Which wire has the most current with the smallest power loss?
a. No. 20
b. No 14
c. No. 16
d. No. 4
e. No. 10

47. The operator in keeping the station record (log) would indicate:
a. Signature on duty
b. Signature off duty
c. Time on duty
d. Maintenance and adjustments performed
e. All of the above

48. A transmitter has a field strength of 120 millivots per meter on a frequency of 2182 kHz., and 1200 microvolts per meter on 4364 kHz. What is the second harmonic attenuation?
a. 10 dB
b. 20 dB
c. 40 dB
d. 80 dB
e. 100 dB

49. When an operator responds to a Notice of Violation, it must be addressed to:
a. FCC office originating the notice
b. Federal District Court
c. Federal Fines Authority
d. any FCC field office
e. Federal Bureau of Investigation

50. The crystalline substance that is widely employed in crystal oscillators is:
a. Carbon
b. Quartz
c. Iron Oxide
d. Silicon
e. Plastic

51. A crystal oscillator sees a reactance tube as:
a. Varying DC source
b. Varying AC source
c. Variable resistance
d. Pure DC
e. Variable inductance or capacitance

52. In frequency modulation, the modulation index means the ratio of:
a. Minimum to maximum frequency swing
b. Modulating frequency to frequency swing
c. Maximum frequency swing to minimum frequency swing
d. Frequency swing to modulating frequency
e. Operating frequency to assigned frequency

53. Identify the diagram below:

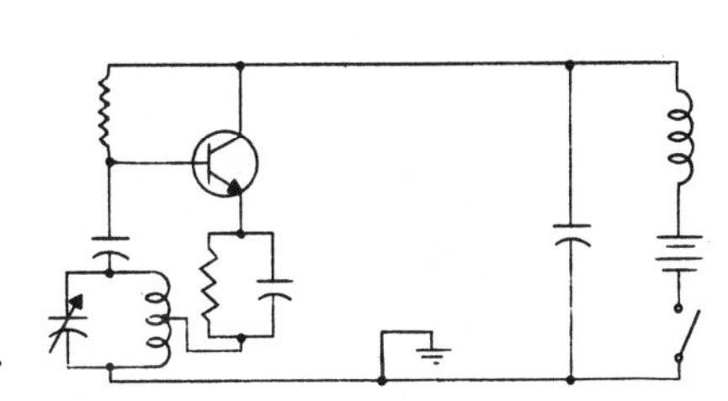

a. Electron coupled oscillator
b. One tube multivibrator
c. Hartley Oscillator
d. Tuned plate tuned grid oscillator
e. Frequency doubler

54. A certain transmitter is designed to operate with a modulation index of 5 at a modulating frequency of 1000 cycles, producing 8 significant sidebands. A modulation meter, used to measure this, must have a minimum bandpass response of:
   a. 5 Kc
   b. 40 Kc
   c. 1 Kc
   d. 16 Kc
   e. 200 Kc

55. Interference to radio receivers in automobiles can be reduced by:
   a. Connecting resistances in series with the spark plugs
   b. Using heavy conductors between the starting battery and the starting motor
   c. Connecting resistances in series with the starting battery
   d. Grounding the negative side of the starting battery
   e. Grounding the positive side of the starting battery

56. Voltage regulation refers to the output:
   a. voltage of a power supply under full load and no load
   b. voltage of an RF amplifier times load frequency
   c. frequency drift of the line voltage supply
   d. power supply noise suppression control
   e. voltage changes of an amplifier to input frequency

57. Class "C" amplifiers have:
   a. Low plate current efficiency
   b. Their use as audio amplifiers
   c. Great output distortion of the input wave shape
   d. Small amount of grid driving power required
   e. Their ability to identically reproduce wave shapes even at high power

58. Compared to high vacuum rectifier tubes, hot cathode mercury vapor rectifier tubes have the advantage of:
   a. Less danger to operator
   b. No parasitic oscillations
   c. Better voltage regulation
   d. Standing greater abuse
   e. Easier filtering

59. What is the type of coupling in the schematic below?
   a. Resistance
   b. Impedance
   c. Capacitance
   d. Transformer
   e. Faraday

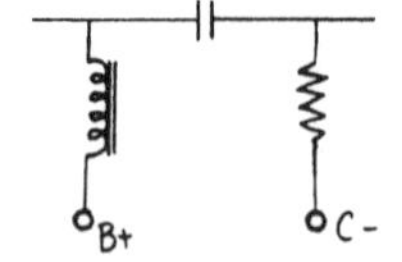


60. The power input to a 52 ohm transmission line is 1,872 watts. The current flowing through the line is:
   a. 6 amps
   b. 144 amps
   c. 0.06 amps
   d. 28.7 amps
   e. 9.6 amps

61. Interference from other stations can be eliminated by use of:
   a. Regenerative feedback
   b. Squelch circuits
   c. Decoupling circuits
   d. Wave traps
   e. Degenerative feedback

62. A certain conductor has an R of 100 ohms per inch with a cross-sectional area of 10 circular mils, the R of 1/2" of a conductor of the same material having a cross-sectional area of 5 circular mils would be:
   a. 100 ohms
   b. 175 ohms
   c. 75 ohms
   d. 250 ohms
   e. 10.0 ohms

63. The crystal microphone is widely used in mobile communications. Care must be taken not to damage it by:
   a. Leaving it to the direct rays of the sun
   b. Whistling into it
   c. Talking closely to it
   d. Maintaining its usual battery voltage too high
   e. All of the above

64. In a series RLC circuit, the inductive reactance is 52 ohms, the capacitive reactance is 40 ohms, and the value of the resistance is 12 ohms. What is the phase angle?
   a. $90^{\circ}$ leading power factory
   b. $90^{\circ}$ lagging power factory
   c. $45^{\circ}$ leading power factor
   d. $45^{\circ}$ lagging power factor
   e. $0^{\circ}$

65. A satisfactory method of determining if oscillation is occuring in an oscillator is to note if:
   a. Plate current is flowing
   b. Grid bias is present
   c. Cathode current is flowing
   d. There is a DC voltage drop across the load resistor
   e. Any of the above

66. Which is a shunt wound generator?
   a. A
   b. B
   c. C
   d. D
   e. E

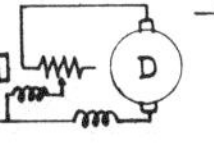


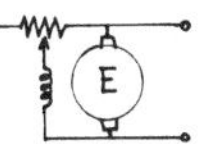


67. Magnetron oscillators are used in the generation of:
   a. AF
   b. Low RF
   c. Super high RF
   d. High VHF
   e. Medium RF

68. Low impedance 'CAN', most satisfactorily be connected to a high impedance source by use of:
   a. Series choke coil
   b. Series condensors
   c. Series resistors
   d. A transformer
   e. A crystal

69. The operating frequency of all radio stations shall be determined in comparison with:
   a. A secondary standard
   b. A Pierce oscillator if power exceeds 25 watts
   c. An approved frequency meter
   d. The standard signals of station WWV
   e. X and Y cut quartz crystals

70. With an AC filter supply, a filament center tap is usually provided for the transmitter tube plate and grid return circuits to:
a. Reduce harmonic outputs
b. Prevent modulation of the emitted signal by the AC filament supply
c. Provide a source of uninterrupted filament supply
d. Control the regulation of filament voltage
e. None of the above

71. A voltmeter with a full-scale of 0-50 volts, with a resistance of 50,000 ohms, has a sensitivity of:
a. 1000 volts per ohm
b. 1000 ohms per volt
c. 10 ohms per volt
d. 25 ohms per volt
e. 50 ohms per volt

72. At series resonance, the impedance of the AC circuit is equal to:
a. The inductive reactance of the circuit
b. 1.414 multiplied by the resistance of the circuit
c. The capacitive reactance of the circuit
d. The resistance of the circuit
e. Infinity

73. The urgency signal is second in priority to what type of message?
a. safety
b. international traffic
c. distress
d. microwave
e. security report

74. What statement is true regarding transistor amplifiers?
a. Emitter is biased in reverse direction
b. Collector is biased in forward direction
c. Collector is biased in reverse direction
d. a and b above
e. All of the above

75. To tune a transmitter first:
a. Turn on all stages
b. Connect a dummy antenna
c. Disconnect the radiating antenna
d. Detune all stages
e. Check on the plate voltage

76. If a 45 megacycle carrier frequency is to be maintained within .002%, it would operate between:
a. 44.0000 Mc and 45.0001 Mc
b. 44.9991 Mc and 45.0009 Mc
c. 44.0000 Mc and 45.0091 Mc
d. 44.0100 Mc and 45.0009 Mc
e. 44.9001 Mc and 45.0900 Mc

77. A buffer amplifier is used to:
a. Provide a more perfect sine-wave
b. Multiple the frequency of the oscillator
c. Provide a stable load for the oscillator
d. Produce harmonics fcr amplification
e. Prevent possible rupture of the oscillator crystal

78. Magnetron oscillators are used for:
a. Generating SHF signals
b. Multiplexing
c. Generating rich harmonics
d. FM demodulation
e. FM transmission

79. An increase of 10 decibels in the output of a power circuit represents what change in the power level:
   a. There is no relationship between decibals and power output
   b. The change cannot be determined
   c. The power is multiplied 100 times
   d. The power is multiplied 10 times
   e. The power is doubled

80. A power supply has a no-load voltage of 660 volts and a full-load voltage of 600 volts. What is the regulation?
   a. 0%
   b. 6.6%
   c. 10%
   d. 96%
   e. 46%

81. When frequency modulation is used in narrow band telephony, the deviation from the modulated carrier shall not exceed plus or minus:
   a. 20 Kc
   b. 15 Kc
   c. 12 Kc
   d. 10 Kc
   e. 5 Kc

82. In an FM receiver, in order to reduce noise to signal ratio:
   a. Use an omni-directional antenna
   b. Employ split tuning
   c. Increase regenerative feedback
   d. Increase coupling between stages
   e. Use automatic volume control

83. A peaked grid current reading when a plate tank circuit is tuned through resonance:
   a. Normal condition
   b. Indicates parasitic oscillations are ocurring
   c. Stage not neutralized
   d. Transit time is too long
   e. Grid leak resistor has too large a value

84. Amplitude of instantaneous voltage induced in a conductor cutting magnetic lines of force is proportional to:
   a. Angle of cutting
   b. Sine of angle of cutting
   c. Conductance of conductor
   d. Skin effect
   e. Temperature

85. Series resistors are used with voltage meters to:
   a. Increase the speed of meter movement
   b. Decrease the speed of meter movement
   c. Decrease the voltage range of the instrument
   d. Increase the voltage range of the instrument
   e. Protect the instrument from induced AC voltages

86. An advantage of frequency modulation over amplitude modulation is:
   a. Greater distance can be covered
   b. Static interference is reduced
   c. Shorter antennas can be used
   d. The ground wave is not attenuated
   e. Signals have straight line propogation characteristics

87. Normally in mobile radio installations the E output of dynamoters is:
   a. Adjusted by armature rheostat
   b. Adjusted by field rheostat
   c. Not adjustable
   d. Adjusted by battery rheostat
   e. Both a and b above

88. This circuit is:
   a. parallel detection
   b. Single-Sideband reduced carrier modulator
   c. half-wave diode detector
   d. full-wave diode detector
   e. phase shift network

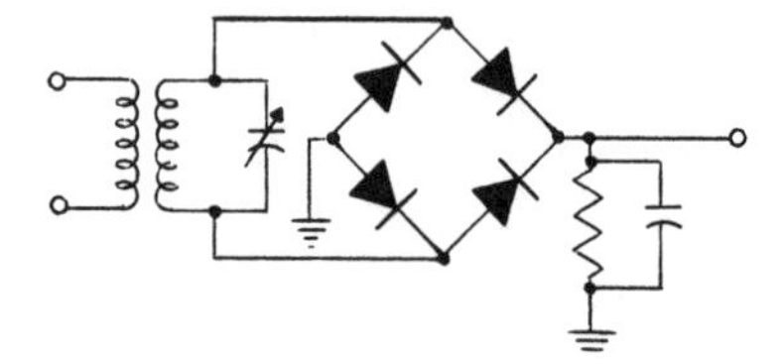

89. If a shunt motor, running with a load, has its shunt field opened, how would this effect the speed of the motor?
   a. Slow down
   b. Stop suddenly
   c. Speed up
   d. Speed up than slow down
   e. Unaffected

90. A 6.3 V battery is charged to 100 ampere hours based on an 8 hour period. Current delivery capacity:
   a. 6.3 amps for 6 hours
   b. 12.5 amps for 8 hours
   c. 100 amps for 1.7 hours
   d. 34 amps for 2 hours
   e. None of the above

91. The state of charge of a Lead Acid storage cell is determined by:
   a. Hydrometer reading
   b. Its open circuit voltage
   c. Its short circuit discharge current
   d. Ohmeter
   e. Plate resistor

92. The circuit shown below would most likely be used as a:
   a. Audio frequency oscillator
   b. Class B AF amplifier
   c. Class C RF amplifier
   d. Class A power amplifier
   e. Half-wave rectifier

-V

93. This circuit is most likely used as:
a. limiter
b. Class B push-pull amplifier
c. Class AB amplifier
d. Class C frequency doubler
e. squelch control

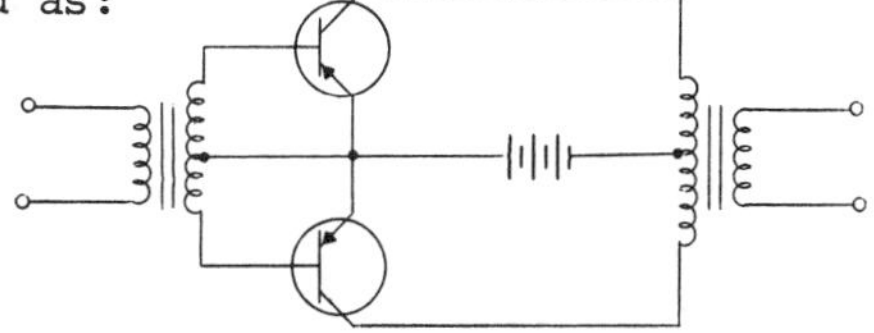

94. VHF is:
a. 30 MHz - 300 MHz
b. 30 KHz - 300 KHz
c. 3 KHz - 30 KHz
d. Very High Frequency
e. both a and d

95. The plate input voltage to the last stage of a transmitter is 600 volts. Plate input current to the last stage is 300 ma. Antenna current is 3 amps. Antenna resistance is 15 ohms. Plate efficiency factor is:
a. 0.25
b. 0.5
c. 0.6
d. 0.7
e. 0.75

The circuit below represents 2 stages in a properly operating FM mobile radiotelephone transmitter. The output drives a frequency tripler stage operating at 15 Mc/s. Questions 96-100 refer to the diagram below:

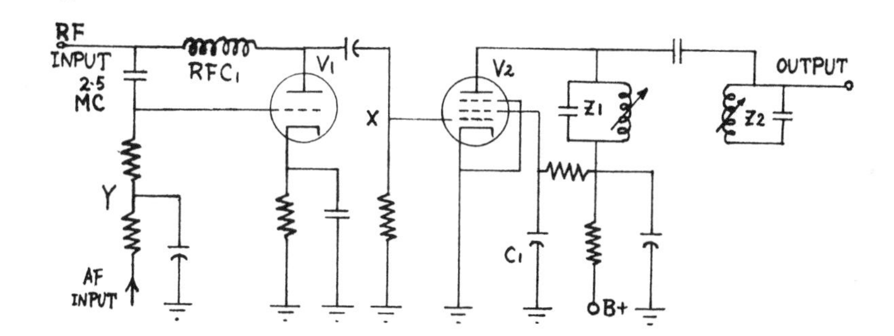


96. In the above circuit:
a. Plate power for V1 is obtained from the second stage
b. The second stage operates as a speech clipper
c. The frequency of current in Z1 is affected by a change in the AF voltage at Y
d. Both V1 and V2 operate as a Class A amplifier
e. None of the above

97. RFC 1 in the circuit above:
a. Attenuates the lower audio frequencies
b. Attenuates the higher audio frequencies
c. Provides a regulated power supply
d. Provides the proper grid bias for the stage
e. Provides the neccessary phase difference between the plate and grid

98. The tuned circuit (Z1) is tuned to:
    a. 5.0 Mc/s
    b. 2.4 Mc/s
    c. 3.5 Mc/s
    d. 20 Mc/s
    e. 50 Mc/s

99. A meter properly connected at point X would measure:
    a. Plate current of the second stage
    b. Bias voltage to the first stage
    c. B+ voltage to the second stage
    d. B+ voltage to the first stage
    e. RF drive to the second stage

100. If the circuit is followed by a frequency tripler, a doubler, and a power amplifier, the transmitter carrier frequency would be:
    a. 50 Mc/s
    b. 25 Mc/s
    c. 10 Mc/s
    d. 44 Mc/s
    e. 30 Mc/s

# Test 3-G Element Three

1. When attempting to contact other vessels on Channel 16:
    a. limit calling to 30 seconds
    b. if no answer is received, wait 2 minutes before calling vessel again
    c. Channel 16 is used for emergency calls only
    d. both a and b
    e. use Channel 16 only if no reply when using 2182 kHz.

2. Which of the following sine waves can a 25 kHz. square wave be formed?
    a. 12.5 kHz., 25 kHz., 50 kHz., 100 kHz.
    b. 25 kHz., 50 kHz., 50 kHz., 25 kHz.
    c. 250 kHz., 500 kHz., 5 MHz., 10 MHz.
    d. 50 kHz., 100 kHz., 150 kHz., 200 kHz
    e. 25 kHz., 75 kHz., 125 kHz., 175 kHz.

3. A system of telecommunications for the transmission of fixed images with a view of their reception in a permanent form is:
    a. Digital Frame System
    b. SSSC
    c. Image-SSB
    d. EPIRB
    e. Facsimile

4. The band fo frequencies used for On-Board ship portable communications in the Marine services:
    a. 9300-9500 MHz.
    b. 1636.5-1644 MHz.
    c. 14.0-14.05 GHz.
    d. 2900-3100 MHz.
    e. 457.525-467.825 MHz.

5. "Stacking" elements on an antenna
   a. Makes for better reception
   b. Makes for poorer reception
   c. Decreases antenna current
   d. Decreases directivity
   e. Has no effect on reception or directivity

6. The feedback occurs in a tuned plate tuned grid oscillator by virtue of:
   a. Plate circuit losses
   b. Interelectrode capacitance
   c. Tank circuit losses
   d. Detuning of plate circuit
   e. Detuning of tank circuit

7. The carrier of an AM transmitter is the:
   a. Output of the transmitter when the modulating wave is zero
   b. Output of the transmitter when the modulating wave is present
   c. Frequency of the master oscillator
   d. The RMS average of the modulated signal
   e. Tone transmitted for testing

8. The reciprocal of conductance is:
   a. Admittance
   b. Susceptance
   c. Inductance
   d. Capacitance
   e. Resistance

9. This diagram is:
   a. VHF final RF amplifier
   b. Balanced ring modulator
   c. RF power amplifier stage
   d. Frequency multiplier
   e. SSB Detector stage

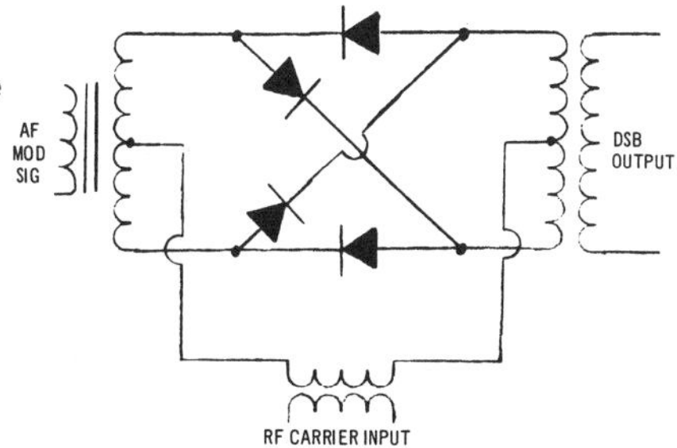


10. What word may be used to say that a message has been received and will be complied with?
   a. mayday
   b. over
   c. security
   d. roger
   e. wilco

11. If the frequency of the input voltage to a single phase, full wave rectifier is 50 c/s the predominant ripple frequency in the output of the rectifier will be:
   a. 1 Kc
   b. 100 c/s
   c. 150 c/s
   d. 15 c/s
   e. 20 c/s

12. The capacitance of a condenser may be increased by:
    a. Decreasing the dielectric constant
    b. Increasing the spacing of the plates
    c. Increasing the electrical resistance of the plate material
    d. Increasing the number of plates
    e. Increasing the conductance of the plates

13. The input voltage to a center tapped power transformer of a full-wave power supply is 120 volts (RMS) at 60 cycles. The transformer turns ratio is 1 to 10. The output of the power supply having capacitance input filter as measured on a DC voltmeter would be approximately:
    a. 850 volts
    b. 1200 volts
    c. 1700 volts
    d. 600 volts
    e. 120 volts

14. If the frequency swing of an FM broadcast station is plus or minus 75 Kc, and the audio tone modulated signal is 30.0 Kc; what is the modulating index?
    a. 2.5
    b. 250
    c. 15
    d. 40
    e. 1

15. The input to a transformer is 100 volts. One side of the center-tap of the secondary to ground is 300 volts. What is the turns ratio?
    a. 1 to 3
    b. 1 to 4
    c. 1 to 6
    d. 1 to 100
    e. 1 to 300

16. An absorption wave meter is useful in measuring:
    a. Field strength
    b. Output frequencies to conform with FCC tolerances
    c. Standing wave frequencies
    d. Crystal tolerances
    e. The resonant frequency of LC tank circuit

17. UHF is:
    a. 30 to 3000 Kc
    b. 30,000 to 300,000 Mc
    c. 300 to 3000 Kc
    d. 3000 to 30,000 Mc
    e. 300 to 3000 Mc

18. Eddy currents in a power transformer are:
    a. Stray currents in core
    b. Same as hysteresis
    c. Reduced by laminating the core
    d. $I^2$
    e. a and c

19. A high vacuum tube full-wave rectifier power supply has 200 volts rms induced in its center tapped transformer secondary. Assuming no voltage across the tube, what would be the approximate minimum voltage rating of its filter capacitors?
    a. 282 volts
    b. 150 volts
    c. 180 volts
    d. 200 volts
    e. 141 volts

20. Radiated energy:
   a. Voltage along a straightened out balanced loop
   b. Voltage along a 1/4 wave Hertz antenna
   c. Voltage along a 1/2 wave Hertz antenna
   d. Current along a 1/4 wave Hertz antenna
   e. Current along a 1/2 wave Hertz antenna

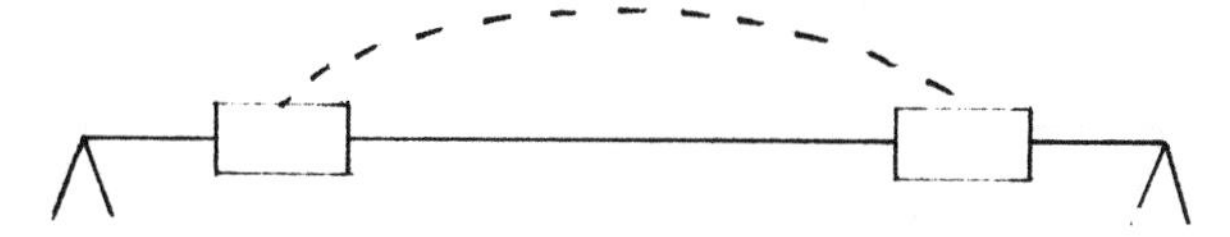

21. The parasitic elements on a receiving antenna:
   a. Increase its directivity
   b. Decrease its directivity
   c. Have no effect on its impedance
   d. Make it more nearly omnidirectional
   e. None of the above

22. In a standard frequency modulation transmitter the deviation ratio is 5. The frequency of the modulating audio frequency is 5000 cycles per second. If there are eight significant sidebands, what is the bandwidth of the transmitter?
   a. 80 Kc
   b. 15 Kc
   c. 150 Kc
   d. 10 Kc
   e. 2 c/s

23. The frequency of a properly operating crystal oscillator can be changed by:
   a. Increasing the grid bias
   b. Connecting a condenser in parallel with the crystal
   c. Connecting a resistor in series with the crystal
   d. Decreasing grid bias
   e. Connecting a resistance in parallel with the crystal

24. While transmitting on a properly adjusted FM transmitter, the DC plate current fluctuates in:
   a. The master control oscillator
   b. Radio frequency doubler stage
   c. None of the transmitter stages
   d. The speech amplifier if single ended
   e. RF tripler stage

25. Impedance of a set of earphones is 15 ohms. To couple them to the plate circuit of a power amplifier with an impedance of 6000 ohms, you would use a matching transformer with a turns ratio of:
   a. 400:1
   b. 15:6000
   c. 40:1
   d. 20:1
   e. 15:1

26. Plate saturation occurs when:
   a. Grid bias is minimum
   b. Plate voltage is maximum
   c. Further increase in plate voltage will not cause an increase in plate current
   d. Grid goes positive
   e. Grid current peaks

27. An air-core choke coil of 1500 turns of #28 copper wire has an inductance of 0.3 henrys. When the air-core is replaced by iron, the inductance becomes:
a. 0 henrys
b. Less than 0.1 henry
c. Negative
d. Greater than 0.3 henrys
e. Less

28. Antenna voltage is:
a. Inversely proportional to the square of its length
b. Proportional to its effective height
c. Measured voltage times length in feet
d. Always proportional to field strength
e. None of the above

29. What is the diagram?
a. frequency doubler stage
b. Push-pull AF amplifier
c. High power RF oscillator
d. Cascaded RF stages
e. Plate modulated AM ampl

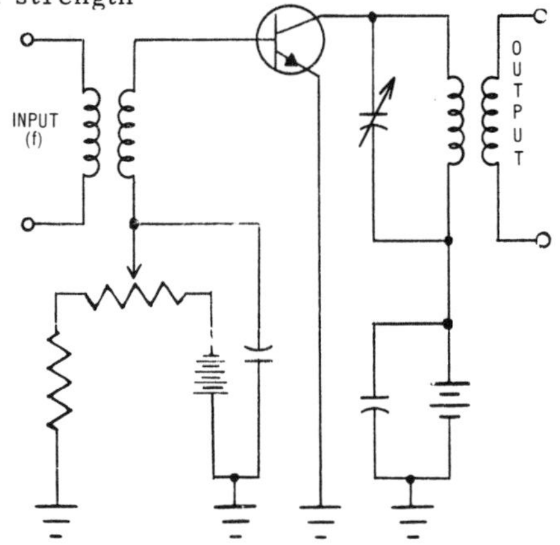


30. Three quarters (3/4) of a pure sine wave cycle would represent how many degrees of one complete cycle:
a. 45
b. 90
c. 180
d. 270
e. 360

31. Atmospheric noise or static is no great problem:
a. In AM receivers
b. At frequencies below 5 Mc
c. At frequencies above 1 Mc
d. At frequencies above 30 Mc
e. At frequencies below 10 Mc

32. A duo-triode:
a. Must be connected in push-pull
b. Is, in effect, 2 (two) triodes in one envelope
c. Is never connected in push-pull
d. Must be connected in cascade
e. Two seperate vacuum tubes always connected in parallel

33. FM equipment used in two way auto communications is designed for modulation index of:
a. 15
b. 5
c. 1.66
d. 10
e. 2.5

34. A vacuum tube amplifier has a gain of 50; this means:
   a. The mu of the tube will not be more than 50 in usual circumstances
   b. Output current is 50 times input current
   c. Output voltage is 50 times input voltage
   d. For every one volt change on the grid there will be a corresponding 50 volt change in the plate output
   e. All of the above

35. The wavelength of a 500 Mc RF wave is approximately:
   a. 500 meters
   b. 0.6 meters
   c. 0.5 meters
   d. 1.0 meters
   e. 10 meters

36. Part of the proper procedure involved in determining frequency swing, on a standard FM modulation monitor, would be (after suitable connections and warm up period) to:
   a. Check the crystal against a frequency standard, then adjust tuning dial, noting minimum and maximum frequency
   b. Check the crystal against a frequency standard, then adjust tuning dial, noting center and maximum frequency
   c. Adjust tuning dial to the center frequency, switch on the instruments internal modulation signal, and note deviation produced
   d. Adjust tuning dial and note frequency difference between each sideband
   e. Adjust tuning dial to all harmonics and measure spacing

37. If a power supply fails, a new high vacuum tube glows red-hot, smoke curls from around the filter choke
   a. The transformer secondary has shorted
   b. The filter choke has an open turn
   c. One of the filter capacitors has shorted
   d. A bleeder resistor has opened
   e. There is a crystalized ground connection

38. A bleeder resistor is across a filter condenser rated at 8 mfds. Resistor is carrying 25 ma. at 450 volts. It dissapates approximately:
   a. 18 watts
   b. 4.5 watts
   c. 11 watts
   d. 2 watts
   e. 33 watts

39. The DC milliammeter shown in the circuit below is used as a voltmeter by the addition of the series resistor $R_s$ which has a value such that a full scale deflection on the meter is equivalent of 120 volts. If $R_1$ is added and 135 volts is now impressed on the circuit and the ammeter reads as indicated, what is the value of the load resistor $R_1$ ?
   a. 18,000 ohms
   b. 13,500 ohms
   c. 8000 ohms
   d. 3000 ohms
   e. 1200 ohms

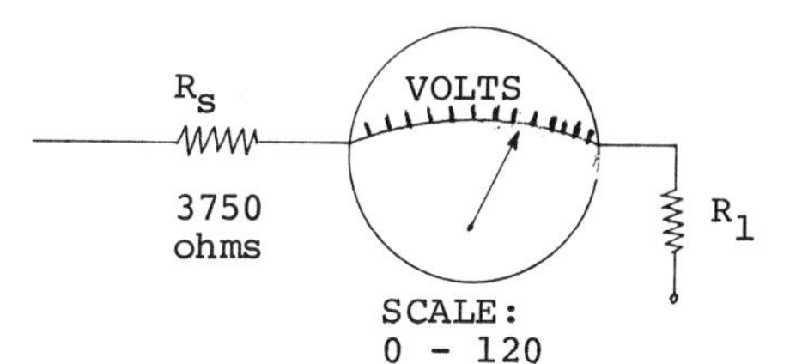

40. Velocity of radio wave propogation in free space does what?
   a. Varies in speed
   b. Is constant
   c. Is always refracted by inosphere
   d. Is same as speed of light
   e. Both b and d above

41. What part of an atom is most concerned with electricity?
   a. Inner electrons
   b. Neutrons
   c. Valence electrons or outer electrons
   d. Protons
   e. Ions

42. Which of these statements is correct?
   a. Class "B" RF amplifiers must be operated push-pull
   b. RF linear operated amplifiers are usually used as linear amplifiers
   c. Class "C" amplifiers are usually used as linear amplifiers
   d. Class "B" AF amplifier stages usually have a minimum of 2 vacuum tubes
   e. All of the above are correct

43. Transmitting equipment that is required to have FCC type acceptance:
   a. May not be adjusted or tampered with in any manner
   b. May not be repaired, except by written request to the Commission
   c. Must be periodically submitted for reappraisal of performance rating
   d. Must have no change whatsoever made in its basic design without authorization from the Commission
   e. Is governed by all of the above

44. The resonant frequency of a Hertz antenna can be lowered by:
   a. Lowering the frequency of the transmitter
   b. Placing a condenser in series with the antenna
   c. Placing a resistor in series with the antenna
   d. Reducing the physical length of the antenna
   e. Placing an inductance in series with the antenna

45. Voltage gain of a triode amplifier with a mu of 100, Rp of .045 meg ohms, operating into a load of 15,000 ohms is:
   a. 1,500
   b. 250
   c. 100
   d. 25
   e. 9

46. What is the approximate total equivalent inductance when connecting X and Y?
   a. 4.4 h
   b. 15 h
   c. 7.5 h
   d. 3.4 h
   e. 5.1 h

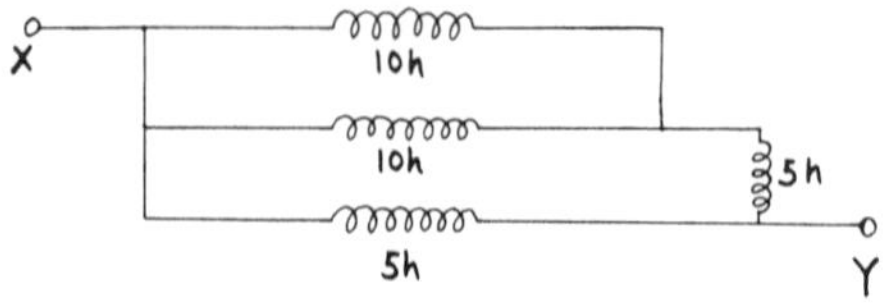

X
10h
10h
5h
5h
Y

47. How does a licensed operator of a ship's radiotelephone station exhibit his authority to operate?
   a. making transmitter inaccessible
   b. knowing FCC regulations
   c. knowing where operating log is located
   d. posting the license at the control point of the station
   e. transmitting the official call sign of the station

48. An AC series circuit composed of an inductive reactance of 10 ohms, and a resistance of 10 ohms, the source voltage current will be out of phase with the source voltage by:
   a. 360 degrees
   b. 180 degrees
   c. 90 degrees
   d. 45 degrees
   e. 0 degrees

49. When an operator tests a transmitter on the air, care should be taken not to:
   a. broadcast call letters
   b. test for a short period of time
   c. turn transmitter on
   d. post his operator license
   e. interfere with other communications

50. Carbon resistors are more desirable than wirewound resistors for bleeder resistors in vacuum tube power supplies because:
   a. Wirewound resistors are more subject to open circuit
   b. Wirewound resistors have short leads
   c. Carbon fuses easily
   d. Carbon is a poor conductor of electricity
   e. Carbon has a negative temperature coefficient

51. A base station is:
   a. An airport traffic control station
   b. A land station handling public correspondence with ships stations
   c. Any fixed station at a land base
   d. Any station operating on a military base
   e. A land station in the land mobile service carrying on a service with land mobile stations

52. In the circuit below what would AC voltmeter read between X and Y? V = 100 V (RMS), $X_L$ = 100 ohms, $X_C$ = 100 ohms, R = 100 ohms.
   a. 0 volt
   b. 1 volt
   c. 10 volts
   d. 100 volts
   e. 1000 volts

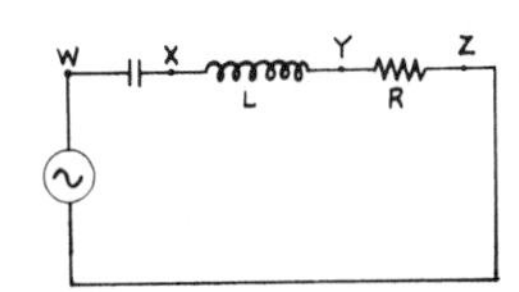


53. A relay coil of 600 ohms operates on .1 amp. It is connected across a 110 volt DC source; how much power is dissipated in the protective resistance?
   a. 60 watts
   b. 50 watts
   c. 0.1 watt
   d. 5 watts
   e. 67.5 watts

54. An electrostatic (FARADAY) screen between the final tank circuit of a transmitter and the antenna circuit will:
   a. Decrease the transfer of harmonic energy from the tank
   b. Decrease the output of the fundamental frequency
   c. Reduce parasitic oscillations
   d. Prevent generation of parasitic oscillations
   e. Increase power output

55. Positive and negative polarity need not be observed when connecting:
   a. Electrolytic condensers
   b. Rectifier units in an AC circuit
   c. Secondary cells of a battery in series
   d. DC bleeder resistors
   e. DC milliammeter

56. A screen grid in a vacuum tube primarily:
   a. Reduces grid-plate electrostatic capacity
   b. Increases grid-plate electrostatic capacity
   c. Increases grid-cathode electrostatic capacity
   d. Decreases secondary emission

57. When connecting an electrolytic condenser:
   a. Observe Polarity
   b. Use large resistors in shunt
   c. Connect ahead of choke coils
   d. Use only in full-wave power supplies
   e. Use small resistors in parallel

58. The number of significant sidebands contained in an FM signal is directly proportional to:
   a. Audio modulation voltage
   b. Audio modulation frequency
   c. Audio quality
   d. Carrier frequency
   e. All of the above

59. When transmissions are not being made, the transmitter should be:
   a. left on the air
   b. dismantled for testing
   c. kept off the air
   d. tuned to 2182 KHz
   e. modulated

60. A high percentage of modulation is desirable in an AM transmitter:
   a. Increase signal to noise ratio
   b. Widen bandwidth
   c. Narrow the bandwidth
   d. Double the power output
   e. Keep antenna current from excessive increase

61. Neutralization of an RF amplifier means:
   a. Tap on the grid coil is properly centered
   b. Tap on the plate coil is properly centered
   c. Net capacitive feedback voltage from plate to grid is zero
   d. Net capacitive voltage from plate to ground is zero
   e. Voltage in the grid circuit is balanced by an equal voltage in screen circuit

62. The function of pre-emphasis in an FM transmitter is:
   a. High audio frequencies are over amplified improving the signal to noise ratio in the receiver
   b. Amplifies low audio frequencies
   c. Amplifies high audio frequencies
   d. Amplifies low radio frequencies
   e. Multiplies high audio frequencies

63. Germanium diodes as compared to most vacuum tube diodes usually:
   a. Cannot withstand as high inverse peak voltages
   b. Are capable of withstanding higher currents
   c. Are capable of withstanding higher voltages
   d. b and c
   e. All of the above

64. A cavity resonator:
   a. Acts as a pure inductance at its resonant frequency
   b. Usually has physical dimensions which are independent of frequency
   c. Acts as a LC circuit at its resonant frequency
   d. Acts as a pure resistance at any frequency
   e. Is usually employed in 60 cycle high power transformers

65. The disadvantage of using a squelch switch on a receiver:
   a. Reduces sensitivity of receiver to a week signal
   b. Difficult to adjust
   c. Cannot be used with AVC
   d. a and c
   e. b and c

66. The last stage of a transmitter is properly designed, but it is desired to increase its output power. You would:
   a. Increase size of load resistor
   b. Feed its output into a voltage step-up transformer
   c. Increase the negative control grid bias
   d. Perform both b and c
   e. Perform none of the above

67. Impedance in a circuit:
   a. Is measured in farads
   b. Is measured in henrys
   c. Is always independent of frequency
   d. Is expressed in ohms
   e. Is inversely proportional to reactance

68. The peak value of a sine-wave, whose RMS value is 20 volts would be approximately:
   a. 19.99 volts
   b. 25 volts
   c. 28.28 volts
   d. 16.4 volts
   e. 20 volts

69. In storing a fully charged battery (lead-acid) for a long period of time (8 to 12 months) one should:
 a. Drain and flush out the electrolyte then refill with distilled water
 b. Keep it in a warm place
 c. Jar it at least once a week to prevent sulfation
 d. Keep at least 50% of it immersed in water
 e. Keep dust cover over it

70. EPIRB batteries are inspected how often?
 a. monthly
 b. every 12 months
 c. daily while at sea
 d. as often as necessary
 e. during normal testing

71. An RC circuit has a .001 microfarad capacitor and a 1-Meg-ohm resistor. What is the impedance if $2\pi F = 1000$?
 a. 1.0 Meg-ohm
 b. 1000 ohms
 c. 10,000 ohms
 d. 2.4 Meg-ohm
 e. 1.4 Meg-ohm

72. AC probes (utilizing 2 diodes) are often used on a VTVM:
 a. To measure higher voltages
 b. In measuring circuits containing high currents
 c. To increase frequency range of instrument
 d. To avoid rectifing measured voltage
 e. To change it from a peak reading to an effective reading instrument

73. A conventional wattmeter:
 a. Measures the amount of current (squared) through it
 b. Measures the amount of voltage (squared) through it
 c. Measures voltage times current times circuit power factor
 d. Measures voltage across it, times current through it, disregarding phase
 e. Has a permanent magnet and one coil

74. A single tone amplitude modulated wave contains the fundamental frequency plus two sidebands. These sidebands are created by:
 a. Distortion of the final amplifier
 b. Variations in antenna impedance during each cycle
 c. The modulating signal
 d. Ionospheric distortion of the carrier
 e. Saturation effect of the output transformer

75. A screen grid resistor burns out after smoking. First thing to check would be:
 a. Short in screen grid by-pass capacitor
 b. An open turn in plate coil
 c. Short in B+ by-pass capacitor
 d. Open grid leak resistor
 e. Open power supply bleeder resistor

76. What is the limiter of an FM receiver?
 a. Is placed ahead of the discriminator
 b. It limits amplitude of the carrier to a given value
 c. Usually a low gain IF amplifier
 d. Uses either grid-circuit limiting or plate circuit limiting
 e. Any of the above is correct

77. The circuit below is:
 a. An AVC
 b. A mixer
 c. A video amplifier
 d. A reinsertion
 e. A discriminator

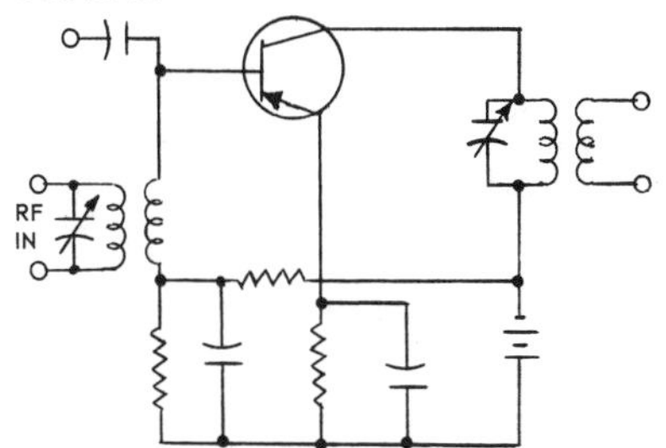


78. As a general rule, increasing the coupling between two tuned circuits up to the critical point:
 a. Increases the bandwidth response
 b. Decreases the bandwidth response
 c. Decreases the power transfer
 d. Decreases the coefficient of coupling
 e. Increases the gain on the following stage

79. An FM transmitter at 5 Mc deviates .002%. What will be the frequency of the fully modulated signal?
 a. 4.000 Mc
 b. 5.002 Mc
 c. 5.010 Mc
 d. No change
 e. 5.100 Mc

80. The purpose of an "M" derived filter is:
 a. Create series resonant band-pass circuit
 b. Create parallel resonant band-pass circuit
 c. Broaden frequency response of a circuit
 d. Create sharper cut-off to the frequency response of a system
 e. Create a broader frequency response to a system

81. A transmitter operating on 16 Mc is allowed a frequency tolerance of ±.02 %. The oscillator operates at 1/8 of the output frequency. What is the maximum allowable deviation in the oscillator frequency?
 a. 32 cycles
 b. 400 cycles
 c. 2.16 cycles
 d. 16 Kc
 e. 64 Mc

82. Neglecting line losses, the RMS voltage along an RF transmission line having no standing waves:
 a. Is equal to the impedance
 b. Is one-half of the surge impedance
 c. Is the product of the surge impedance times the line current
 d. Varies sinusodially along the line
 e. Is the quotient of the maximum current to the minimum current

83. Waveguides are:
   a. A hollow tube that carries RF
   b. Solid conductor of RF
   c. Coaxial cables
   d. copper wire
   e. AF conductor

84. When a vacuum tube operates at VHF or higher as compared to lower frequencies:
   a. Transit time of electrons becomes important
   b. It is necessary to make larger components
   c. It is necessary to increase grid spacing
   d. Only a pentode is satisfactory
   e. All of the above

85. Grounding the center tap on the secondary transformer will have the effect of:
   a. The voltage between center tap and one side of the secondary will be half that of the total induced voltage
   b. The voltage induced in the secondary will be doubled
   c. Open circuit
   d. The voltage in the secondary will be halved
   e. The induced voltage in the secondary will always be positive with respect to ground

86. In general, which of the following can be said of voltage and power amplifiers
   a. Power amplifiers usually employ tubes with high plate
   b. Power amplifiers usually employ low-mu tubes capable of withstanding high plate current
   c. Voltage amplifiers usually employ low-mu tubes for greater amplification
   d. Power amplifiers usually employ hi-mu tubes for greater amplification
   e. Preamps usually employ power rather than voltage stages

87. Identify the unmarked stage in this Heterodyne Frequency Meter block diagram:
   a. Buffer amplifier
   b. Converter
   c. Mixer
   d. Detector
   e. RF filter network

RF INPUT FROM TRANSMITTER
VARIABLE OSCILLATOR
?
AUDIO AMPLI-FIER
CALIBRATE SWITCH ON / OFF
CORRECTOR
CRYSTAL OSCILLATOR

88. This circuit:
   a. Reactance modulation oscillator circuit
   b. will operate properly if C2 is shorted
   c. both a and b
   d. will operate properly if C1 is removed
   e. both a and d

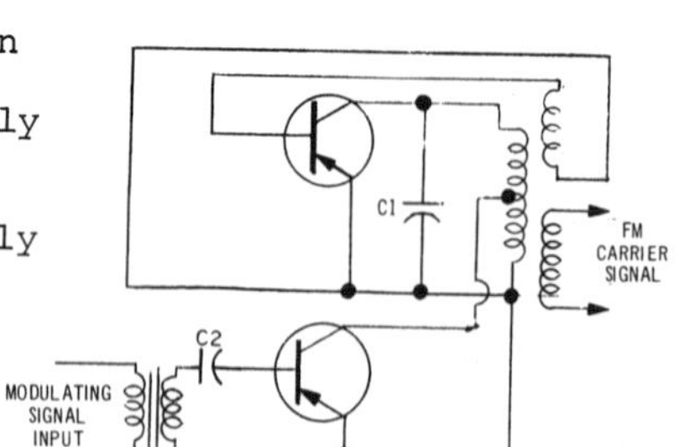

89. A mobile FM, 50 watt, transmitter has just been received in shipment. All stages are assumed to be untuned. After proper connections to the power supply and installation of a dummy antenna, you should first:
a. Turn on power to all stages and speak into the microphone while adjusting the final tank circuit
b. Turn on power to all but final amplifier, activate microphone very briefly while tuning each stage
c. Turn on power to all stages and adjust the oscillator frequency
d. Turn on power to all stages and adjust each stage to its correct frequency
e. Turn on power to oscillator stage, tune it, turn on power to final amplifier, then tune multiplier stages

90. Wires connecting amplifier stages can sometimes pick up noise from an external source by virtue of:
a. Saturation of immobile area
b. DC component in external source voltage
c. The fluctuations of surrounding field of flux
d. The rectifying action of the connecting wires
e. Any batteries associated with external source equiptment

91. What should the value of the load resistor (RL) be if it is to dissipate the most power?
a. 1 ohm
b. 10 ohms
c. 20 ohms
d. 22 ohms
e. 30 ohms

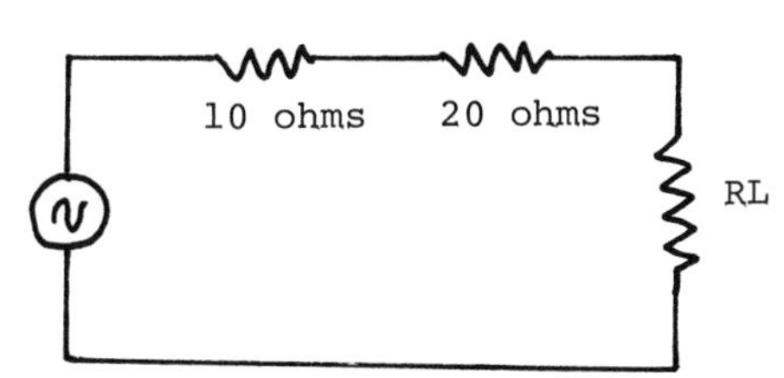


92. The resonant frequency of a series circuit having C of 20 mfds, and an L of 0.25 h and R of 6 ohms is:
a. 1.5 Kc
b. 120 c/s
c. 71 c/s
d. 6 Kc
e. 30 c/s

93. A transmitter using a crystal oscillator, a doubler stage and a Class C power amplifier ceases to operate. Meter readings are as follows. Antenna current is zero; power amplifier plate current and doubler plate current are high; the crystal oscillator plate current is increased over normal. The failure is probably due to a:
a. Burned out power amplifier tube
b. Broken antenna lead
c. Burned crystal oscillator tube
d. Burned out bleeder resistor in the power supply
e. Fractured crystal

94. What is the disadvantage of wideband FM as compared to narrow-band FM?
a. Shorter range
b. Requires more power to operate
c. Cannot be used with directional antenna
d. Occupies more space in the radio spectrum
e. Uses more expensive equiptment

95. The collector of a transistor is analogous to the following part of a vacuum tube
a. Plate
b. Cathode
c. Control grid
d. Screen grid
e. Normal grid

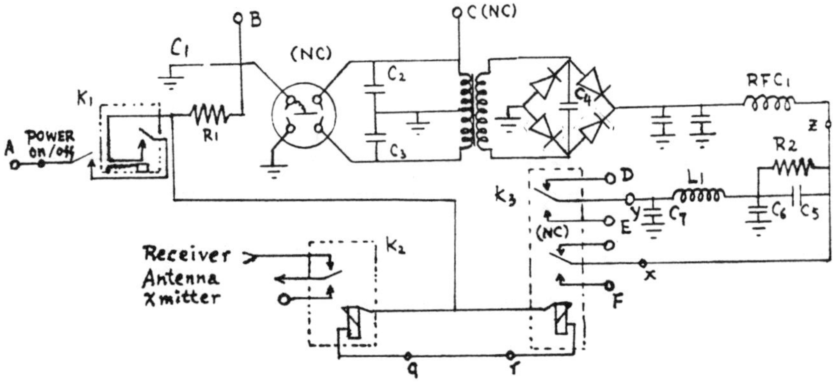

Note: (NC) means that no connections are normally made to this point. All relays (K1, K2, K3) operate on 6 volts and are shown in their inactivated positions. The voltage source is assumed to be a 6 volt lead-acid battery. The above circuit represents a possible power supply for a mobile communications transmitter and receiver. It is assumed to be properly connected to external equiptment and capable of operation.

96. If the transmitter were operating (power ON and press to talk switch closed) and capacitor C2 should open or become detached from ground, an ammeter inserted in the circuit at point Z would read (compared to normal):
a. Very high
b. A reversed reading
c. Nearly normal
d. Very low
e. Zero

97. If, with power ON and the press-to-talk switch closed, capacitor C4 should short:
a. The voltage at Terminal A would drop to zero
b. The voltage at Terminal B would drop to a very low value
c. Relay K3 would probably burn out
d. The vibrator would be damaged after a short period of time
e. The current at point X would be excessive

98. With power ON and the press-to-talk switch closed, the terminal with the highest voltage would be:
a. TERMINAL F
b. TERMINAL E
c. TERMINAL C
d. TERMINAL B
e. TERMINAL D

99. To determine the amount of plate current being drawn by the final power amplifier (power ON, press-to-talk switch closed) an ammeter would be inserted in the circuit at:
a. Point P
b. Point Q
c. Point Y
d. Point Z
e. Point X

100.

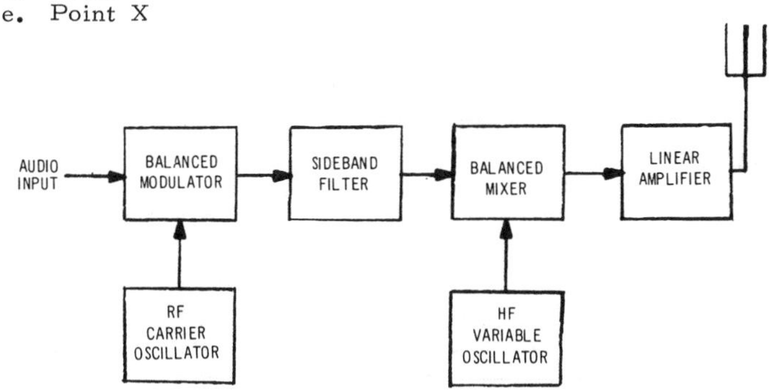

The diagram above represents:
a. Single-Sideband receiver
b. VHF-FM reciever
c. Channel 13 - 16 transmitter
d. Full wave amplitude modulated UHF transmitter
e. Single-Sideband transmitter

# Test 3-H Element Three

1. What is the emission designator for a VHF-FM station having an authorized bandwidth of 20 kHz., frequency deviation of + or - 5 kHz. in the 156-162 MHz. band?

   a. 2K80R3E (previously A3A)
   b. 16K0F3E (previously F3)
   c. 2K80J3E (previously A3J)
   d. 6K00A3E (previously A3)
   e. none of the above

2. How do you check an emergency transmitter, such as survival craft radio equipment, for proper operation?

   a. by official FCC authorization
   b. by use of a dummy antenna
   c. with 1000 Hz. test tones modulated 100% on 2182 kHz.
   d. by activating the auto-alarm signal
   e. all of the above

3. When is it required to give station identification when using portable hand-held 'Marine Utility' transmitters on-board a ship?

   a. When vessel is within 20 miles of any coastline
   b. when traveling is busy shipping channels or when communications are likely to be heard on another vessel in your vacinity
   c. both a and b above
   d. at all times
   e. only while unloading cargo on shore and signal may interfere with land communications

4. During daytime hours, how far must a passenger ship transporting more than 12 people be capable of transmitting a signal by radiotelephone?

   a. 500 miles
   b. 300 miles
   c. 250 miles
   d. 150 miles
   e. 50 miles

5. Under what circumstances are you allowed more than one watt while operating portable VHF-FM transmitters?

   a. distress or sinking of vessel
   b. intership safety or medical emergency
   c. liaison with U.S. Coast Guard
   d. all of the above
   e. never

6. What all inputs are 0 and the output is 0, what input could be made high to provide a high output?

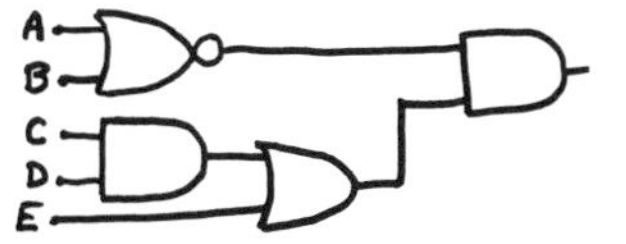


a. A
b. B
c. C
d. D
e. E

7. An FM transmitter operating on a carrier frequency of 25 Mc has a modulation index of five, producing eight significant sidebands above the carrier. When modulated by a 5 khz tone, the frequency bandwidth response must be:

a. 5 khz
b. 8 khz
c. 16 khz
d. 40 khz
e. 80 khz

8. This circuit is a:

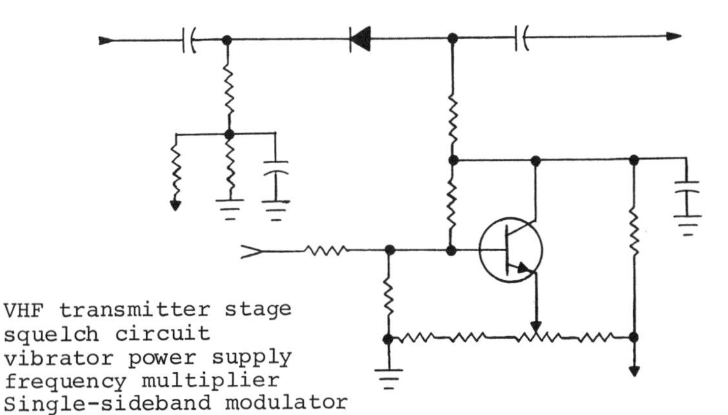

a. VHF transmitter stage
b. squelch circuit
c. vibrator power supply
d. frequency multiplier
e. Single-sideband modulator

9. In single sideband suppressed carrier transmissions:

a. Sidebands and carrier are suppressed
b. Both sidebands are present without the carrier
c. One sideband is heterodyned with a fixed frequency
d. The carrier is modulated by a fixed frequency
e. None of the above

10. Polarity may be ignored in connecting:

a. Electrolytic capacitors
b. E-meters
c. Silicon controlled rectifiers
d. DC bleeder resistors
e. transformer secondary stages

11. Only a person holding a valid General Radiotelephone Operator License may do maintenance on:

    a. low power 10-watt educational broadcast stations
    b. taxi-communications
    c. amateur radio transmitters
    d. marine and aeronautical transmitters
    e. all of the above

12. The phrase "bandwidth occupied by an emission" means:

    a. All frequencies and sidebands for the type of emission and frequency authorized by the FCC
    b. All emissions, including spurious harmonics, radiated by an FCC-licenced station
    c. The width of the band containing 99 % of the energy of the emission
    d. The width of the band whose frequencies contain 99 % of the energy, including any frequency of at least .25 % power
    e. None of the above

13. If the RMS value of an AC voltage is 20 V, the peak value is:

    a. 28.28 volts
    b. 14.14 volts
    c. $1/14.14^2$ volts
    d. 12.72 volts
    e. 24.24 volts

14. What value should $R_L$ be to permit maximum power dissapation?

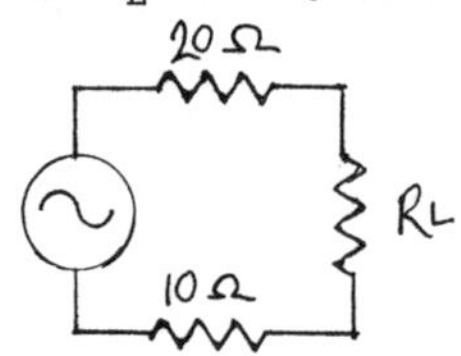


    a. 10 ohms
    b. 20 ohms
    c. 30 ohms
    d. As low as is practical
    e. As high as is practical

15. When measuring the frequency of a station,

    a. The results must be entered in the station log
    b. The measuring device must bear an FCC seal
    c. Prior approval must be obtained from the district FCC engineer-in-charge
    d. Both a and b
    e. Both b and c

16. A 5 Mc FM transmitter has a 5 kc frequency deviation. What will the higest frequency in the transmitter be?

    a. 5.005 Mc
    b. 10.050 Mc
    c. 25 Mc
    d. 50 Mc
    e. Cannot be determined from information given

17. In this circuit, total inductance between X and Y is:

a. 5.2 henrys
b. 7.5 henrys
c. 12.5 henrys
d. 3.4 henrys
e. 64 henrys

18. To see if an oscillator is producing a signal,

a. Check to see if plate resistance is high
b. Check to see if plate current is flowing
c. Check to see if grid current is flowing
d. Measure the plate supply voltage
e. Measure the grid bias

19. A wavelength of 500 MHz. is:

a. 6 meters
b. 60 cm
c. 0.6 cm
d. approx. 0.5 meters
e. 5 meters

20. This circuit is used as:

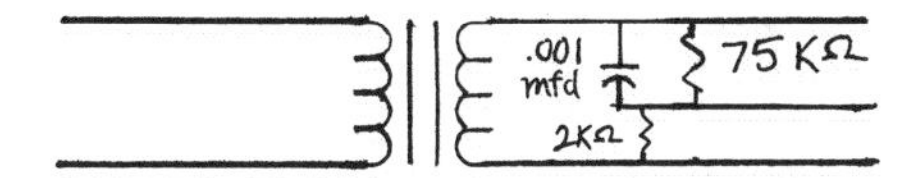


a. An FM transmitter pre-emphasis circuit
b. An FM receiver de-emphasis circuit
c. An FM receiver discriminator
d. An FM receiver peak limiter
e. An FM receiver power supply

21. If the input level to this circuit stayed constant, but the input frequency decreased steadily, the output would:

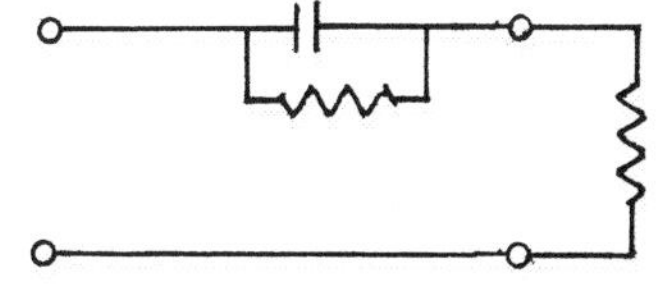

a. Remain constant
b. Increase steadily
c. Decrease steadily
d. Go down, then up
e. Go up, then down

22. When may you utilize and repeat information heard on a private radiotelephone transmission?
a. only if you are a licensed operator
b. when the information is transmitted on 2182 kHz.
c. when listening on a ship in international waters
d. always because radio emission are never private
e. never

23. Output power from a stage compared to input power is:

a. usually smaller
b. equals input power times effieiency
c. always higher
d. neutralized
e. both a and b

24. The strength of a carrier wave on 102.4 Mc measures 120 millivolts-per-meter. The second harmonic strength is 1,200 microvolts-per meter. How attenuated is the second harmonic compared to the fundamental?

a. 10 db
b. 20 db
c. 30 db
d. 40 db
e. 50 db

25. As compared to a full-wave rectifier, a bridge rectifier:

a. Will provide better regulation
b. Will not require a power transformer with a center tap connection on its secondary winding
c. Will provide twice the voltage
d. Will provide .414 times the voltage
e. Will provide .707 times the voltage

26. Parasitic elements are useful in a receiving antenna for:

a. Increasing directivity
b. Increasing selectivity
c. Increasing sensitivity
d. Both a and c
e. None of the above

27. The oscillator crystal of a 24 MHz. transmitter has a positive temperature coefficient of 10 Hertz/C°. If the oscillator frequency is 2 MHz., and the temperature of the crystal should increase by 20° C, the transmitter carrier frequency would shift to:

a. 24,999,000 Hertz
b. 24,002,400 Hertz
c. 25,000,600 Hertz
d. 24,000,000.040 Hertz
e. 24,008,040 Hertz

28. How is this circuit used?

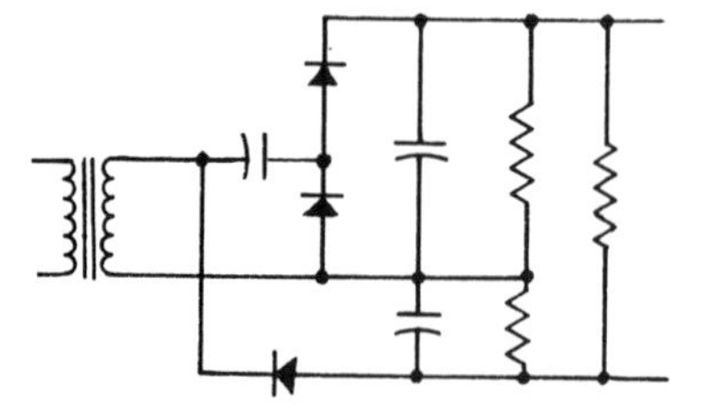

a. frequency doubler
b. voltage tripler
c. frequency tripler
d. phase inverter
e. squelch control

29. A battery has a 100 amper-hour rating based on an eight hour rating period. The amount of current that could be supplied continuously by this battery is:

a. 100 amps for 1 hour
b. 50 amps for 2 hours
c. 12.5 amps for 8 hours
d. 10 amps for 10 hours
e. Any of the above

30. A 36-foot conductor with a resistance of 12 ohms-per-foot is replaced by another made of the same material, but 1/3 the size. What is the resistance of the replacement?

a. 144 ohms
b. 432 ohms
c. 1296 ohms
d. 3888 ohms
e. 6778 ohms

31. The 'Q' of a circuit is the ratio of the:

a. Coil's inductance to the coil's resistance
b. Coil's resistance to the coil's reluctance
c. Coil's reluctance to the coil's inductance
d. Coil's reactance to the coil's resistance
e. None of the above

32. Two ammeters are connected in series in a circuit. Their sum will be:

a. Total current flowing
b. Half the current flowing
c. Twice the current flowing
d. Determined by the power factor of the circuit

33. What change could be made to improve the operation of this oscillator?

a. remove R1
b. remove C2
c. short C4
d. short RFC
e. remove C3

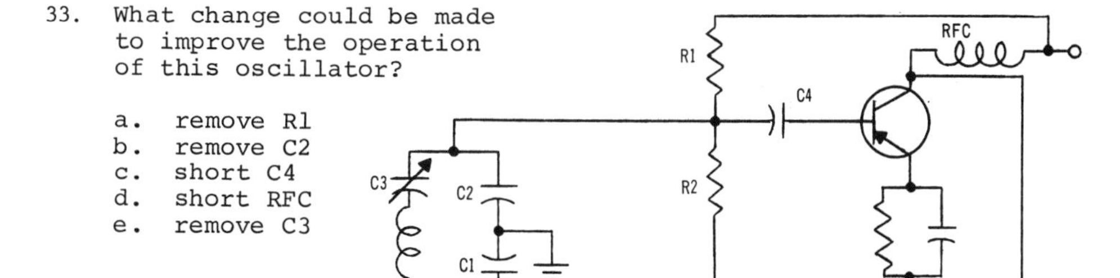


34. The unit of electromotive force is the:

a. Ampere
b. Volt
C. Watt
d. Farad
e. Oersted

35. A superheterodyne receiver is tuned to 1 Mc. A spurious image is obtained from a station at 1910 kc. Assuming an IF of 455 kc, what frequency must the injection oscillator be operating on?

a. 455 kc
b. 545 kc
c. 1,910 kc
d. 1,455 kc
e. 1,545 kc

36. A full-wave high vacuum rectifier circuit uses a center-tapped transformer with a turns ratio of 1:10, step up, and a high capacity pi-type filter. If 120 volts at 60 cycles is applied across the primary, the normal voltage across the load will be about:

a. 424 volts
b. 1680 volts
c. 1410 volts
d. 850 volts
e. 1200 volts

37. This diagram most nearly indicates the:

a. Voltage along a 1/2 wave Hertz antenna
b. Current along a 1/2 wave Hertz antenna
c. Voltage along a 1/4 wave Marconi antenna
d. Current along a 1/4 wave Marconi antenna
e. Resistance along a 1/4 wave Marconi antenna

38. In a Class A amplifier, plate current flows:

a. For 360 degrees
b. For 180 degrees
c. For less than 180 degrees
d. Only on peaks
e. At no time

39. If a marine radiotelephone receiver uses 75 watts of power and a transmitter uses 325 watts, how long can they both operate before discharging a 50 ampere-hour 12 volt battery?

a. 40 minutes
b. 1 hour
c. 1 1/2 hours
d. 6 hours
e. 12 hours

40. What is the highest radiated harmonic frequency of a transmitter operating on 750 kHz?

a. 850 kHz.
b. 5240 kHz.
c. 2250 kHz.
d. 3550 kHz.
e. 750.5 kHz.

41. Neutralization is sometimes not necessary:

a. when operated with center-tapped transformers
b. when a circuit is operated at high RF frequencies
c. when operating the circuit as a grounded grid amplifier
d. when wires are kept as short as possible
e. all of the above

42. A receiver will never be completely silent, even lacking signal voltage.

a. Due to inherent circuit noise within the receiver stages
b. Due to thermal radiation in the atmosphere
c. Due to electrostatic fields in circuit components
d. Due to microphonic tubes
e. Due to improper shielding

43. As a test instrument, an AC VTVM:

a. Is most accurate at the upper end of the scale
b. Decreases in accuracy as frequency rises
c. Has a high sensitivity
d. Has a high selectivity
e. Must use low impedence probes

44. Public Safety Radiotelephone Stations operating in the 50-1000 Mc band have a frequency tolerance of:

a. .0005 %
b. .005 %
c. .0002 %
d. .002 %
e. Either b or d depending on type of emission

45. This circuit is a(n):

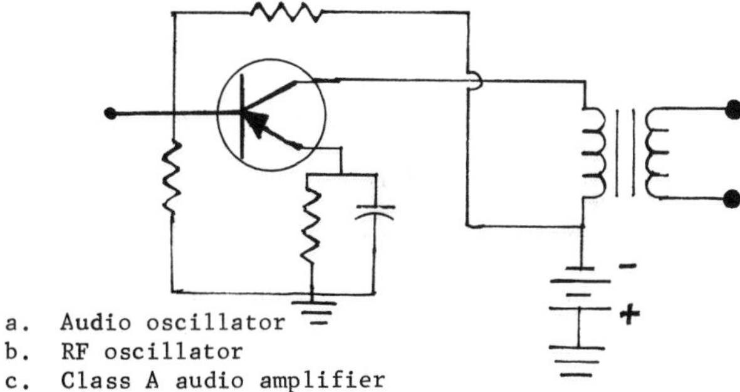


a. Audio oscillator
b. RF oscillator
c. Class A audio amplifier
d. Class B audio amplifier
e. Not enough detail given

46. When replacing components in RF amplifiers

a. leave space for future modifications
b. replace filter and bypass capacitors regularly
c. fill out all appropriate FCC forms
d. keep wire leads as short as possible
e. increase bias voltage as transistors lose output power rating

47. The FCC may suspend an operator license upon proof that the licensee:

a. has assisted another to obtain a license by fradulent means
b. has transmitted superfluous calls
c. has willfully damaged transmitter equipment
d. has transmitted obscene language
e. all of the above

48. What change is needed in order to correct the grounded emitter amplifier shown?

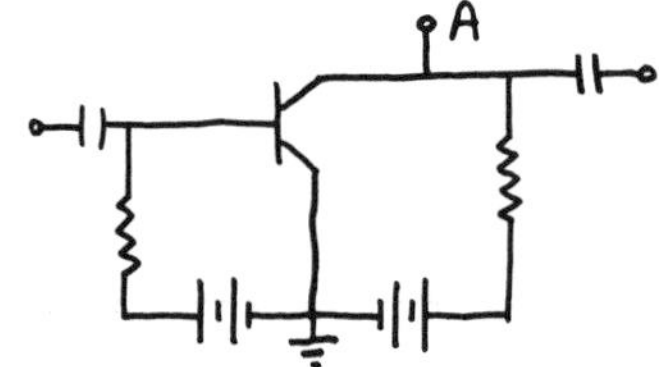


a. no change is necessary
b. polarities of emitter-base battery should be reversed
c. polarities of collector-base battery should be reversed
d. point A should be replaced with a low value capacitor
e. polarities of both batteries should be reversed

49. If a signal is received and passes through port #1 by an RB filter in a circulator multiplex antenna, what occurs at the other ports in the system?

a. signal is reflected
b. signal is passed to transmitter
c. signal is passed to receiver
d. signal is phase-shifted 90°
e. antenna buffer amplifier burn-out results

50. What is the proper method of determining if the operating frequency of a transmitter is being maintained within a specified tolerance?

a. zero-beat a known frequency against the transmitter frequency
b. attach a field strength meter to the antenna input
c. zero-beat the oscillator with FCC radio station WWV
d. zero-beat the output frequency against a suitable source
e. attach a frequency counter to the master oscillator

51. In a properly operating tranmitter, if the power supply bleeder resistor opens, the effect could be:

a. harmonic radiation
b. overload; causing transmitter failure
c. parasitic oscillations
d. filter capacitors might short from voltage surge
e. phase-shift of output

52. AC probes utilizing two diodes are often used on a VTVM to:

a. increase the current range of the meter
b. increase the voltage range of the meter
c. increase the frequency range of the meter
d. decrease the voltage range of the meter
e. both a and b above

53. What is the voltage drop across R1 in this circuit?

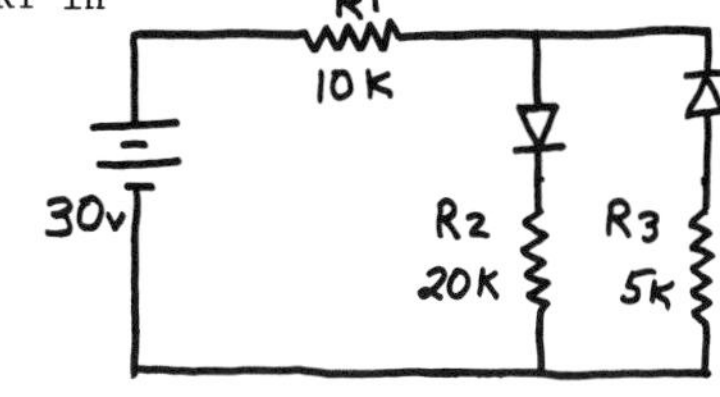


a. 5 volts
b. 7.5 volts
c. 10 volts
d. 20 volts
e. 24.3 volts

54. In an amplifier stage, the output power is equal to:

a. signal voltage and output current
b. square of the current times the power factor
c. square of the current times the impedance
d. square of the current and the resistance
e. none of the above

55. The output voltage of a separately excited AC generator (running at a constant speed) could be controlled by:

a. changing the dilectric constant of the armature
b. changing the material of the armature
c. the field current
d. operating the generator in a no-load condition
e. both b and d

56. What is the effect of a tightly coupled tuned circuit in an amplifier stage?

a. increases bandwidth and selectivity
b. increases bandwidth and decreases selectivity
c. decreases bandwidth and increases selectivity
d. increases selectivity and decreases bandwidth
e. poor frequency response; causing parasitics and harmonics

57. This circuit is:

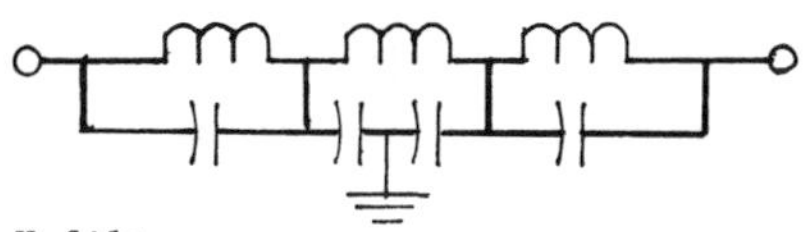

a. a constant-K filter
b. an M-derived filter
c. two M-derived filters
d. two constant K filters
e. none of the above

58. Frequency multiplier circuits:

a. Require Class AB1 operation
b. Require capacitive feeback circuitry
c. Require push-pull doublers
d. inefficient at RF frequencies
e. Do not require linear operation

59. In this circuit C1=C2 and L1=L2. At resonance, if M reads 1.25 ma the applied voltage must be:

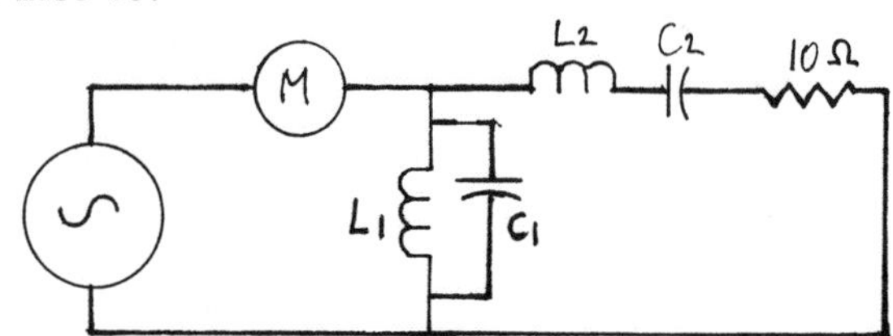


a. .0125 volts
b. .0036 volts
c. .125 volts
d. 1.5625 volts
e. Cannot be determined from given information

60. In a parallel LC circuit having no resistance,

a. If resistance is placed across the circuit, impedance will increase
b. If resistance is placed across the circuit, impedance will decrease
c. Impedance will be infinite
d. Impedance will depend on distributed effects only
e. Impedance will be absent

61. Which class of amplifier will have the least distortion?

a. Class A
b. Class $AB_1$
c. Class $AB_2$
d. Class B
e. Class C

62. In radio circuits, the component most apt to break down is the:

a. Resistor
b. Crystal
c. Transformer
d. Wiring
e. Capacitor

63. Where would these components be found: audio amplifier, RF amplifier, limiter and mixer?

a. FM receiver
b. FM transmitter
c. single-sideband transmitter
d. double-sideband transmitter
e. VHF phase-shift transmitter

64. Voltage applied between two points without current flow produces:

a. Counter EMF
b. Arcing
c. No effect
d. Electrostatic lines of force
e. Both b and d

65. Who is authorized to maintain a continuous and efficient watch on Bridge-to-Bridge Channel 16; 156.65 MHz.?

a. anyone authorized by Master of ship
b. person who pilots or directs movement of vessel
c. FCC licensed Radiotelephone operators only
d. FCC licensed Radiotelegraph operators only
e. anyone holding an FCC Marine Operator Permit

66. The amplitude of voltage induced in a conductor cutting magnetic lines of force is determined mainly by:

a. Permiability of the magnet
b. Conductivity of the armature
c. Cross-sectional area of the conductor
d. Rate of cutting the lines of force
e. Material the windings are made of

67. At or near resonance, a parallel inductance-capacitance circuit has a bandwidth determined by the:

a. Resonant frequency of the circuit
b. "Q" of the circuit
c. Distributed capacitance of the circuit
d. Total resistance of the circuit
e. Both b and d

68. A circulator:

a. cools DC motors during heavy loads
b. allows two or more antennas to feed one transmitter
c. allows one antenna to feed two separate microwave transmitters and receivers at the same time
d. insulates UHF frequencies on transmission lines
e. an antenna attached to a motor; turning constantly

69. Marine transmitters with a 16K0F3E or 16K0G3E emission designator in the 156-162 MHz. band shall not be capable of emitting a carrier power more than:

a. 25 watts
b. 50 watts
c. 150 watts
d. 500 watts
e. 1500 watts

70. A Dynamotor:
a. measures the 'state of charge' of a battery
b. steps up AC voltage
c. operates at 37% efficiency
d. steps up DC voltage
e. steps down DC voltage

71. The most common application of the M-derived filter is:

a. To broaden the frequency response of a circuit
b. To sharpen the frequency response of a circuit
c. To pass a band of frequencies in a series circuit
d. To pass a band of frequencies in a parallel circuit
e. To attenuate unwanted harmonics

72. A wattmeter indicates:

a. E x I x Power Factor
b. I squared x E x Power Factor
c. I squared x Power Factor
d. Power output in watts without regard to phase angle
e. Power output in watt-hours

73. If signal amplitude is greater than noise, the signal-to-noise ratio of an FM system could be improved by:

a. Using Wide Band FM with F1 emissions
b. Using Narrow Band FM
c. Using a narrow frequency swing
d. Using a wide frequency swing
e. Eliminating frequency swing

74. Static and interference from motors can be eliminated by:

a. Grounding the battery with a 2" copper strip
b. Installing Faraday shields around connectors
c. Installing RF chokes across power line to ground
d. Installing bypass capacitors from the power line to grounded parts
e. Installing bypass capacitors between stages

75. A limiter circuit:

a. Protects sensitive circuit elements from high voltage spikes
b. Is a low-gain amplifier with a constant output
c. Limits primarily low frequencies in a circuit
d. Limits primarily high frequencies in a circuit
e. Limits all ranges equally in FM transmitters

76. Two .1 mfd capacitors are connected in series across 120 volts. They are removed, placed in parallel, and a third .1 mfd capacitor is added in parallel. What voltage appears across the third capacitor?

a. 0 volts
b. 30 volts
c. 40 volts
d. 60 volts
e. 120 volts

77. What is the required channel for all VHF-FM equipped vessels to monitor at all times the station is operated?

a. channel 8; 156.4 MHz.
b. channel 16; 156.8 MHz.
c. channel 5A; 156.25 MHz.
d. channel 1A; 156.07 MHz.
e. channel 6; 156.3 MHz.

78. If someone interferes with your transmission, you should:

a. out shout the other signal
b. notify the FCC immediately
c. contact the US CoastGuard
d. increase transmitter power
e. stop transmitting

79. When testing is conducted within the 2170-2194 kHz. and 156.75-156.85 MHz. bands, test transmitters should not continue for more than _______ in any 15 minute period.

a. 15 seconds
b. 1 minute
c. 5 minutes
d. 10 minutes
e. no limitation

80. Waveguides are not used at frequencies below UHF because:

a. poor standing wave ratios result
b. physical size would be too large
c. skin effect
d. high resistance of materials
e. wavelengths at UHF and higher do not require shielding

81. In this circuit all inputs are high and the output is low. If the output is to remain low, what could occur?

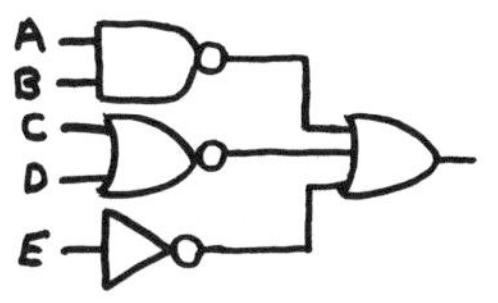

a. A changes to low
b. A and B change to low
c. C and E change to low
d. E changes to low
e. C changes to low

82. To increase the bandwidth of a Class C bandpass amplifier:

a. increase the capacitance of the tank circuit
b. increase the inductance of the tank circuit
c. decrease the "Q" of the tank circuit
d. increase the "Q" of the tank circuit
e. decrease capacitance and inductance of the tank circuit

83. The function of a line equalizer:

a. decrease low frequencies
b. decrease high frequencies
c. increase low frequencies
d. increase mid-range frequencies
e. both a and b

84. Split-tuned IF receiver stages can be corrected by:

a. decrease coupling
b. increase coupling
c. remove link coupling
d. increase the "Q"
e. lower the "Q"

85. In an air core IF (intermediate frequency) transformer, energy is transferred from the primary to the secondary windings by:

a. Electrostatic coupling
b. Capacitive coupling
c. Motion of the electromagnetic field of the primary
d. Eddy currents
e. Hysteresis

86. Which of these circuits offers the best high-pass filter?

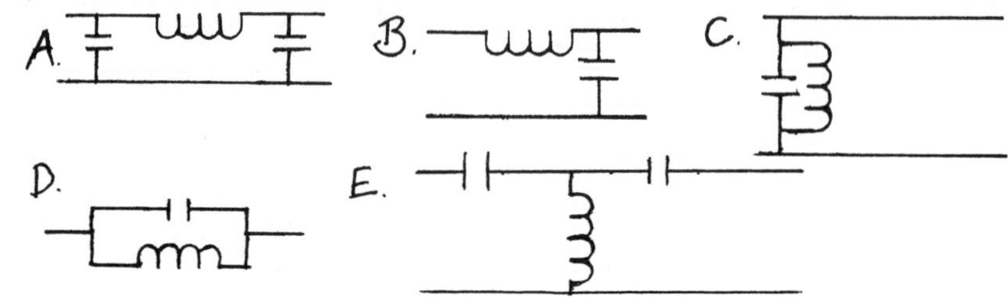


87. Frequency tolerance of 8364 kHz. Survival Craft stations:

a. 20 PPM
b. 50 PPM
c. 100 PPM
d. 1 kHz.
e. no limitation

88. Comparing a vacuum tube to a transistor,

a. The base is comparable to the cathode
b. The base is comparable to the plate
c. The base is comparable to the control grid
d. The collector is comparable to the screen grid
e. None of the above

89. In a purely reactive circuit (no resistance) at non-resonance:

a. Power dissipation will be zero
b. The Power Factor will be infinite
c. Resistance will be zero
d. Current will be zero
e. Reactance will be infinite

90. Motorboating (low frequency oscillations) in an amplifier can be stopped by:

a. Grounding the screen grid
b. Bypassing the screen grid resistor with a .1 mfd capacitor
c. Connect a capacitor between the B+ lead and ground
d. Grounding the plate
e. Grounding the grid-leak

91. Eddy currents are defined as:

a. Currents that are restored in flywheel circuits
b. Currents formed within electrostatic modulation
c. Currents formed when cutting lines of force
d. Currents formed within transformers
e. Currents formed when using positive feedback

92. Radio wave propagation speed is:

a. Dependant on dielectric
b. Increased with frequency
c. Decreased with frequency
d. Constant
e. None of the above

93. What is the turns ratio of this transformer?

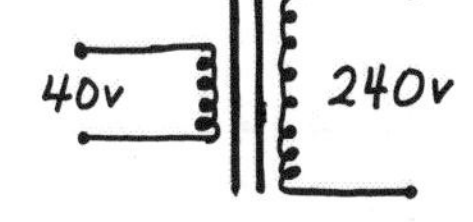


a. 1:6
b. 24/4
c. 6:2.2
d. 1:60
e. cannot be determined

94. A hetrodyne frequency meter beats the second harmonic of a signal at dial marking 3001. The tables for the meter show that a dial reading of 3000 equals 3243 kHz; 3002 equals 3244 kHz. The signal is:

a. 1621.175 kHz.
b. 1621.75 kHz.
c. 3243.50 kHz.
d. 3243.75 kHz.
e. 3243.25 kHz.

95. What is the relationship between input and output power in an amplifier?

a. output power is always higher than input power
b. input and output are always unity gain
c. efficiency determines the difference in values
d. output power is always 120° out of phase with input
e. both c and d

96. A loop antenna:

a. is omnidirectional at all times
b. is always phase vertically
c. will not receive VHF or higher frequencies
d. receives horizontal signals when placed horizontal
e. receives vertical signals when placed horizontal

97. What is the frequency of a signal that completes 5 cycles in 1/50th second?

a. 25 Hz.
b. 250 Hz.
c. 2,500 Hz.
d. 2.5 kHz.
e. 0.02 kHz.

98. Auto interference to radio reception can be eliminated by:

a. Installing resistive spark plugs
b. Installing capacitive spark plugs
c. Installing resistors in series with the spark plugs
d. Installing two copper-braid ground strips
e. Using a faraday screen around the receiver

99. DC series motor speed is affected by:

a. The load
b. The ripple frequency
c. The number of brushes
d. Atmospheric conditions
e. Stray RF fields

100.

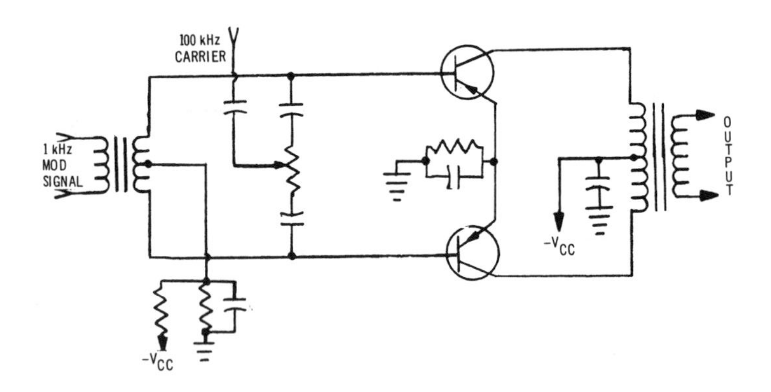


The diagram above is:

a. ratio detector
b. balanced modulator
c. squelch circuit
d. buffer amplifier stage
e. RF phase shift inverter

# Test 3-I Element Three

1. An FM receiver limiter circuit is used to:

   a> reduce amplitude
   b> modulate FM
   c> demodulate FM
   d> respond to frequency shift variations
   e> limit all signals to the same amplitude level
   to minimize noise interference

2. A 122.5 MHz. 100 watt transmitter was emitting spurious emissions at 490 MHz. with 5 watts of radiated power. If a 490 MHz. filter with 7 dB attenuation was attached to the system, what would be the power of the spurious signals?

   a> 0.01 watt
   b> 0.1 watt
   c> 1 watt
   d> 1.3 watts
   e> 1.8 watts

3. In regards to shipboard satellite dish antenna systems, azimuth is:

   a> vertical aiming of the antenna
   b> horizontal aiming of the antenna
   c> 0 - 90 degrees
   d> North to East
   e> both a and b

4. A copper wire conductor has a certain resistance. If the diameter of the same length of wire is increased by double, what would the resistance be?

   a> doubled
   b> halved
   c> quartered
   d> quadrupled
   e> the original resistance

5. One nautical mile is equal to how many statue miles?

   a> 1.5
   b> 8.3
   c> 1.73
   d> 1.15
   e> 1.0

6. Where should a Heat Sink or Heat Shunt (such as a clamp or pliers) be placed when desoldering an IC chip?

a> on the tip of the soldering iron
b> between the IC chip terminal and the soldering iron
c> place clamp across all terminals
d> between solder iron tip and the solder connection
e> underneath circuit board

7. Which is pin number 10 on the IC ship pictured below?

a> A
b> B
c> C
d> D
e> E

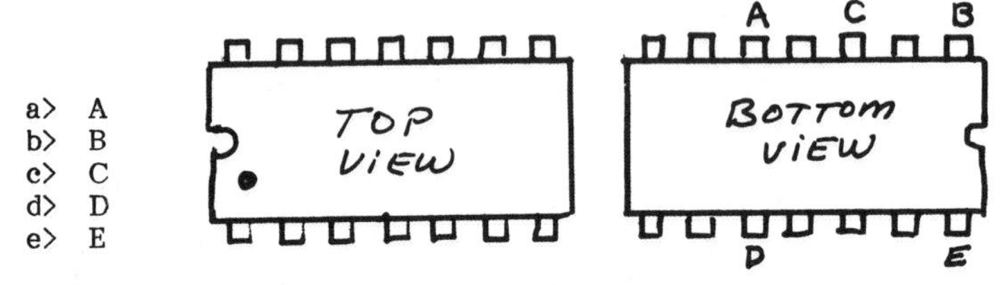


8. An antenna radiates a primary signal of 500 watts output. If there is a 2nd harmonic output of 0.5 watt, what attenuation of the 2nd harmonic has occured?

a> 3 dB
b> 10 dB
c> 20 dB
d> 30 dB
e> 40 dB

9. What type of semiconductor device controls capacitance with a voltage?

a> a Junction diode
b> a Mosfet diode
c> a Tunnel diode
d> a Zener diode
e> a Varactor diode

10. On runway approach, an ILS Localizer shows:

a> deviation left or right of runway center line
b> deviation up or down from ground surface
c> deviation percentage from authorized ground speed
d> wind speed along runway
e> runway boundary via blue marker lights

11. Which emission has the widest bandwidth?

a> 2K70A3E
b> 2000A3E
c> 700A3E
d> 900A3E
e> 200H0A3E

12. Increasing the coupling between two tuned circuits up to the critical point will usually:

a> decrease the power transfer
b> increase the bandwidth response
c> decrease the coefficient of coupling
d> reduce the frequency response
e> limit the passage of frequencies

13. Omega radio navigation operates at what frequency?

a> 10.2 kHz.
b> 100 kHz
c> 121.5 MHz.
d> 243 MHz.
e> 1200 - 2300 kHz.

14. What is the effect of adding a capacitor in series to an antenna?

a> resonant frequency will decrease
b> resonant frequency wiil increase
c> resonant frequency will remain same
d> electrical length will be longer
e> an inductor will need to be added in parallel

15. If a transmission line has a power loss of 6 dB per 100 feet, what is the power at the feed point to the antenna at the end of a 200 foot transmission line fed by a 100 watt transmitter?

a> 70 watts
b> 50 watts
c> 25 watts
d> 12 watts
e> 6 watts

16. What is an example of angular modulation?

a> amplitude modulaiton
b> frequency modulation
c> single sideband
d> vestigial sideband
e> lower end of Broadcast TV channel

17. Waveguides are:

a> used exclusively in high frequency power supplies
b> ceramic couplers attached to antenna terminals
c> high-pass filters used at low radio frequencies
d> hollow metal conductors used to carry high frequency current
e> always used in neutralizing Class C amplifiers

18. What is the frequency of the sine wave?

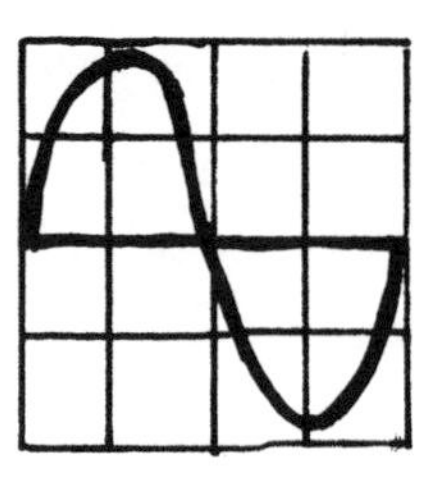

Vertical = 10 mV per division
Horizontal = 50 uS per division

a> 60 Hz.
b> 500 Hz.
c> 5 kHz.
d> 50 MHz.
e> 100 MHz.

19. The RMS (Root Mean Square) value of a sine wave is:

a> peak value divided by the square root of 2
b> average value divided by the square root of 2
c> average value
d> peak value
e> none of the above

20. Which of the following represents the best SWR?

a> 1:1
b> 1:2
c> 1:15
d> 2:1
e> 10:1

21. What is the value and tolerance of a resistor with the color bands: Brown, Black, Red and Silver?

a> 1 K ohm ± 10%
b> 100 K ohm + 10%
c> 10 ohms ± 5%
d> 2 K ohms ± 20%
e> 100 ohms ± 10%

22. What three words represent the first three letter of the phonetic alphabet?

a> Alpha Bravo Charlie
b> Adam Baker Charlie
c> Alpha Baker Crystal
d> Adam Brown Chuck
e> Alpha Bravo Crystal

23. What iss the very low frequency range?

a> 30 - 3000 Hz.
b> 30 - 3000 kHz.
c> 3 - 30 kHz.
d> 30 - 300 kHz.
e> 300 - 3000 kHz.

24. In this circuit:

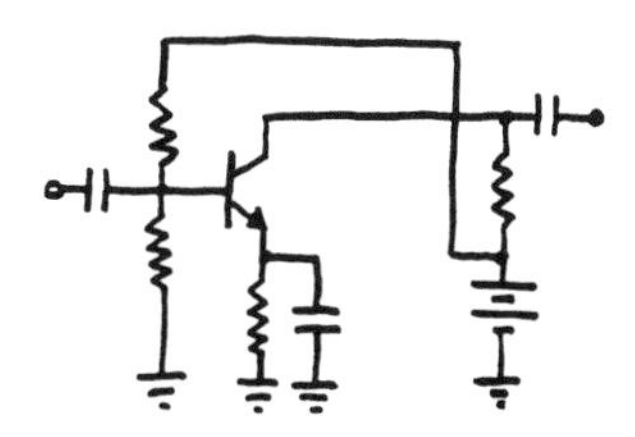

a> no phase reversal occurs
b> causes 180 degree phase reversal
c> transistor is common collector
d> transistor is common base
e> battery polarity must be changed

25. What is true for the amplifier diagram shown above?

a> high input impedance and low gain
b> low input impedance and high gain
c> high input impedance and unity gain
d> low input impedance and 70% gain loss
e> high input impedance; no phase change; unity gain

26. What is the emission designator for a SSSC radiotelephone transmitter with an authorized bandwidth of 3 kHz.?

a> 20KG3E
b> 900R3E
c> 2K80J3E
d> 2K70F3E
e> 20KG3E

27. What should the load resistance be for greatest power transfer?

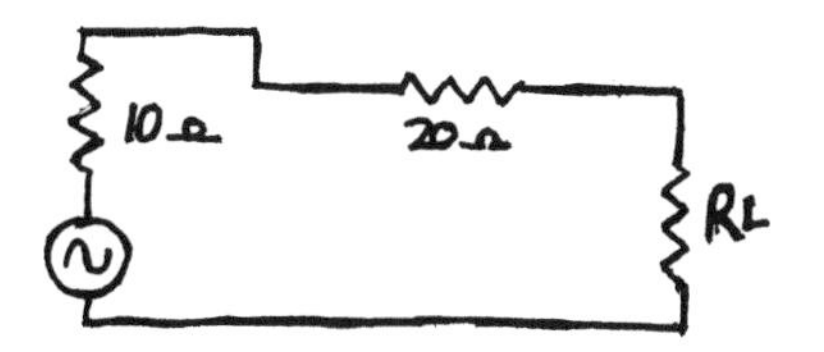


a> as small as is practical
b> 10 ohms
c> 20 ohms
d> 30 ohms
e> 14.14 ohms

28. A varistor:

a> is useful for preventing high voltages from destroying semiconductor components
b> regulates voltage
c> holds voltage constant when load current changes
d> resistance varies with voltage
e> all of the above

29. What is the decimal number 11 in binary form?

a> 2
b> 1011
c> 11010
d> 2X00
e> 10001101

30. What are the frequency tones of the Auto Alarm>

a> 2200 Hz. and 1300 Hz.
b> 1400 Hz. and 2600 Hz.
c> 2500 Hz. and 300 Hz.
d> 100 Hz. and 1100 Hz.
e> 1000 Hz. and 2300 Hz.

31. The output of a transmitter is 25 watts and the standing wave ratio (SWR) is 5 watts. What output power is written in the transmitter log?

a> 20 watts
b> 25 watts
c> 30 watts
d> 15.6
e> 0 watts

32. Referring to the diagram, if circuit voltages is constant, and input frequency increases steadily, output will:

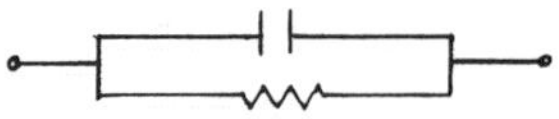

a> increase, then drop
b> remain constant
c> decrease
d> increase
e> cannot be determined from given information

33. What type of antenna ststem allows you to receive and transmit aat the same time?

a> simplex
b> duplex
c> multiplex
d> digital diplex
e> SSSCX

34. At 100 MHz., what offer the least impedance?

a> silver wire, 1 mil - 6 inches long
b> aluminum wire, 1 mil - 6 inches long
c> sheet of copper, 2 inches by 6 inches
d> 1 megohm resistor
e> 1 mfd. capacitor

35. If a 1 MHz. carrier is modulated by a 200 Hz. audio tone, the output waveform wll contain:

a> 1000.2 kHz., 1000 kHz., and 999.8 kHz.
b> all frequencies between 999.8 MHz. and 1000.2 kHz.
c> 1200 kHz. and 800 kHz.
d> 1 MHz. only
e> 1000.2 MHz. only

36. This truth table is correct for which logic gate symbol?

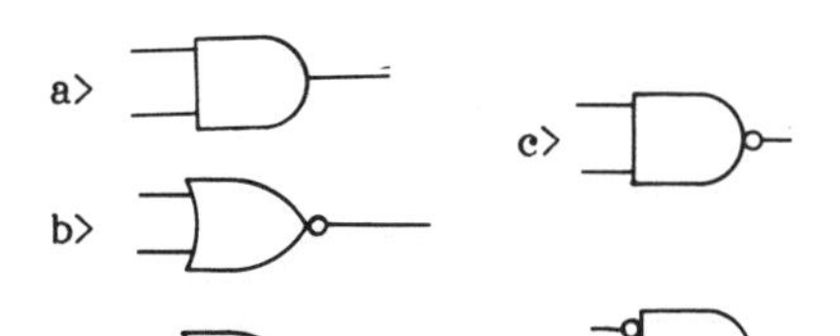


| D̄ | S | NO DUTY |
|---|---|---|
| TRUE | TRUE | TRUE |
| TRUE | FALSE | TRUE |
| FALSE | TRUE | TRUE |
| FALSE | FALSE | FALSE |

37. At 156.8 MHz., how many Hertz may the carrier frequency vary for a 0.002% tolerance?

a> 30,136 Hz.
b> 3,136 Hz.
c> 313 kHz.
d> 30 Hz.
e> 0.3 Hz.

38. Residual magnetism is:

a> magnetism which remains in the core of an electromagnet after the operating circuit has been opened
b> magnetism which becomes activated when voltage is applied to circuit
c> magnetism which remains in the wires of an electromagnet after core is removed
d> magnetism which is induced in a conductor via lines of force from an electromagnet
e> none of the above

39. A microwave device which allows RF energy to pass through in one director with very little loss but absorbs RF power in the opporite direction:

a> circulator
b> wave trap
c> multiplex
d> SWR trap
e> isolator

40. What are the maim characteristics of the amplifier shown?

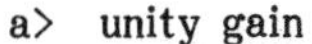

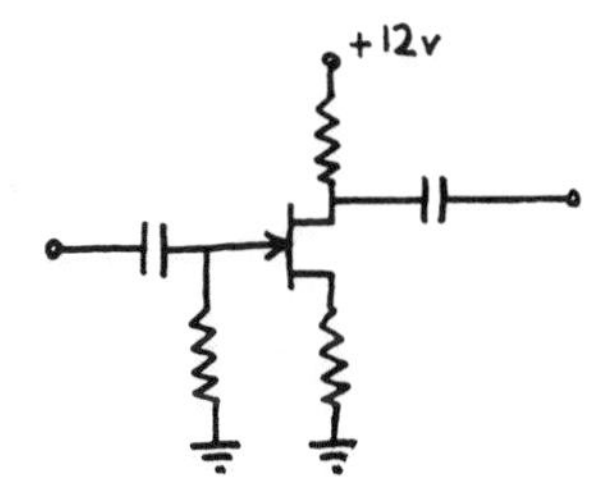


a> unity gain
b> low input impedance
c> high input impedance
d> low output impedance
e> low stage gain

41. A 520 kHz. signal is fed to a 1/2 wave Hertz antenna. The fifth harmonic will be:

a> 2.65 MHz.
b> 2650 kHz.
c> 2600 kHz.
d> 104 kHz.
e> 104 Hz.

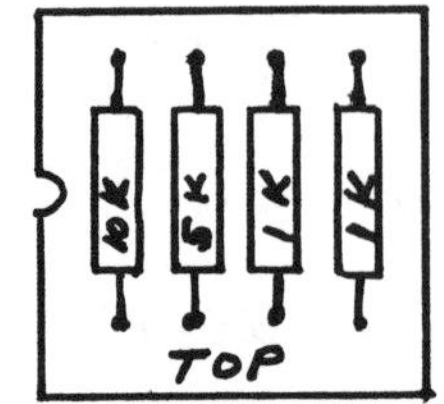


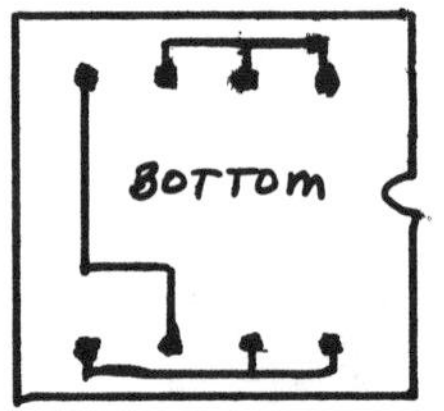


42. Which schematic best represents the circuit pictured above?

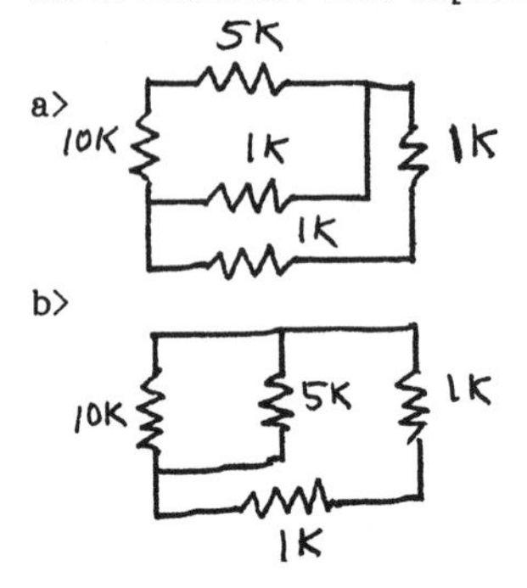


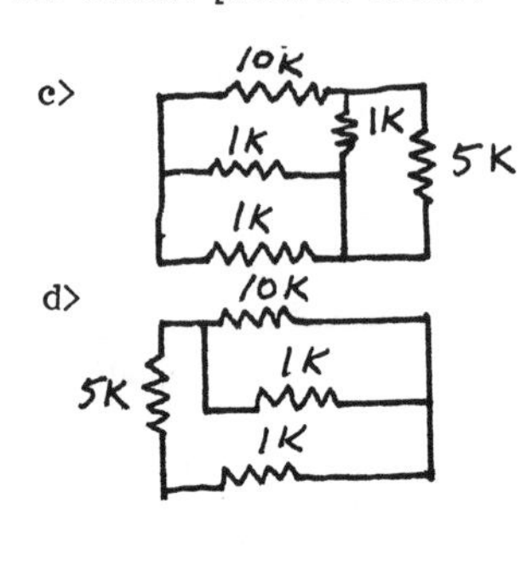


43. Selectivity in a receiver will be greatest when:

a> loose coupling is used between stages
b> tight coupling is used between stages
c> high voltages activate tuned tank circuits
d> multiple stages of audio amplification are employed
e> tight coupling and multiple RF tant circuits are employed

44. One Hertz equals:

a> 1 cycle per minute
b> 1 pi times radiant/second
c> 2 pi times radiant/second
d> pi times power factor
e> volt per meter

45. What is the decimal value of the binary number 1101?

a> 3
b> 9
c> 13
d> 16
e> 64

46. What is the operating frequency of Loran C?

a> 100 MHz.
b> 100 kHz.
c> 243 MHz.
d> 1200 GHz.
e> 1900 kHz.

47. The signal shows on this Spectrum Analyzer is:

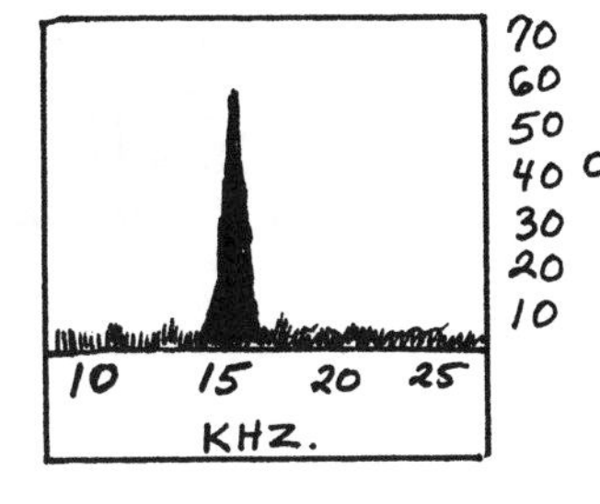


a> 15 kHz. sine wave
b> 15 kHz. square wave
c> 15 kHz. triangle wave
d> 15 kHz. sawtooth wave
e> 25 kHz. sine wave

48. The waveform shown on the Spectrum Analyzer represents:

a> 270 degree square wave
b> 180 degree sine wave
c> 90 degree sine wave
d> 90 degree square wave
e> 120 degreee triangle wave

49. What is the unit of electrical potential?

a> kilowatt
b> kilovolt
c> kilohertz
d> ampere
e> wattage

50. When a capacitor is connected in series with a Marconi antenna:

a> an inductor of equal value must be added
b> no change occurs to antenna
c> antenna open circuit stops transmission
d> antenna resonant frequency decreases
e> antenna resonant frequency increases

51. If a 50 MHz. transmitter is actually operating at 50.010 MHz., by what percentage is it off frequency?

a> 0.002%
b> 0.01%
c> 2.02%
d> 0.005%
e> 0.02%

52. A transmitter has an output power reading of 100 watts and a reflected power of 1 watt. It is connected to a 50 foot transmission line with a loss of 6 dB per 100 feet. What is the E.R.P. signal reading at the antenna?

a> 100 watts
b> 94 watts
c> 88 watts
d> 49.5 watts
e> 10.5 watts

53. What is the maximum power that can be dissipated by the parallel circuit below, compared to the series diagram?

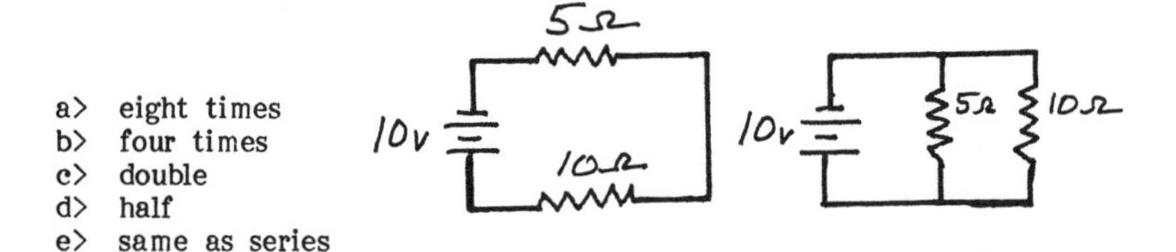


a> eight times
b> four times
c> double
d> half
e> same as series

54. If the frequency tolerance is 10 parts per million, how many Hertz can the carrier of a 2182 kHz. transmtter drift?

a> 2182 Hz.
b> 218 Hz.
c> 10.91 Hz.
d> 21.82 kHz.
e> 20 Hz.

55. Time Constant of resistance capacitance circuit:

a> time required for capacitance to discharge completely after voltage is applied
b> time required for the caplacitor to reach 63.2% of full charge after a voltage is applied
c> time required for the capacitor to reach 36.8% of total voltage supply in one time constant
d> time required for the resistance to reach 22.5% of full charge after voltage is removed
e> time required for the capacitor to reach 37% of full charge after a voltage is removed

56. If a computer memory chip has stored 4096 words, with eight bits for each word, what is the minimum number of address lines that would be necessary?

a> 4096
b> 64K
c> 2048
d> 512
e> 12

57. How do you increase the electrical length of an antenna?

a> add an inductor in parallel
b> add an inductor in series
c> add a capacitor in series
d> add a resistor in series
e> add a capacitor in parallel

58. A coaxial cable has 7 dB of reflected power when the input is 5 watts. What is the output of the transmission line?

a> 5 watts
b> 2.5 watts
c> 1.25 watts
d> 1 watt
e> 0.6 watt

59. What is the circuit impedance?

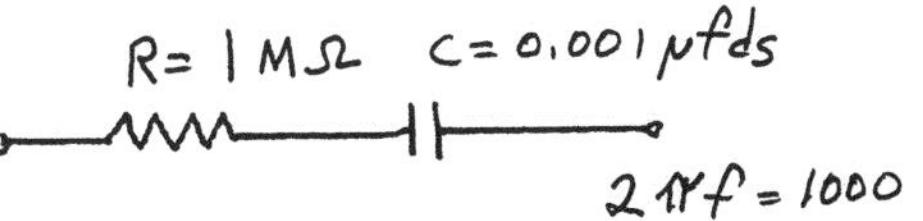


a> 0.5 megohm
b> 2 megohm
c> 3 megohms
d> 4 megohms
e> square root of 2 megohms (1.414 megohms)

60. A limiter:

a> a high gain, constant output amplifier used in AM receivers, placed immediately before the IF stage
b> a low gain, constant output amplifier used in FM receivers, placed immediately before discriminator
c> a low gain, constant output amplifier used in FM receivers, placed between the RF amplifier and the mixer
d> a high gain, contant output amplifier used in FM receivers, placed between the discriminator and audio ampifier
e> a low gain amplifier stage inside the squelch control stage

61. A series circuit has a resistance, inductance and capacitance. The resistance is 12 ohms, and inductive reactance is 52 ohms, and the capacitive reactance is 40 ohms. If 130 VAC at 50 Hz. is applied, the phase relationship between voltage and current will be:

a> 0 degrees
b> 45 degrees
c> 90 degrees
d> 180 degrees
e> 270 degrees

62. What is the symbol for a Mosfet transistor?

a> 
b> 
c> 
d>

63. If a tuned circuit initially had a 12 MHz. frequency, what change in the original value of the capacitor should be made to obtain a 24 MHz. signal output?

a> 1/4
b> 1/2
c> double
d> quadruple
e> cannot be determined

64. What is the image frequency of a receiver tuned to 156.8 MHz. and has an IF frequency of 10.7 MHz.?

a> 21.4 kHz.
b> 159.2 MHz.
c> 135.4 MHz.
d> 178.2 MHz.
e> 167.5 MHz.

65. When an air core coil of 2800 turns of wire is replaced by ferrite, the inductance will:

a> increase
b> decrease
c> not change
d> be infinite
e> require more windings of wire to retain same inductance

66. A 1 KW transmitter has a field strength of 560 microvolts at a 1/4 mile distance. What would be the approximate field strength at one mile away?

a> 1000 microvolts
b> 480 microvolts
c> 250 microvolts
d> 140 microvolts
e> 70 microvolts

67. Grounded base or common base amplifiers:

a> input and output areout of phase
b> high input impedance and low output impedance
c> low input impedance and high output impedance
d> current gain and no voltage gain
e> input and output impedances are the same; 50 K-ohms

68. Wha is the 7th harmonic of 450 kHz. when fed through a 1/4 wavelength vertical antenna?

a> 3150 Hz.
b> 3150 MHz.
c> 787.5 kHz.
d> 3.15 MHz.
e> 30.2 MHz.

69. In this Comparator circuit, what is the output?

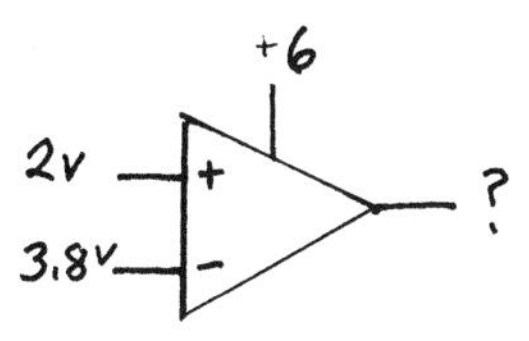


a> 0 volt
b> 2 volts
c> 1.8 volts
d> 3.1 volts
e> -4.2 volts

70. The frequency range of Loran-C is:

a> LF
b> MF
c> HF
d> VHF
e> UHF

71. A logic probe indicates:

a> high and low logic states in a digital circuit
b> intemodulation distortion
c> carrier frequency of an rf transmitter
d> out of phase relationships of current vs. voltage
e> digital short circuit failures

72. If the elapsed time for a radar echo is 62 microseconds, what is the distance in nautical miles to the object?

a> 115
b> 87
c> 37
d> 11.5
e> 5

73. What is the equivalent value in the decimal system (base 10) of the binary number 1101 (base 2) or hexadecimal D (base 16)?

a> 9
b> 64
c> 13
d> 23
e> 111

74. 1.73 nautical miles equals how many statue miles?

a> 2
b> 1.5
c> 1.73
d> 1
e> 0.57

75. A resistor is color coded: Brown, Black, Black and Gold. What is the highest resistance this resistor may have and still be within coded tolerance?

a> 1.5 K-ohms
b> 150 ohms
c> 104 ohms
d> 14 ohms
e> 10.5 ohms

76. Two way communications with both stations operating on the same frequency is:

a> radiotelephone
b> duplex
c> simplex
d> multiplex
e> multipath

77. What is the 5th harmonic of a 450 kHz. transmitter carrier fed to a 1/4 wave antenna?

a> 562.5 MHz.
b> 1125 kHz.
c> 2250 MHz.
d> 562.5 kHz.
e> 2.25 MHz.

78. Why do we use squelch?

a> to eliminate phase problems with FM reception
b> to activate the Auto Alarm signal and gain the attention of other ships at sea
c> to quiet a receiver gain when no signal is received
d> to activate a receiver speaker when alarm is received
e> to limit volume for high signal to noise ratio

79. A buffer amplifier:

a> isolates a preceding circuit from the effects of a following circuit
b> protects a frequency-sensitive stage from variations in the load of another stage
c> protects equipment from over-load spikes from AC line voltage
d> equalizes the amplitude of a wave-form to enable low volume segments to be amplified equally with high voltage signals
e> both a and b

80. Solder is:

a> 50% lead 50% tin
b> 40% lead 60% tin
c> 60% lead 40% tin
d> 70% lead 30% tin
e> 90% lead 5% tin 5% silver

81. What ferrite device can be used instead of a duplexer to isolate a microwave transmitter and receiver when both are connected to the same antenna?

a> isolator
b> circulator
c> magnetron
d> simplex
e> multiplex transmission line

82. What material is a crystal usually made from?

a> mica
b> selenium
c> carbon
d> quartz
e> diamond

83. If is is 3:00 PM Pacific Standard Time, what time is it U.T.C. (Universal Coordinated Time)?

a> 3 PM
b> 11 AM
c> 0300
d> 2300
e> 1500

84. What frequency deviation is allowed for aviation communication?

a> 5 PPM
b> 10 PPM
c> 20 PPM
d> 50 PPM
e> 5000 PPM

85. Marine transmitters should be grounded by a:

a> high guage number wire
b> wire guage #18 to #24
c> short multi-strand wire
d> short solid single-strand wire
e> both a and d

86. A beam radio navigation transmitter at the threshold of a runway that provides signals for guiding aircraft onto the center line of the runway for I.L.S. instrument landing system:

a> Glide Path
b> Localizer
c> EPIRB
d> ELT
e> Beam frequency

87. What is the symbol for a Zener diode?

a>

c>

b>

d>

88. Zener diode:

a> 2.4 to 200 volts
b> voltage regulation
c> voltage reference
d> provides constant voltage during varying current
e> all of the above

89. How often do you check tower lights at an aeronautical station?

a> daily; once every 24 hours
b> hourly; during first 3 minutes of each hour
c> every quarter hour
d> continuously
e> never

90. High power ship transmitters using VHF FM must be capable of reducing carrier power to:

a> 0.5 watt
b> 1 watt
c> 50 watts
d> 100 watts
e> 500 watts

91. Under the new rules, the General Radiotelephone Operator License is needed for repairing:

a> CB Radios
b> ambulance and police radios
c> cellular car phones
d> satellite receivers
e> none of the above

92. According to the Commission, every marine transmitter must have a name plate label showing what information?

a> name of manufacturer and model number
b> official "seal of approval"
c> operating frequency
d> operating power
e> all of the above

93. When the ownership of a ship changes, what happens to the FCC license for the marine transmitter?

a> new owner must apply for a new license
b> after present license expires a new license must be applied for from the Commission
c> FCC inspectiion of equipment is required
d> old license is valid until is expires
e> continue to operate; license automatically transfers with boat ownership

94. How many days in advance must the owner or representative of a vessel apply for yearly FCC transmitter inspection?

a> 120 days
b> 60 days
c> 30 days
d> 10 days
e> 3 days

95. In the marine mobile service, to prevent radio interference what should the operator do?

a> use low power to avoid interference with distant stations
b> check to determine if anyone is on the same frequency before you transmit
c> transmit "C.Q." several times to assure that the channel is available
d> use maximum power to avoid cross-modulation interfering with your signal at the receiver
e> always transmit on long range 2182 kHz. for maximum coverage

96. What is the second order of priority communications?

a> urgent
b> distress
c> safety
d> mayday
e> security

97. Portable ship units, hand-helds, walkie-talkiies and associated ship units:

a> use ship station license
b> operate with 1 watt and must be able to transmit on Channel 16 156.8 MHz.
c> may communicate only with the mother ship and other portable units and small boats belonging to mother ship
d> must not transmit from shore or to other vessels
e> all of the above

98. What class of EPIRB has the longest transmitter range?

a> Class A EPIRB; automatically activates when emersed and has a transmitting range of 100-200 miles at 121.5 MHz. and 243 MHz.
b> Class B EPIRB; manually activated by operator only and has a transmitting range of 100-200 miles at 121.5 MHz. and 243 MHz.
c> Class C EPIRB; Authorized for use within the effective 20 miles coverage range on VHF-FM channels 15 and 16, 156.75 MHz. and 156.8 MHz.
d> both a and b above
e> 2162 kHz. Class 1 EPIRB International; 2000-3000 miles

99. When it is not required to post your operator license, you are required to carry a copy with you under what circumstances?

a> when soley on board ship to service equipment
b> when servicing a transmitter not required for a ship
c> when servicing a portable transceiver
d> when you work for a maintenance facility and are performing service at a remote location
e> all of the above

100. All flashing, rotating beacons and light control devices at aviation ground airport facilities must be inspected how often to assure that equipment is functioning properly?

a> daily
b> sunrise and sunset
c> once per month
d> every 3 months
e> once per year

# Test 3-J Element Three

1. What is the carrier power transmitted by a marine UHF antenna with a 3 dB gain and a transmitter output power of 12.5 Kilowatts

   a> 12.5 KW
   b> 15.5 KW
   c> 25 KW
   d> 50 KW
   e> 100 KW

2. Telephone communication is what type of transmission?

   a> simplex
   b> duplex
   c> multiplex
   d> digital/diplex
   e> SSSCX

3. What is the wavelength of a signal at 500 MHz.?

   a> 0.062 cm
   b> 6 meters
   c> 60 cm
   d> 60 meters
   e> 0.0006 cm

4. The ILS Localizer measures what deviation of an aircraft?

   a> horizontal
   b> vertical
   c> ground speed
   d> distance between aircraft
   e> wind speed and directon

5. 3:00 PM Central Standard Time is:

   a> 1000 UTC
   b> 2100 UTC
   c> 1800 UTC
   d> 0300 UTC
   e> 0030 UTC

6. A varistor is a:

   a> frequency regulator
   b> volume control
   c> variable capacitor
   d> capacitance controller
   e> voltage regulator

7. 10 statue miles per hour equals how many knots?

   a> 11.5
   b> 8.7
   c> 5
   d> 3
   e> 2

8. What gate circuit does this represent?

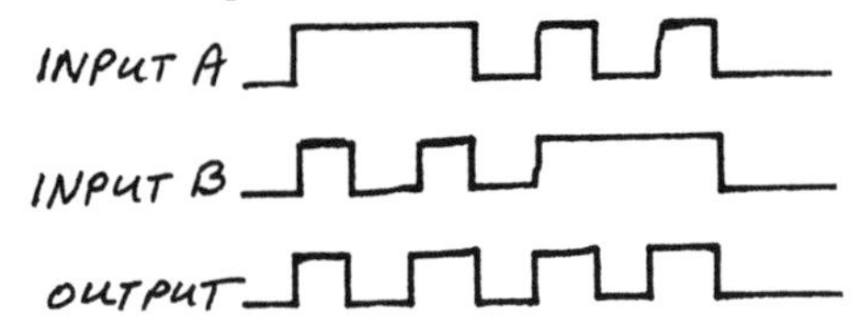


a> AND
b> NOR
c> Exclusive OR
d> OR
e> NAND

9. Which of the following is an acceptable method of solder removal from holes in a printed circuit board?

a> compressed air
b> toothpick
c> soldering iron and a suction device
d> power drill
e> stainless steel wire

10. 100 statue miles equals how many nautical miles?

a> 87
b> 108
c> 173
d> 13
e> 115

11. If a transmitter output is 30 watts and is connected to an antenna line with 10 watts of reflected power, what is the actual radiated power of the system?

a> 40 watts
b> 30 watts
c> 25 watts
d> 20 watts
e> 4 watts

12. Waveguide construction:

a> should not used silver plating
b> should not use copper
c> should have short vertical runs
d> should not have long horizontal runs
e> should allow room for coaxial cables placement

13. 6:00 PM PST is equal to what time in UTC?

a> 0200
b> 1800
c> 2300
d> 1300
e> 0300

14. The symbol of a Thyristor Bidirectional Triode:

a>  c>

b>  d>

15. A frequency tolerance of 0.01% is how many parts per million?

a> 10 PPM
b> 100 PPM
c> 1000 PPM
d> 10,000 PPM
e> 100,000 PPM

16. This drawing indicates:

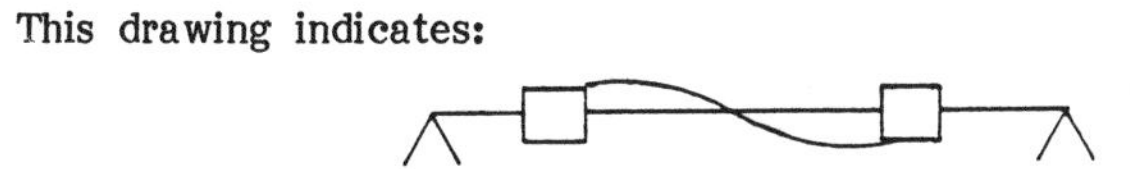

a> current along a 1/2 wave Marconi antenna
b> current along a 1/4 wave Hertz antenna
c> voltage along a 1/2 wave Hertz antenna
d> voltage along a 1/4 wave Hertz antenna
e> voltage along a 1/4 wave Marconi antenna

17. The main advantage of using a Logic Probe over a voltmeter is:

a> small size
b> simplified readout
c> circuit protection
d> reduced loading
e> both a and b above

18. Identify pin number 10 on the dip switch:

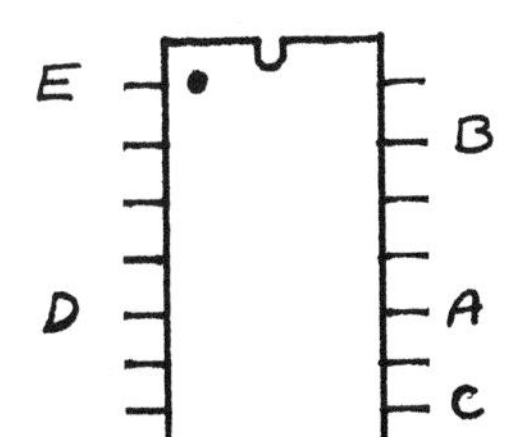


a> A
b> B
c> C
d> D
e> E

19. Which emission has the greatest bandwidth?

a> 70A3E
b> 700A3E
c> 90A3E
d> 900A3E
e> 40A3E

20. What inputs would give a high output?

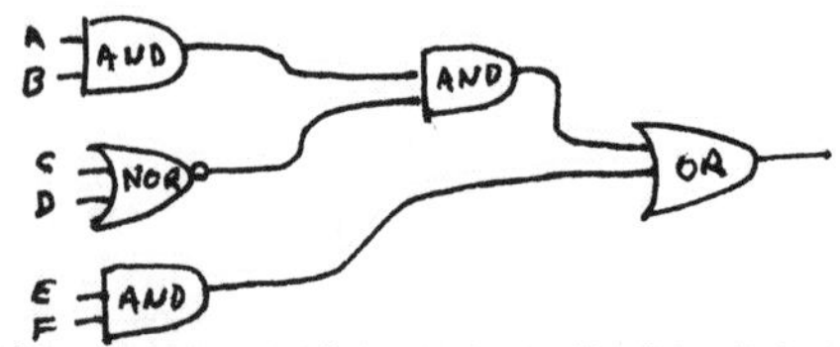


a> A-high, B-low, C-high, D-low, E-high, F-low
b> A-high, B-low, C-low, D-low, E-high, F-low
c> A-low, B-high, C-low, D-high, E-low, F-low
d> A-high, B-high, C-low, D-high, E-high, F-low
e> A-high, B-low, C-low, D-low, E-high, F-high

21. Auto Alarm consists of two sine wave audio tones transmitted alternately at what frequencies?

a> 121.5 and 243 MHz.
b> 500 and 1000 kHz.
c> 1300 and 2200 kHz.
d> 2000 and 2300 kHz.
e> none of the above

22. What is the value and tolerance of a resistor with the color bands: Brown, Black and Red?

a> 100 K-ohms
b> 10 K-ohms $\pm$ 5%
c> 1 K-ohm $\pm$ 20%
d> 100 ohms
e> 10 ohms $\pm$ 5%

23. The output voltage of a separately excited AC generator with constant frequency is dependant upon the adjustment of:

a> iron or ferrite choke core
b> field current
c> brush position
d> phase angle
e> time constant

24. What kind of filter is this?

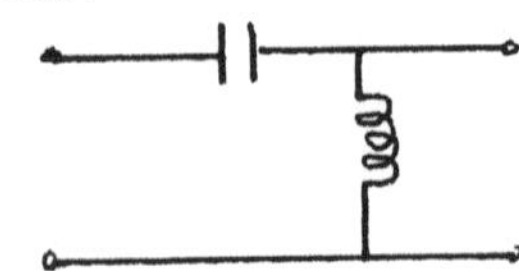

a> low pass
b> high pass
c> medium pass
d> T-Section
e> M-Derived

25. What is the output voltage?

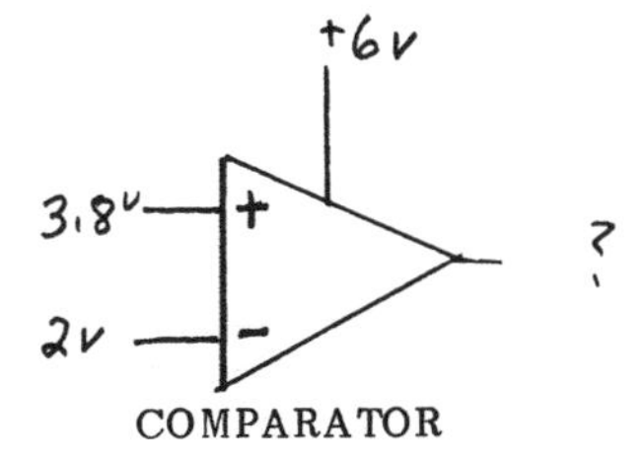

COMPARATOR

a> 0 volt
b> -3.8 volts
c> 1.8 volts
d> 2 volts
e> 6 volts

26. Two relays connected in series are best represented by:

a> AND gate
b> OR gate
c> NAND gate
d> NOR gate
e> Exclusive NOR gate

27. What radio navigation aid determines the distance from a transponder beacon by measuring the length of time the radio signal took to travel to the receiver?

a> Radar
b> Loran C
c> Distance Marking (DM)
d> Distance Measuring Equipment (DME)
e> Transponder Travel Time (TTT)

28. What emission has the widest bandwidth and highest frequency?

a> 280J3E (previously A3J)
b> 900R3E (previously A3A)
c> 2K80J3E (previously A3J)
d> 2K50H3E (previously A3H)
e> 2000H3E (previously A3H)

29. The MF (medium frequency) range is:

a> 0.3 - 3 MHz.
b> 300 - 3000 kHz.
c> 3 - 30 MHz.
d> 300 - 3000 MHz.
e> either a or b

30. A choke coil with 4,000 turns of #28 wire is compared with the same coil wound around a ferrite core:

a> coil winding will short due to iron added to core
b> ferrite is not used as core material
c> ferrite core increases inductance
d> ferrite decreases inductance
e> inductance will not change

31. What is the output waveform for the circuit below?

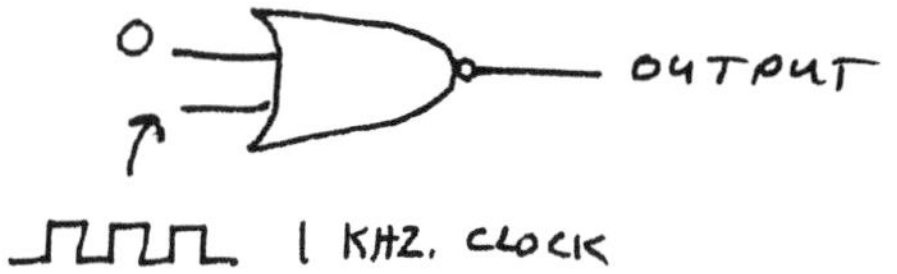

0

OUTPUT

1 KHZ. CLOCK

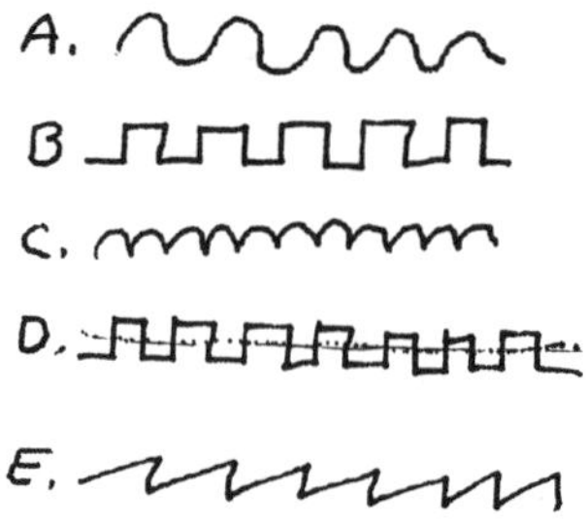

A.

B

C.

D.

E.

32. A limiter is:

a> a high frequency limiter
b> a low frequency limiter
c> an amplitude limiter
d> reduces high gain signals and increases low gain signals
e> a bandwidth wave trap for specific RF frequencies

33. How many memory locations can be specified with a twelve bit address?

a> 256
b> 512
c> 1024
d> 2048
e> 4096

34. A transmitter has an output frequency of 16 MHz. with a frequency tolerance of $\pm$ 200 PPM. The oscillator operates at 1/8 of the output frequency. What is the maximum permitted deviation of the oscillator allowed?

a> 3,200 Hz.
b> 1,600 Hz.
c> 400 Hz.
d> 40 Hz.
e> 3,200 Hz.

35. To lengthen an antenna electrically, add a:

a> coil
b> resistor
c> battery
d> conduit
e> capacitor

36. If a receiver has a local oscillator operating at a frequency of 167.8 MHz., and it is tuned to a carrier signal of 156.7 MHz., what is the IMAGE frequency (assume IF is 10.7 MHz.)?

a> 157 MHz.
b> 11 MHz.
c> 178.4 MHz.
d> 135.4 MHz.
e> 21.4 MHz.

37. The radar range in nautical miles to an object can be found by measuirng the elapsed time during a radar pulse and dividing this quantity by:

a> 0.87 seconds
b> 1.15 microseconds
c> 12.36 microseconds
d> 1.73 microseconds
e> 2 microseconds

38. What occurs when the signals of two transmitters in close proximity mix together in the final RF amplifier at either transmitter and cause signals of the sum and difference of the originals?

a> intermodulation interference
b> intermodulation injection
c> cross-modulation
d> image rejection effect
e> adjacent carrier interference

39. What is the third harmonic of 2182 kHz. when the signal is transmitted from a half-wavelength Hertz antenna?

a> 3273 kHz.
b> 6546 MHz.
c> 6.55 MHz.
d> 654.6 Hz.
e> 21.82 MHz.

40. What will be the maximum power that can be dissipated by the series circuit below, compared to the parallel circuit, if the voltage and resistance values remain the same?

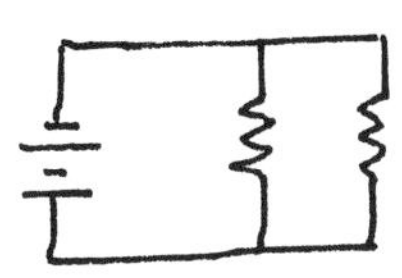

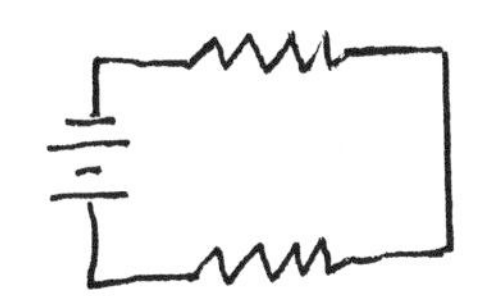

a> 4 times more
b> double
c> one half
d> one quarter
e> same as parallel

41. When calculating read wattage (true power) what must be considered?

a> RMS voltage and current
b> phase angle
c> peak current and voltage
d> average current and voltage
e> both a and b

42. Which of the following is a feature of an ILS instrument landing system?

a> Localizer: shows aircraft deviation horizontally from center of runway
b> Glide Slope (or Glide Path): shows aircraft vertical altitude of an aircraft during landing
c> lprovides communication to aircraft
d> ground speed controller
e> both a and b

43. A 2nd harmonic of a signal is reduced by a filter circuit 40 dB. If the main emission is 1000 watts, what is the power of the 2nd harmonic?

a> 0.1 watt
b> 1 watt
c> 5 watts
d> 40 watts
e> 0.4 watt

44. To find the supply power with only a voltmeter, measure voltage between:

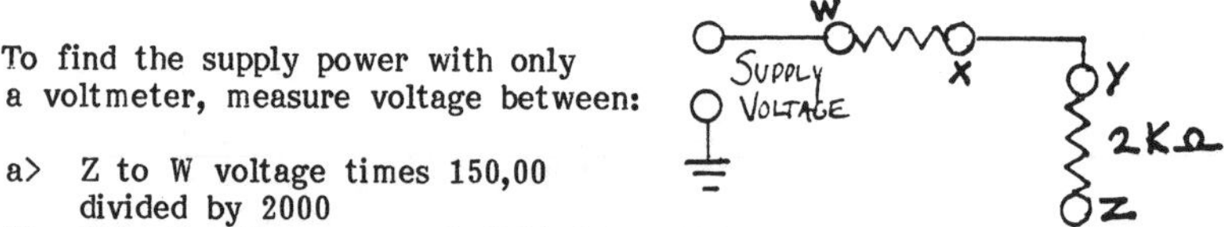


a> Z to W voltage times 150,00 divided by 2000
b> Y to Z voltage squared divided by 2000
c> W to Y voltage divided by 150
d> W to X voltage divided by 150,000 times W to Z voltage
e> W to X voltage divided by 150,000 times W to Y voltage

45. What is azimuth on a radar antenna>

a> diameter
b> degrees elevation
c> degrees horizon
d> impedance
e> frequency

46. How do you electrically decrease the length of an antenna?

a> add an inductor in series
b> add an inductor in parallel
c> add a capacitor in series
d> add a resistor in series
e> add a fiilter in parallel

47. Convert 150 nautical miles to statue miles:

a> 172.5
b> 130.5
c> 75
d> 73.6
e> 68.3

48. What logic circuit does this represent?

a> AND
b> NOR
c> Exclusive OR
d> OR
e> NAND

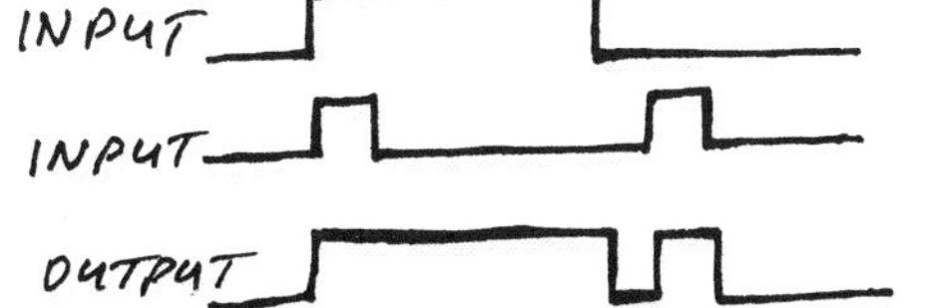


49. A frequency tolerance of 0.001% is how many parts per million?

a> 10 PPM
b> 100 PPM
c> 1000 PPM
d> 10,000 PPM
e> 100,000 PPM

50. What operating frequency is used in modern Loran radio navigation systems?

a> Loran A 1900 kHz.
b> Loran B 121.5 MHz.
c> Loran C 100 kHz.
d> Sat-Nav 243 MHz.
e> Omega 2300 kHz.

51. A transmission line has a 20 dB loss. If the signal entering the line is 1000 watts, what is the power of the signal entering the antenna?

a> 980 watts
b> 500 watts
c> 100 watts
d> 10 watts
e> 1 watt

52. What is the total inductance?

a> 25 H
b> 100 H
c> 2.5 H
d> 15 H
e> 500 H

53. A varactor diode can be used to vary frequency of resonance of an LC circuit. What is another use?

a> frequency control
b> amplify
c> multiply
d> switch
e> all of the above

54. A 500 watt radiotelephone transmitter is connected to a coaxial cable transmission line 200 feet long. If the cable has a line loss of 3 dB per 100 feet, what is the output power of the system if the antenna has a gain of 9 dB?

a> 625 watts
b> 900 watts
c> 800 watts
d> 1000 watts
e> 500 watts

55. What is NOT a good soldering practice in electronic circuits?

a> use adequate head
b> clean parts sufficiently
c> prevent corrosion by never using flux
d> make mechanical connection between parts
e> be certain parts do not move while silder is cooling

56. Operation of communication with a signal in one director and one in the opposite direction is:

a> duplex
b> multiplex
c> stereo
d> simplex
e> Double Sideband

57. A 50.0 MHz. transmitter ERP is 100 watts. There is a 5 watt spurious emission at 49.9 MHz. If a 7 dB filter is added to the system, what will be the new ERP at 49.9 MHz.?

a> 2.5 watts
b> 1.0 watt
c> 0.5 watt
d> 0.1 watt
e> 0.07 watt

58. Waveguides are not utilized at VHF or UHF frequencies because:

a> characteristic impedance
b> resistance to high frequency waves
c> large dimensions of waveguide are not practical
d> grounding problems
e> all of the above

59. If the period of a complete waveform is four divisions on an oscilloscope and the horizontal scale is 50 microseconds per division, what is the frequency of the sine wave?

a> 200 kHz.
b> 2 MHz.
c> 20 Hz.
d> 5 MHz.
e> 5000 Hz.

60. 2300 UTC time is:

a> 2 PM CST
b> 3 PM PST
c> 10 AM EST
d> 6 AM EST
e> 4 AM PST

61. At 156.8 MHz., how many Hertz may frequency for a tolerance of 20 PPM?

a> 0.16 Hz.
b> 313.6 Hz.
c> 784 Hz.
d> 1,568 Hz.
e> 3,136 Hz.

62. When making your preliminary radiotelephone call, it must be limited to:

a> 15 minutes, then not repeated for 30 minutes
b> one minute, then not repeated for 30 minutes
c> 30 seconds, then not repeated for 2 minutes
d> the first 3 minutes of the hour and half hour, then not repeated for 27 minutes
e> one watt

63. If the length of an antenna is changed from 1.5 feet to 1.6 feet, its resonant frequency will:

a> decrease
b> increase
c> be 6.7% higher
d> be 6% lower
e> remain the same

64. Why do we tin component leads?

a> it helps to oxidize the wires
b> prevents resting of circuit board
c> decreases heating time and aids in connection
d> provides ample wetting for good connection
e> both a and b above

65. Transmitters using F3E and G3E emissions in the 156 to 162 MHz. band may have a maximum frequency deviation of plus or minus how many Hertz during 100% modulation>

a> 1 kHz.
b> 2 kHz.
c> 3 kHz.
d> 5 kHz.
e> 10 kHz.

66. What emission has the greatest bandwidth?

a> 6K00A3E
b> 16K0G3E
c> 15KG3E
d> 7K50A3E
e> 3000HA3E

67. 100 nautical miles equals how many statue miles?

a> 87
b> 108
c> 172
d> 130
e> 115

68. The HF (high frequency) range is:

a> 3 - 30 MHz.
b> 30 - 300 MHz.
c> 300 - 3000 MHz.
d> 3 - 30 GHz.
e> 30 - 300 Ghz.

69. Omega operates in what frequency band?

a> below 3 kHz.
b> 3 - 30 kHz
c> 30 - 300 kHz.
d> 300 - 3000 kHz.
e> 30 - 300 GHz.

70. If the voltage of a DC series circuit is doubled, what change in resistance must occur to dissipate the same power?

a> eight times the original
b> four times the original
c> 50% of the original
d> 25% of the original
e> cannot be determined

71. A 1000 watt transmitter output is connected to a transmission line with a 7 dB attenuatiion. If the antenna has a gain of 3 dB, what is the output of the system?

a> 770 watts
b> 400 watts
c> 300 watts
d> 125 watts
e> 50 watts

72. What is the purpose of using a small amount of solder on the tip of a soldering iron just priior to making a connection?

a> removes oxidation
b> burns up flux
c> increases solder temperature
d> aids in wetting the wires
e> all of the above

73. One statue mile equals how many nautical miles?

a> 3.8
b> 1.5
c> 0.87
d> 0.7
e> 1.0

74. Ship board transmitters using F3E emission may not exceed what carrier power?

a> 500 watts
b> 250 watts
c> 100 watts
d> 25 watts
e> 1 watt

75. If the required frequency tolerance of an aircraft ELT transmitter is 50 ppm, which of the following would be within authorized specifications?

a> 243.014 MHz.
b> 243.012 MHz.
c> 242.988 MHz.
d> 242.986 MHz.
e> 0.2428 GHz.

76. When can you use more than one watt of transmitter output power on the Bridge-to-Bridge radio frequency?

a> when rounding a bend in a river; blind situation or emergency
b> when in a rendezvous with the Coast Guard
c> when the Captain deems it necessary
d> it is never permitted
e> all of the above

77. Loran C operates in what frequency band?

a> 30 - 300 MHz.
b> 3 - 30 MHz.
c> 300 - 3000 kHz.
d> 30 - 300 kHz.
e> 3 - 30 kHz.

78. When performing maintenance work, an FCC General Radio-telephone License is required at which of the following?

a> two-way mobile radio
b> police radio
c> public paging system
d> satellite Broadcast Network
e> none of the above

79. What has more priority:

a> urgent
b> distress
c> safety
d> security
e> priority

80. Where is the type of emission for a transmitter listed?

a> in Part 83 of the FCC Rules and Regulations.
b> on the transmitter name place
c> on the station license
d> on the station operating log
e> all of the above

81. When can a power greater than one watt be used in Bridge to Bridge communication?

a> during an emergency
b> when rounding a bend in a river
c> failure of another vessel being called to respond to your second call
d> in a blind situation when your restricted view of waterway could be dangerous
e> all of the above

82. When may a Class B EPIRB be tested without the coordination of the U.S. Coast Guard?

a> between midnight and 1 AM U.T.C.
b> between midnight and 6 AM local time
c> between 0000 and 0600 U.T.C. time
d> during the official FCC Silent Period
e> during the first 5 minutes of the hour, not to exceed three audible sweeps or one second

83. An airport ILS instrument landing Localizer transmitter sends what guidance signals to incoming aircraft?

a> lateral axis approach
b> horizontal axis approach
c> vertical axis approach
d> control town landing instructions
e> runway wind speed in knots

84. When listening to non-distress radiotelephone communications directed to others, you may:

a> use all of the information, except U.S. military communications
b> report all conversations to the master of the ship
c> use none of the information you hear for personal gain and do not repeat the conversation to others
d> use and relay all other information because of "Freedom of Speech" statues
e> both a and d above

85. In the aviation services, an emergency locator transmitter (ELT) should be tested:

a> with an internal test circuit having a manually activated test switch
b> if a dummy load equivalent to the ELT antenna is affixed to eliminate radiation
c> under the control of the Federal Aviation Administration if ELT is not fitted with test circuit
d> if brief opeating tests are authorized, tests must be conducted within the first 5 minutes of any hour and not longer lthan 3 audio sweeps into a dummy antenna
e> all of the above

86. Marine transmitters should be modulated between:

a> 60% - 99%
b> 70% - 105%
c> 75% - 100%
d> 85% - 100%
e> 90% - 100%

87. When a ship is authorized to transmit within the 1605 kHz. to 3500 kHz. band, and other frequencies, listening must be maintained which of the following?

a> 156.8 Mhz.
b> 2182 MHz.
c> 121.5 MHz.
d> 2200 kHz.
e> 1300 kHz.

88. When soldering electronic circuits be sure to:

a> use sufficient heat
b> use maximum heat
c> heat wires until sweating begins
d> use minimum solder
e> wet wires with flux after soldering

89. What is Channel 16?

a> Loran: 100 kHz.
b> distress, calling: 100 kHz.
c> distress, calling: 156.8 MHz.
d> Bridge to Bridge: 157.4 MHz.
e> monitoring, calling: 2162 kHz.

90. When and how may Class A and Class B EPIRB's be tested?

a> within the first 5 minutes of the hour; tests not exceed 3 audible sweeps or one second, which ever is longer
b> within first 3 minutes of hour; tests not to exceed 30 seconds
c> within first 1 minute of hour, test not to exceed 1 minute
d> at any time ship is at sea.
e> when necessarly to maintain proper transmitter alignment

91. The band of frequencies least susceptible to atmospheric noise and interference is:

a> 30 - 300 kHz.
b> 300 - 3000 kHz.
c> 3 - 30 MHz.
d> 30 - 300 MHz.
e> 300 - 3000 MHz.

92. Logs which contain communications that are being investigated by the Commission must be retained:

a> one year
b> three years
c> seven years
d> until the Commission authorizes the logs to be destroyed
e> logs are not required for marine transmitters

93. What happens to the radio license when a vessel is sold?

a> nothing, if license is valid
b> it must be renewed
c> it is automatically transfered with vessel
d> new owner of vessel receives license and call sign sehn license is renewed at espiration
e> new owner of vessel must apply for a new license

94. Who must sign an application for a station license?

a> person applying for the license
b> vessel owner, master or operating agency
c> officer of corporation that owner the ship
d> offical of a government branch which operates the ship
e> all of the above

95. When is the Silent Period on 2182 kHz., when only emergency communications my occur?

a> for the first three audio sweeps of every hour
b> for one minute at the beginning of every hour and half hour
c> at all times
d> never; only observe silence when a distress call is received
e> for three minutes at the beginning of every hour and half hour

96. Radiotelephone transmitters according to section 80 - 83 must have a durable nameplate mounted on transmitters and receivers showing:

a> name of manufacturer
b> type or model number
c> must be type approved and listed in the FCC "Radio Equipment List"
d> all of the above
e> none of the above

97. 2.3 statue miles equals how many nautical miles?

a> 2
b> 1.5
c> 1.73
d> 1
e> 0.57

98. What is the frequency range of UHF?

a> 0.3 to 3 GHz.
b> 0.3 to 3 MHz.
c> 3 to 30 kHz
d> 30 to 300 MHz.
e> 30 to 300 kHz.

99. What is the range of marine VHF distress transmissions?

a> 10 miles
b> 20 miles
c> 50 miles
d> 150 miles
e> 500 miles

100. What is the purpose of flux?

a> removes oxides from surfaces to be joined
b> prevents oxidation during soldering
c> acid cleans printed circuit connections
d> causes wetting of leads for solid connection
e> both a and b

# Test 3-K Element Three

1. If the reactance of a coil is 75 ohms at 500 Kc., what is the reactance at a frequency of 2500 Kc.?
   a. 15 ohms
   b. 75 ohms
   c. 150 ohms
   d. 375 ohms
   e. 650 ohms

2. The lower Class radiotelephone license of an operator who qualifies for a higher Class license:
   a. may retain both licenses
   b. may retain the lower Class license for five years
   c. may retain the lower Class license for 10 days
   d. may operate without a license
   e. is automatically cancelled

3. What is the final output of the three stages?

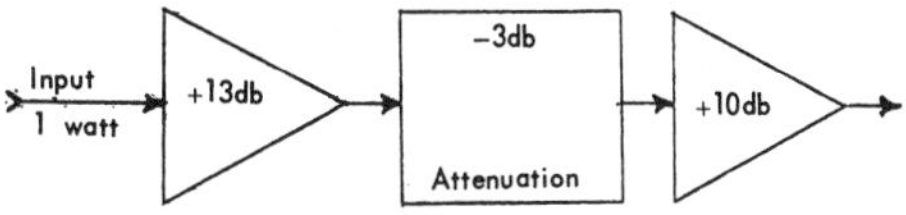

   a. 20 watts
   b. 25 watts
   c. 50 watts
   d. 100 watts
   e. 250 watts

4. The power gain of an amplifier is 40 db and the rated output is 20 watts. If the zero db reference level is 2 milliwatts, the input signal level will be:
   a. 0 db
   b. 40 db
   c. -40 db
   d. 2 db
   e. 20 db

5. A decrease in RF excitation of a class C amplifier may cause a:
   a. increase in grid current
   b. decrease in grid current
   c. no change in grid current
   d. amplifier short circuit
   e. any of the above

6. What type of RF amplifier has an approximate efficiency of 65%?
   a. Foster-Edison
   b. Parasitic
   c. Ratio
   d. Wheatstone
   e. Doherty

7. The schematic diagram shown is:
   a. triode oscillator
   b. voltage doubler power supply
   c. full wave vibrator
   d. voltage divider
   e. ratio detector

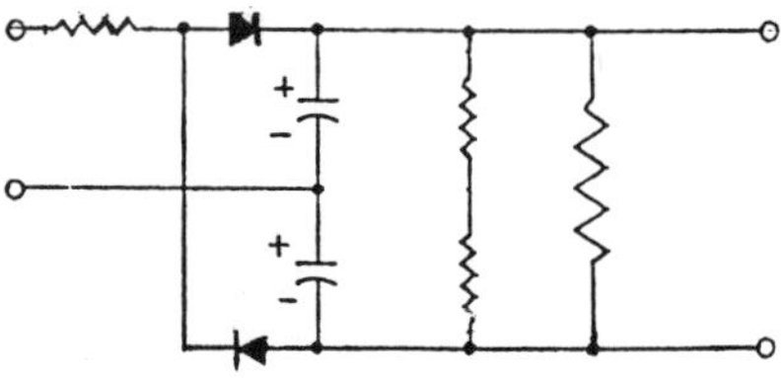

8. A transformer is being used to match a 500 ohm program line to a 150 ohm load. The turns ratio should be approximately:
   a. 1.3
   b. 1.8
   c. 3.3
   d. 11.1
   e. 3.14

9. If the power output from a modulator is reduced from 50 watts to 0.5 watts, the power loss will be:
   a. 5 db
   b. 10 db
   c. 20 db
   d. 50 db
   e. 100 db

10. If a 3/4 wavelength transmission is shortened at one end, impedance at the open end will be:
    a. zero
    b. infinite
    c. decreased
    d. increased
    e. cannot be determined without additional information

11. What is Class C noted for?
    a. high output power; moderate distortion
    b. distortion of the input waveform shape and high harmonic output
    c. low output power and low distortion of input wave
    d. 10% more distortion than Class B operation
    e. 20% more distortion than Class A operation

12. If a radio-frequency amplifier is operated push-pull and the outputs are connected in parallel, the resulting output will be:
    a. out-of-phase and cancelled
    b. the fundamental frequency only
    c. odd harmonics of the input frequency
    d. even harmonics of the input frequency
    e. 50% of the input power

13. A balanced push-pull amplifier will:
    a. suppress the fundamental frequency
    b. suppress the fundamental and all odd harmonics
    c. suppress all even harmonics
    d. generate sub-harmonic frequency
    e. have the same putput as a single-ended amplifier

14. A 0 to 10 DC milliammeter is used with a resistor connected in series to measure full scale voltage up to 1000 volts. What is the ohm-per-volt sensitivity of the voltmeter?
    a. 10
    b. 100
    c. 1000
    d. 50
    e. 500

15. The most accurate tool for measuring AVC voltages in a receiver is:
a. low impedance voltmeter
b. VU meter
c. absorption wavemeter
d. VTVM
e. Thermasistor-meter

16. The schematic diagram shown is:
a. push-pull audio amplifier
b. carrier shift indicator
c. RC coupling
d. impedance coupling
e. squelch circuit

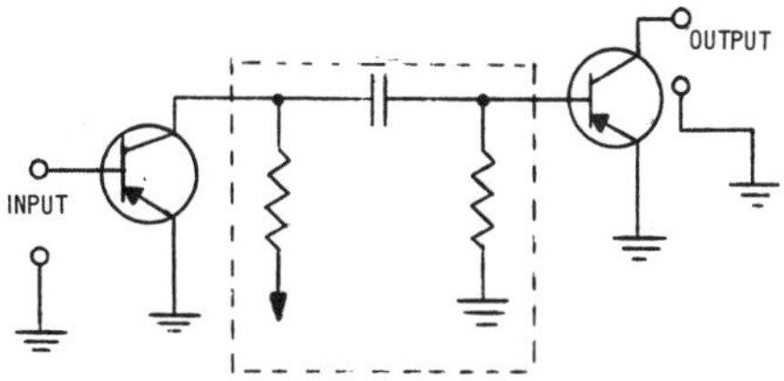

17. To correct split tuning:
a. tune to resonance
b. use resistance feedback
c. correct phase reversal
d. increase coupling between stages
e. decrease coupling between stages

18. The system of connections for a three-phase, three transformer circuit that provides the maximum secondary voltage is:
a. delta series
b. full load
c. delta induction
d. delta Y
e. variable ratio

19. The "Q" of a tank circuit is a measurement of:
a. frequency response
b. resonance reactance
c. resistance in coil
d. capacitance
e. inductance

20. What is a slight change in plate voltage to a slight change in control grid voltage called?
a. mhoconductance
b. transconductance
c. plate conductance
d. sinusoidal factor
e. amplification factor

21. A dummy antenna is a:
a. non-directional receiver antenna
b. wide bandwidth directional receiver antenna
c. transmitter test antenna designed for minimum radiation
d. transmitter non-directional narrow-band antenna
e. VHF short range non-directional receiving antenna

22. Where can parasitic oscillations occur?
a. final amplifier
b. buffer
c. frequency multiplier
d. crystal oscillator
e. all of the above

23. What is the input power of an audio amplifier having a gain of 40 db and the output is 6 watts?
a. 600 watts
b. 60 watts
c. 6 watts
d. 6 milliwatts
e. 0.6 milliwatt

24. This diagram is:
    a. Radar receiver
    b. AM transmitter
    c. AM receiver
    d. FM Transmitter
    e. FM receiver

25. If a turned resonant circuit is resonant and parallel with another circuit, each at 100.1 MHz, what is the frequency of the combination of both circuits?
    a. 200.2 MHz
    b. 10,2020.01 MHz
    c. 100.1 MHz
    d. 1550 KHz
    e. 97.1 Mhz

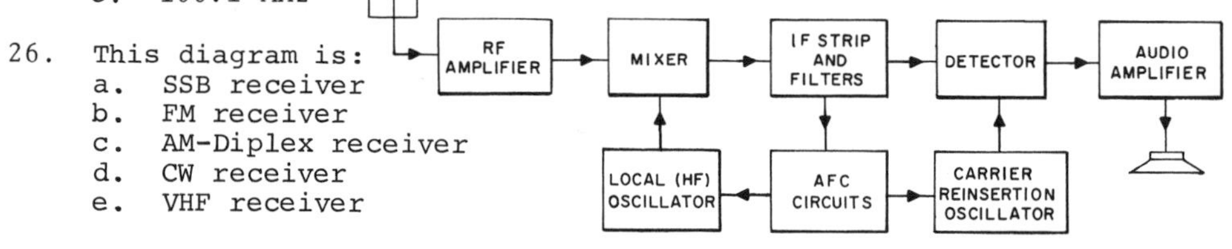


26. This diagram is:
    a. SSB receiver
    b. FM receiver
    c. AM-Diplex receiver
    d. CW receiver
    e. VHF receiver

27. What is the gain of this operational inverting amplifier?
    a. infinate
    b. 10
    c. 100
    d. 1,000
    e. cannot be determined

28. The cause of a high standing wave ratio could be caused by:
    a. carrier shift
    b. poor ratio detection
    c. de-tuned antenna coupling
    d. skin effect
    e. all of the above

29 Upon receipt of a Notification of Suspension from the commission, the suspension becomes effective:
    a. immediately upon receipt
    b. within 15 days
    c. within 10 days
    d. within 5 days

30. The "shielding" of coaxial transmission lines are usually:
    a. ac voltage conductors
    b. full wave
    c. grounded
    d. neutralized
    e. all of the above

31. The purpose of a transmitter buffer state is:
    a. increase the output of the oscillator
    b. prevents loss of a-f frequencies
    c. prevents load changes from affecting the oscillator
    d. both a and b above
    e. both b and c above

32. Except for emergencies, maximum Bridge-to-Bridge power is:
a. 1 watt
b. 5 watts
c. 25 watts
d. 100 watts
e. no limitation

33. To obtain an output power of 6 watts from an audio amplifier having a gain of 30 db, the amplifier input level should be:
a. 1 watt
b. 2 watts
c. 60 milliwatts
d. 30 db
e. 0 db

34. What is a ratio of a small change in plate current to a small change in grid voltage with no change in plate voltage:
a. mutual inductance
b. mutual conductance
c. dynamic plate resistance
d. grid inductance
e. grid amplification ratio

35. When two inductors of equal inductance are connected in phase with coefficient of coupling 0.5, the total circuit inductance is:
a. same value as any one inductance
b. three times any one inductance
c. two times any one inductance
d. five times any one inductance
e. four times any one inductance

36. What is the speed of a 220 volt, 6 pole, 3 phase motor obtaining current at 60 hertz per second?
a. 600 rpm
b. 1200 rpm
c. 1800 rpm
d. 2400 rpm
e. 3000 rpm

37. This schematic contains:
a. ratio detection
b. frequency multipliers
c. impedance coupling
d. direct coupling
e. phase modulation

INPUT
RFC
OUTPUT

38. The FCC requires modulation to be from:

a. 75 to 100%
b. 85 to 105%
c. 50 to 90%
d. 65 to 99%
e. always 100%

39. What is the reactance of a 0.09 millihenry coil in series with another 0.01 millihenry coil with no mutual inductance if 3,000 kHz is applied to the circuit?
a. 300 ohms
b. 300 kilo-ohms
c. 18 ohms
d. 1.88 ohms
e. 1.88 kilo-ohms

40. A balanced push-pull amplifier suppresses:
   a. over modulation
   b. harmonic r-f excitation
   c. only odd harmonics
   d. even harmonics
   e. standing wave radio

41. If a series circuit has a capacitive reactance of 44 ohms, an inductive reactance of 27 ohms, resistance equals 17 ohms, and the voltage equals 100 volts:
   a. voltage leads applied current
   b. current leads applied voltage
   c. voltage is equal to current squared
   d. current is equal to voltage squared
   e. not enough information given

42. A power supply has good voltage regulation when:
   a. input voltage varies slightly under a varying load
   b. output voltage varies slightly under a varying load
   c. output power is adjustable over a varying range
   d. output voltage varies slightly to a minimum load
   e. remains the same

43. What is the peak value of a 20 volt RMS sine wave?
   a. 7.07 volts
   b. 22.5 volts
   c. 28.28 volts
   d. 66.22 volts
   e. 400 volts

44. If a class C r-f amplifier is connected with grids in both tubes in push-pull, the output frequency is:
   a. double input frequency
   b. equal to input power
   c. equal to input frequency
   d. equal to input voltage
   e. reduced 50%

45. If a two micro-farad capacitor is discharged down to 37 volts through a one meg-ohm resistor from 100 volts, how long will the discharge take?
   a. 0.2 seconds
   b. 2 seconds
   c. 20 seconds
   d. 200 micro-seconds
   e. 37 micro-seconds

46. When A3j single-sideband suppressed carrier is used, carrier must be at least ____ below peak envelope power.
   a. 40 dB
   b. 30 dB
   c. 20 dB
   d. 10 dB
   e. 0 dB

47. Class C amplifiers are noted for:
   a. high efficiency
   b. poor reproduction of input waveform
   c. low distortion of input waveform
   d. low efficiency and high quality reproduction
   e. both a and b above

48. How is this curcuit used?
    a. to match tube to antenna impedance
    b. to reduce antenna current
    c. to double voltage
    d. to reduce modulation index
    e. to match tube plate to the input of the bridge input of the buffer output stage

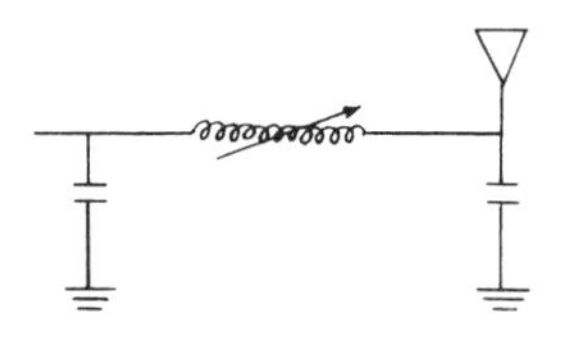

49. When the input frequency of a full-wave rectifier is 60 hertz the output ripple frequency is:
    a. 360 hertz
    b. 240 hertz
    c. 180 hertz
    d. 120 hertz
    e. 60 hertz

50. A push-pull final amplifier operates at 2182 kHz. Which of the following harmonic frequencies contains the greatest power?
    a. 2183 kHz.
    b. 2181 kHz.
    c. 4364 kHz.
    d. 6546 kHz.
    e. 8728 kHz.

51. A Foster-Seeley discriminator:
    a. detects amplitude modulated signals
    b. detects frequency modulated signals
    c. detects carrier shift signals
    d. regulates de-emphasis voltages
    e. induces FM detection voltage

52. If a heterodyne frequency meter, having a straight-line relationship between frequency and dial reading has a dial reading of 32.2 for a frequency of 2390 kHz and a dial reading of 35.8 for a frequency of 2408 kHz, what is the frequency corresponding to a scale reading of 34.6?
    a. 2390.876 kHz
    b. 2395.696 kHz
    c. 2398.851 kHz
    d. 2401.980 kHz
    e. 2404.697 kHz

53. What is the purpose of negative feedback?
    a. reduce distortion
    b. increase gain
    c. reduce harmonics
    d. lower final input power
    e. cancel even harmonics

54. Two coils are connected in series with fields opposing $180^{o}$ and the mutual inductance between the coils is 0.3 henries. If the inductance values are 0.9 henry and 0.5 henry, the total inductance of the circuit is:
    a. 0.9 henry
    b. 0.8 henry
    c. 0.7 henry
    d. 0.5 henry
    e. 0.3 henry

55. A resistor is connected in series with a milliammeter which reads from 0 to 100 milliampers and indicates full scale voltages up to 250 volts. The meter sensitivity is:
a. 1.0 ohm-per-volt
b. 10 ohms-per-volt
c. 100 ohms-per-volt
d. 2.50 ohms-per-volt
e. 25 ohms-per-volt

56. A parallel circuit is composed of resistance, inductance and capacitance. The resistance is 25 ohms, the inductive reactance is 10 ohms and the capacitive reactance is 50 ohms. When 100 volts is imposed on the circuit, the total current will be:
a. 4.5 amperes
b. 8.9 milliamperes
c. 8.9 amperes
d. 81 amperes
e. 1.5 amperes

57. Saturation of a single-ended audio output transformer will cause:
a. higher modulation
b. lower modulation
c. better carrier wave coverage
d. distortion
e. skin effect

58. A crystal oscillator frequency can be changed by:
a. connecting a capacitor in parallel with the crystal
b. connecting a resistor in series with the crystal
c. connecting a resistor in parallel with the crystal
d. increasing pressure on the crystal with screw adjustment
e. increase voltage across crystal

59. Transformers with grounded center taps are used in audio lines:
a. to increase hum
b. to cancel out noise or hum
c. to lower line efficiency
d. to cancel even harmonics of r-f current
e. to increase skin effect

60. When will a frequency doubler circuit operate best?
a. during high plate current distortion
b. during low plate current distortion
c. at low audio frequencies
d. during phase modulation
e. at microwave frequencies

# Test 8-A Element Eight

1. When handling silicon crystal rectifier cartridges care should be taken to:
   a. discharge any static charge before touching the crystal
   b. avoid strong winds
   c. wear gloves and goggles
   d. de-magnetize magnetron
   e. avoid magnetic fields

2. When may a Ship Radar station be operated by operators without an FCC license?
   a. never
   b. only when a licensed operator is on duty nearby
   c. if the transmitter is under 1000 watts peak input power
   d. if no internal adjustments are necessary to operate pulse magnetron
   e. if transmitter uses a reflex Klystron

3. What determines the timing duration and shape of the radar pulse?
   a. parabolic reflector
   b. artifical transmission line
   c. anti - TR box
   d. detector
   e. reflex Klystron

4. Range markings are produced on a PPI radar scope by:
   a. applied pulses to cathode of CRT
   b. applied pulses to the grid of CRT
   c. painted on the PPI class screen cover
   d. aquadag coating
   e. etched circular markings on CRT glass

5. When listening to a radiotelephone receiver a high level of "hash" noise is usually caused by:
   a. magnetron arcing
   b. radar motor generator or poor grounding or shielding
   c. air leaks in the waveguide
   d. radar beam hitting metal sections of ship
   e. de-tuned antenna coupling

6. Before making repairs or adjustments to Ship Radar equipment the maintenance person should first:
   a. request approval by ship's Mate
   b. disconnect magnetron
   c. shut off all power
   d. discharge capacitors
   e. check all radar frequencies for possible interference

7. The sensitivity time control circuit:
   a. lowers the sensitivity of the receiver when receiving nearby target signals
   b. increases the sensitivity of the receiver when receiving nearby target signals
   c. controls magnetron current
   d. triggers blocking oscillator
   e. controls CRT "focus coil"

8. A radar installation has a maximum range of 20 miles. The radar beam will travel this distance to a target and bounce back to the receiving antenna in approximately:
   a. 24.6 microseconds
   b. 0.0009 second
   c. 250 microseconds
   d. 1231 microseconds
   e. 1/600 second

9. What is the steady-tone heard on radiotelephone receivers?
   a. emergency auto-alarm
   b. adjust waveguide echo box for minimum reading
   c. magnetron feedback to radar receiver
   d. radar transmitter pulse or harmonic
   e. LORAN signal

10. What should be checked to eliminate steady-tone interference to a LORAN receiver?
    a. echo box
    b. grounding
    c. magnetron
    d. crystal
    e. direction finder

11. What license is required for replacement of fuses and receiving tubes in a ship radar set in actual use?
    a. none
    b. First or Second class Radiotelephone license
    c. Ship radar endorsement only
    d. First class radiotelegraph license only
    e. either B or D above

12. A band of frequencies that Ship Radar operate:
    a. 10 GHz
    b. 30 to 60 MHz
    c. 2100 to 2900 MHz
    d. 9300 to 9500 MHz
    e. 500 KHz

13. What determines the operating frequency of a self-blocking oscillator?
    a. magnetron
    b. input resonant tank circuit
    c. cathode bias LC values
    d. plate tank circuit
    e. grid circuit time constant

14. What precautions should be taken to prevent damage to the magnet of a magnetron?
    a. strong breezes
    b. high electric fields
    c. excessive heat, shocks or magnetized metal filings
    d. "Spikes", "Hash", and "Sea Return"
    e. all of the above

15. A TR box:
    a. reduces modulator tube arching
    b. protects video amplifier of receiver
    c. creates "Heading Flash"
    d. hollow copper rectangular tubes used to transmit radar signals
    e. two electrodes in a resonant cavity with a spark gap

16. In radar signal reception, target information is displayed on:
    a. cathode-ray tube fluorescent screen
    b. Auto-Alarm receiver
    c. radar tube
    d. reflex Klystron
    e. Radiotelephone or Radiotelegraph receiver

17. What type of modulation causes the radar transmitter carrier to be turned on and off at regular intervals?
    a. pulse
    b. phase
    c. blocking
    d. echo
    e. reflex Kylstron

18. What frequencies are used for IF amplifiers in radar sets?
    a. 9300 Mc
    b. 2300 Kc
    c. 131 Mc
    d. 500 Kc
    e. 30 or 60 Mc

19. When adjusting a radar set with an echo box, the serviceman adjusts:
    a. blocking oscillator
    b. TR and anti-TR boxes
    c. to obtain the longest "ringingtime" and longest "spokes" on radar screen
    d. to obtain the minimum "ringing time" and shortest "spokes" on radar screen
    e. magnetron current for maximum reading

20. What portion of the magnetron is operated at negative potential?
    a. emitter
    b. cathode
    c. anode
    d. heater
    e. gride tank

21. The rotation position of the radar trace line is determined by:
    a. antenna phase current
    b. "sweep" amplifier current
    c. grid input signal
    d. rotation of deflection coil
    e. magnetron current reading

22. What is the duty cycle of a 1.0 microsecond radar pulse if the repetition rate is 1000 and the average power is 20 watts?
    a. 1,000,00
    b. 20,000
    c. 30
    d. 0.09
    e. 0.001

23. What type of transmission line is used most often after the diplexer circuit?
    a. directional
    b. parabolic reflector
    c. coxial cable
    d. waveguide
    e. artificial transmission line

24. What should be checked when all targets look unusually weak on a radar screen?
    a. magnetron
    b. mixer crystal
    c. cathode-ray tube
    d. reflex Klystron
    e. antenna reflector

25. When installing waveguides it is a good practice to avoid:
    a. motors and generators
    b. all radiotelephone equipment
    c. long horizontal distances
    d. long vertical distances
    e. strong electric fields

26. TR and anti-TR tubes act as what type of circuits during transmission?
    a. video amplifiers
    b. limiter circuits
    c. rotating deflection servo amplifier
    d. short circuits
    e. artificial transmission line

27. What simulates an artificial target utilized to test a radar receiver:
    a. waveguide oscillations
    b. TR tube
    c. echo box
    d. repeller plate
    e. artificial transmission line

28. What components may be replaced in ship radar equipment by an unlicensed operator?
    a. crystals
    b. magnetron
    c. fuses and receiving tubes
    d. broken waveguide sections
    e. nothing

29. What is a typical front-to-back resistance ratio for a radar receiver mixer crystal?
    a. 1:2
    b. 12.3:1
    c. 1:1
    d. 10:1
    e. 20:1

30. What entries are required in the maintenance record of a ship radar station?
    a. place and date of installation
    b. nature of complaints and remedy steps taken to reduce interference
    c. listing of component failures, reason for trouble and date remedial measures taken
    d. name, license number, and date of ship radar endorsement of licensed operator performing maintenance work
    e. all of the above

31. "Sea Return" on a radar scope is caused by:
    a. the reflection of the radar pulse "echoing" of the waves of the sea long distances from the ship
    b. the reflection of the radar beam bouncing off waves of the sea near the ship
    c. arcing of motors and generators
    d. a defective magnetron
    e. simply range and bearing markings

32. A waveguide can be terminated at the radar antenna reflector:
    a. "Horn" radiator
    b. parabolic reflector
    c. echo box
    d. resonant cavity
    e. either a or b above

33. Who makes entries in the installation and maintenance log of a ship radar station?
    a. Radiotelegraph First or Second Class operator only
    b. first or second class radiotelephone or radiotelegraph operator with radar endorsement
    c. anyone approved by ship's Mate
    d. U.S. citizens licensed by FCC only
    e. person responsible for operator activity

34. Interference to commercial radiotelephone receivers:
    a. is always eliminated by adjusting receiver
    b. is louder on some frequencies than others
    c. is eliminated by grounding waveguides
    d. is usually a problem below 30 KHz
    e. is never a problem above 60 KHz

35. When working with crystals, to avoid possible damage:
    a. place metal foil over crystal
    b. always avoid static discharge to the crystal
    c. keep it away from strong breezes
    d. wear protective gloves and goggles
    e. keep it away from strong fields

36. What is the pear power of a radar installation having a pulse width of 1.0 microsecond, average power of 18 watts, and the pulse repetition rate is 900?
 a. 50 watts
 b. 0.0162 kilowatts
 c. 16,200 watts
 d. 20,000 watts
 e. 100,000 watts

37. What sound is heard when radar interference is picked up on a radiotelephone receiver?
 a. steady tone
 b. a tone that changes frequency when receiver is tuned
 c. high speed pounding sound of pulse emissions
 d. pulsed tones
 e. "Hash" and low frequency "Spikes"

38. Bright flashing pie sections appearing on a radar PPI scope may be caused by:
 a. defective reflex Klystron
 b. defective crystal in radar receiver
 c. adjustment of echo box through resonant frequencies
 d. targets on scope less than one mile
 e. "Grass"

39. What is the average power of a 1.0 microsecond radar pulse, when the pulse repetitition rate is 900 and the peak power is 25,000 watts?
 a. 0.001111
 b. 25 watts
 c. 225 watts
 d. 500 watts
 e. 1,100 watts

40. When do anti-TR and TR tubes deionize?
 a. during the receiving interval when transmitter is inactive
 b. during the receiving interval when no transmission occurs
 c. during the transmission interval
 d. never
 e. both a and b above

41. When there are sweep and range marks with no targets and low magnetron current, this indicates:
 a. deflection coil of CRT malfunctioning
 b. grid voltage loss
 c. defective magnetron
 d. waveguide gas leakage
 e. normal condition

42. Flanges and waveguide components such as a parabolic reflector may be physically separated by:
 a. 5 inches
 b. 2 cm
 c. 3 millimeters
 d. 1/2 wavelength
 e. 12.3 micrometers

43. What should be checked when steady-tone interference occurs on communication receivers?
 a. directional antenna
 b. waveguide choke connections
 c. auto-alarm
 d. grounding connections and shielding
 e. blocking oscillator

44. To reduce a condensed moisture inside of a waveguide:
    a. check for scratches in the silver plating
    b. fill the waveguide with nitrogen gas
    c. remove all oxides with FCC approved cleaners, then refill waveguide with gas
    d. drill a small 1/8" hole at the lowest point of the waveguide
    e. change all problem sections with weather resistant coax

45. The schematic diagram is:
    a. magnetron
    b. Klystron oscillator
    c. crystal mixer
    d. duplexer
    e. modulator

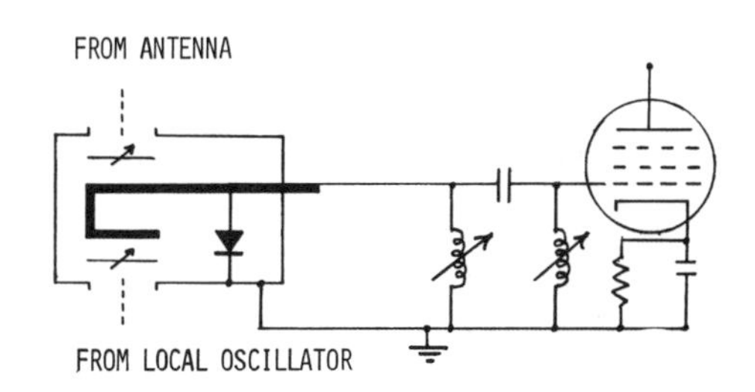


FOR QUESTIONS #46 - #50 REFER TO THE BLOCK DIAGRAM BELOW:

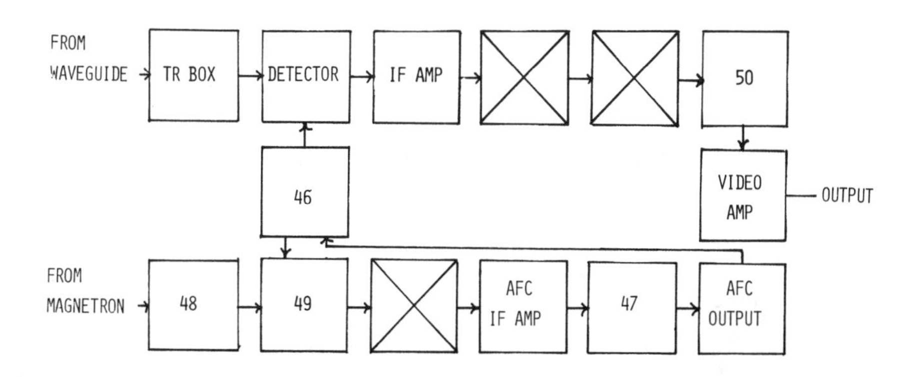


HERE ARE THE POSSIBLE ANSWER CHOICES FOR QUESTIONS #46 - #50:

a. RF attenuator
b. duplexer
c. detector
d. discriminator
e. local oscillator

# Test 8-B Element Eight

1. When may an unlicensed operator operate a radar station?
   a. if the radar set can be operated by use of internal controls and approval given by ship's Mate
   b. when a First or Second Class Radiotelegraph operator is on duty
   c. during emergency situations only
   d. if the radar set can be operated in accordance with the rules and regulations of the commission by use of external controls
   e. never

2. What is the average power of a 1.0 microsecond radar pulse when the pulse repetition rate is 900 and the peak power is 20 Kw?
   a. 20 watts
   b. 180 watts
   c. 400 watts
   d. 1,000 watts
   e. 1,800 watts

3. "Sea Return" can be reduced by:
   a. increasing antenna gain in areas at maximum distance from radar set
   b. lowering receiver gain for areas close to radar set
   c. increasing transmitter power for areas at maximum distance from radar set
   d. lowering receiver gain for areas at maximum distance from radar set
   e. good waveguide and magnetron grounding

4. What maintenance work may be done by unlicensed operators to ship radar equipment?
   a. "Range" and "Bearlag" plastic overlays for cathode-ray tube
   b. magnetron or Klystron plug-in circuits
   c. replacement of fuses and receiving tubes
   d. line cords and antenna plugs
   e. any of the above

5. How does radar interference appear on a LORAN?
   a. dark intensified areas in center of screen
   b. flashing range markings
   c. narrow vertical "spikes" moving across screen
   d. out of focus bearing markings
   e. rotation of "Spoke" markings

6. What is utilized as a local oscillator of a radar receiver?
   a. Magnetron
   b. reflex Klystron
   c. LORAN
   d. TR
   e. Aquadag

7. Ship radar transmitters operate on which band of frequencies?
   a. 2900 - 3100 MHz
   b. 3460 - 9200 MHz
   c. 9100 - 9200 MHz
   d. 9600 - 9850 MHz
   e. 30 - 60 MHz

8. Range marking signals are applied to:
   a. grid circuit of CRT
   b. first anode of CRT
   c. deflection coil of CRT
   d. range marker blocking oscillator anode
   e. video shaper amplifier cathode

9. Who may write entries in the maintenance record of a ship radar station?
   a. a First or Second Class Radio telephone or Radio-telegraph operator
   b. the person who supervises and is responsible for the actual maintenance work
   c. a First or Second Class Radiotelephone or Radiotelegraph operator with Ship Radar Endorsement
   d. the ship's Mate
   e. the chief radio operator

10. A Magnetron is:
   a. frequency doubler
   b. range marker oscillator
   c. diode
   d. triode
   e. pentode

11. What precautions should be observed when handling a cathode-ray tube?
   a. radar set should be turned off
   b. high voltage capacitors should be discharged with a well-insulated screwdriver
   c. avoid CRT breakage
   d. the fluorescent material of a broken CRT may cause serious poisoning of the bloodstream
   e. all of the above

12. The FCC requires waveguides between the transmitter and antenna to be:
   a. horizontal only
   b. 18 guage copper pipe
   c. silver coat interior
   d. minimum length as practical
   e. less than 10 feet long

13. "Heading Flash" is produced on a CRT radar screen by:
   a. radar beam hitting front mast
   b. reflex Klystron pulses
   c. momentary closing of a microswitch located on antenna assembly when the antenna points "dead ahead".
   d. etching marks on CRT face
   e. painting on screen

14. To avoid high-voltage shocks and to reduce insulation problems, the magnetron in a radar transmitter should be:
    a. wear protective gloves
    b. operated at low current
    c. at ground potential
    d. attached with heavy duty "flanges" to the waveguide
    e. operated with magnet 180° out of phase with modulator network

15. How is radar interference detected in auto-alarm equipment?
    a. by listening to earphones plugged into the auto-alarm and listening for interference or a steady-tone
    b. with a directional antenna
    c. by the ringing of auto-alarm
    d. vertical "spikes" across screen
    e. pulsed tones ranging from 30-60 Mc

16. What forms the burst of microwave RF energy which is fed to a radar antenna?
    a. Klystron
    b. magnetron
    c. TR box
    d. local oscillator
    e. control transfomer

17. What is the length of a waveguide antenna stub of a ship radar installation?
    a. 8 cm
    b. 1/4 wavelength
    c. 1/2 wavelength
    d. 2 inches
    e. 0.01111 inch

18. What equipment aboard ship is affected by radar interference?
    a. Auto-Alarm
    b. direction finder
    c. LORAN
    d. Radiotelephone receivers and public address system
    e. all of the above

19. The technician who performs or supervises the installation, servicing and maintenance of the ship radar equipment must hold:
    a. First or Second Class Radiotelephone or Radiotelegraph license
    b. FCC Element #8 Ship Radar Endorsement
    c. any class commercial operator license
    d. only a Radiotelegraph license with special Ship Radar endorsement
    e. First or Second Class Radiotelegraph or Radiotelephone license with Ship Radar endorsement

20. A narrow width radar beam:
    a. is less able to separate targets at the same radial distance
    b. is more able to separate targets in the same direction
    c. may cause serious damage from the high energy concentrated on the high velocity wave
    d. is more able to separate targets at the same range but different azimuth
    e. reduces signal-to-noise ratio in receiver

21. What is the peak power of a 1.0 microsecond radar pulse, when the pulse repetition rate is 900 and the average power is 14 watts?
    a. 0.001111
    b. 15,500 watts
    c. 12,600 watts
    d. 1,000 kw
    e. 155.555 watts

22. What is the preferred type of transmission conductor of microwave energy in most ship radar installations?
    a. circular shaped waveguides
    b. rectangular shaped waveguides
    c. coaxil cable
    d. copper plated 2" steel pipe with silver plated interior
    e. parabolic reflector

23. A high magnetron current reading and a change in oscillator frequency indicates:
    a. defective magnetron magnet
    b. imporoper waveguide coupling
    c. defective synchronizer stage
    d. anti-TR box short circuit
    e. normal condition

24. What is an advantage of using a waveguide over coaxial cable
    a. less expensive to install
    b. create less "Hash" and "Spikes"
    c. easier to connect to a parabolic reflector
    d. attenuates less RF energy
    e. all of the above

25. What is logged in the radar maintenance log?
    a. an interference problem description and details about any repairs made
    b. time and date when repair work began
    c. FCC transmitter license number
    d. magnetron current meter reading
    e. when steady-tone signals are received

26. What indication on a LORAN scope indicates radar is causing interference?
    a. "Grass"
    b. narrow vertical "Spike" pulses moving across screen
    c. steady-tone audio
    d. rotation of "Spokes" on screen
    e. both a and b above

27. What determines the operating frequency of a self-blocking oscillator?
    a. reflex Klystron
    b. B+ resistor
    c. gride transformer tank
    d. bias capacitor and resistor
    e. changing diode

28. A radar installation has a maximum range of 30 miles. The radar beam will travel to the target and bounce back to the receiving antenna in approximately:
a. 12.3 microseconds
b. 123 microseconds
c. 184.5 microseconds
d. 244.8 microseconds
e. 370 microseconds

29. What type of voltage is applied to the TR tube electrodes to keep gas in the tube at the point of ionization?
a. 1,500 volts
b. 30 to 60 KHz
c. out-of-phase
d. high frequency
e. keep-alive voltage

30. Who may operate Ship Radar equipment?
a. any person licensed by the marine operators bureau of the FCC
b. any operator with a FCC commercial grade license
c. any person with a ship radar endorsement
d. a First or Second Class Radiotelegraph or Radiotelephone license only
e. the Master or any person assigned to the job by the ship's Mate

31. To prevent moisture from entering a choke-coupling flange:
a. tighten all bolts to 12.3 pounds torque
b. keep flange air tight
c. drill several 1/8" holes in flange hose
d. tightly join flanges with suitable gasket
e. fill waveguide with gas

32. A weak magnetron magnet:
a. will decrease range mark circle size
b. will make targets to appear "fuzzy"
c. will cause deflection beam to move to outer edge of cathode-ray tube
d. cause CRT to distort
e. will cause high current

33. What type of detector is used most often in radar receivers?
a. magnetron
b. crystal diode
c. reflex Klystron
d. TR box
e. duplexer

34. The distance to a target when it takes 123 microseconds for a radar pulse to travel to the target and bounce back to the antenna:
a. 12.3 miles
b. 0.12 miles
c. 30 miles
d. 20 miles
e. 10 miles

35. If a TR box malfunctions during the transmission pulse:
a. "spokes" may appear fuzzy
b. magnetron current will increase
c. possible damage to the receiver could occur
d. possible damage to the transmitter could occur
e. oscillation may stop

36. The radar antenna should be installed aboard a ship in such a way as to:
    a. avoid shock to persons making adjustments to antenna ammeter
    b. be placed a minimum of 100 feet from radiotelephone receiving antenna
    c. be $180^{0}$ out-of-phase with radiotelephone receiver
    d. transmit the maximum power
    e. avoid the maximum number of scanning obstructions

37. How is radar interference located with direction finding equipment?
    a. tune receiver to resonance with use of D/F loop antenna
    b. rotate D/F loop antenna until source is detected
    c. listen to earphones plugged into radiotelephone receiver
    d. rotate parabolic reflector until interference is reduced
    e. turn receiver until a sharp steady-line appears on CRT

38. After a serviceman turns off all power when making repairs to a radar set:
    a. notify the ship's first Mate
    b. pull circuit breakers
    c. discharge all high voltage capacitors
    d. discharge the magnetron magnet
    e. discharge the crystal

39. The "Bearing Resolution" of a radar set is the ability to distinguish:
    a. the minimum range distance between two targets on the same CRT "Spoke"
    b. the minimum range distance between two targets at the same bearing
    c. the minimum angular distance between two targets at the same range
    d. the maximum distance between two targets at the same range
    e. the maximum distance between two targets at the same bearing

40. To minimumize signal loss, what should be done to the interior to waveguides?
    a. painted with rust proof paint
    b. use rounded corners
    c. fill with gas
    d. apply oil to all surfaces
    e. keep as clean as possible

41. An artificial target used to check and allign radar sets:
    a. direction finder
    b. artificial transmission line
    c. anti-TR box
    d. LORAN
    e. echo box

42. Gas diodes which ionize and arc during excitation of the transmitter pulse are called:
  a. chock joint
  b. magnetron
  c. heading flash diodes
  d. TR and anti-TR boxes
  e. reflex Klystron tubes

43. To reduce interference caused by radar and prevent possibility of shock to operators:
  a. enclose waveguide in heavy insulation
  b. adjust receiver with D/L Loop
  c. attach all metal components thoroughly to the ship's electrical ground
  d. adjust transmitter for minimum B+ leakage
  e. keep receiving and transmitting antenna maximum distance apart

44. What generates corrective voltage frequency?
  a. magnetron
  b. discriminator
  c. duplexer
  d. blocking oscillator
  e. AFC video amplifier

45. One of the three bands of frequencies that ship radar transmitters operate:
  a. 950 - 1100 MHz.
  b. 5460 - 5650 MHz.
  c. 16,000 - 20,000 MHz.
  d. 40 - 50 GHz.
  e. 30 - 60 GHz.

46. If long length radar transmission lines are not shielded or terminated properly, a possible result could be:
  a. interference to radio reception
  b. overmodulation
  c. non-directional radiation
  d. improper "Sea Return"
  e. repeller plate damage

47. This schematic diagram is:
  a. RF attenuator
  b. detector
  c. timing amplifier
  d. Klystron oscillator
  e. Magnetron

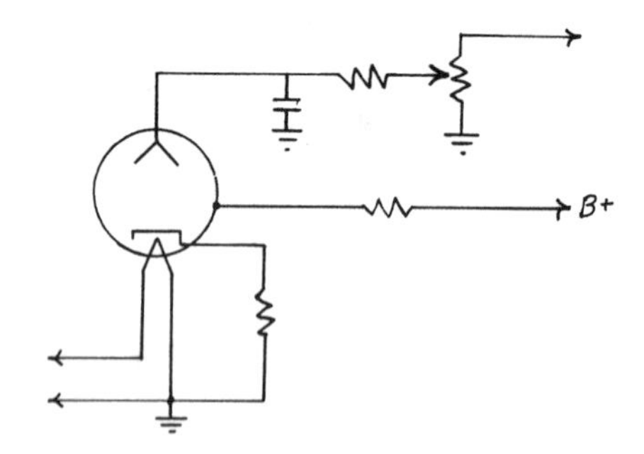

48. This schematic diagram is:
    a. detector
    b. discriminator
    c. TR box
    d. local oscillator
    e. radar modulator

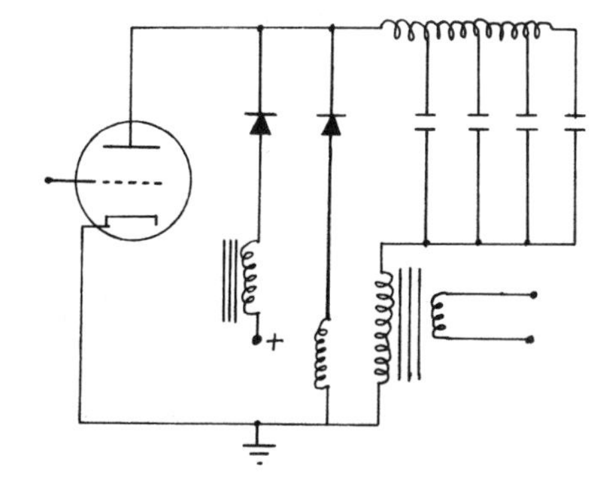

49. In this diagram, what is the approximate distance of "X"?
    a. 8 cm
    b. 1/2 inch
    c. 1/4 wavelength
    d. 1/2 wavelength
    e. 1 wavelength

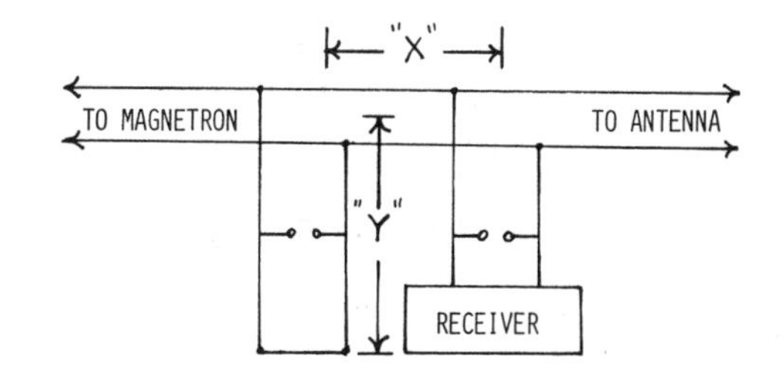


50. This schematic diagram is:
    a. RF attenuator
    b. detector
    c. Klystron oscillator
    d. Magnetron oscillator
    e. Blocking oscillator

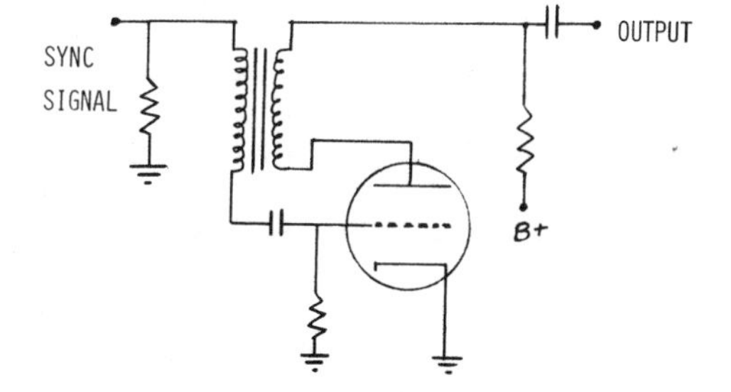

# Self-Study Ability Test
# Answers

| | | | | |
|---|---|---|---|---|
| 1. 393.51 | 12. 4,000 | 22. A | 33. E | 44. E |
| 2. 3/4 | 13. 0.64 | 23. E | 34. D | 45. D |
| 3. 298.72 | 14. 18 | 24. E | 35. E | 46. B |
| 4. 1/4 | 15. 1 | 25. A | 36. B | 47. E |
| 5. 13,396 | 16. 20 | 26. C | 37. C | 48. A |
| 6. 6.048 | 17. 0.707 | 27. A | 38. D | 49. E |
| 7. 2 | 18. $I = \sqrt{\frac{P}{R}}$ | 28. D | 39. B | 50. E |
| 8. 4/25 | | 29. B | 40. B | |
| 9. 7.22 | 19. 141.4 | 30. A | 41. C | |
| 10. 0.0392 | 20. 144 | 31. B | 42. C | |
| 11. 1/2 | 21. B | 32. D | 43. A | |

45 to 50 correct — EXCELLENT electronic background, well adapted for self-study. Your forecasted study time should be from 75 to 100 hours.

35 to 45 correct — ABOVE AVERAGE electronic background. With aid from good reference books, and the tests in this book, your forecasted study time: 100 to 300 hours.

25 to 35 correct — AVERAGE score for a person with limited electronic background. Consider the advantages of a resident school, unless you have great drive and determination. Forecasted study time: 300 to 600 hours.

BELOW 25 correct — BELOW AVERAGE score. The advantages of going to a resident school out number the ones for self-study. FCC study on your own would be a long and difficult battle. Forecasted study time +600!

# Test Answers

## TEST 3-A

| | | | | |
|---|---|---|---|---|
| 1. B | 21. E | 41. C | 61. D | 81. E |
| 2. D | 22. A | 42. D | 62. C | 82. E |
| 3. A | 23. B | 43. E | 63. C | 83. D |
| 4. C | 24. C | 44. C | 64. D | 84. B |
| 5. E | 25. D | 45. C | 65. E | 85. D |
| 6. D | 26. E | 46. E | 66. A | 86. D |
| 7. D | 27. B | 47. A | 67. C | 87. B |
| 8. A | 28. A | 48. A | 68. E | 88. C |
| 9. D | 29. D | 49. B | 69. B | 89. E |
| 10. A | 30. B | 50. A | 70. E | 90. B |
| 11. D | 31. C | 51. C | 71. A | 91. C |
| 12. D | 32. B | 52. A | 72. E | 92. A |
| 13. D | 33. E | 53. D | 73. C | 93. E |
| 14. B | 34. D | 54. B | 74. E | 94. C |
| 15. E | 35. A | 55. E | 75. B | 95. A |
| 16. A | 36. B | 56. B | 76. C | 96. A |
| 17. D | 37. A | 57. A | 77. B | 97. E |
| 18. E | 38. E | 58. E | 78. B | 98. C |
| 19. E | 39. B | 59. D | 79. E | 99. A |
| 20. A | 40. D | 60. E | 80. E | 100. B |

## TEST 3-B

| | | | | |
|---|---|---|---|---|
| 1. D | 21. B | 41. D | 61. C | 81. D |
| 2. D | 22. B | 42. C | 62. A | 82. C |
| 3. C | 23. C | 43. E | 63. A | 83. E |
| 4. B | 24. A | 44. E | 64. E | 84. D |
| 5. B | 25. E | 45. C | 65. B | 85. D |
| 6. E | 26. D | 46. B | 66. B | 86. A |
| 7. B | 27. D | 47. C | 67. E | 87. C |
| 8. C | 28. D | 48. D | 68. A | 88. A |
| 9. C | 29. B | 49. C | 69. D | 89. E |
| 10. A | 30. E | 50. D | 70. C | 90. A |
| 11. B | 31. C | 51. E | 71. C | 91. D |
| 12. D | 32. C | 52. C | 72. D | 92. E |
| 13. C | 33. D | 53. C | 73. A | 93. C |
| 14. B | 34. B | 54. E | 74. C | 94. A |
| 15. C | 35. C | 55. E | 75. C | 95. C |
| 16. A | 36. C | 56. D | 76. E | 96. C |
| 17. C | 37. C | 57. A | 77. D | 97. E |
| 18. A | 38. A | 58. D | 78. A | 98. A |
| 19. E | 39. A | 59. C | 79. D | 99. B |
| 20. C | 40. A | 60. A | 80. B | 100. B |

## TEST 3-C

| | | | | |
|---|---|---|---|---|
| 1. B | 21. A | 41. C | 61. D | 81. A |
| 2. D | 22. D | 42. E | 62. D | 82. B |
| 3. B | 23. D | 43. C | 63. B | 83. C |
| 4. B | 24. D | 44. D | 64. C | 84. C |
| 5. E | 25. E | 45. B | 65. C | 85. A |
| 6. B | 26. D | 46. B | 66. C | 86. C |
| 7. C | 27. A | 47. C | 67. B | 87. C |
| 8. C | 28. A | 48. B | 68. A | 88. B |
| 9. A | 29. C | 49. D | 69. B | 89. D |
| 10. C | 30. D | 50. E | 70. E | 90. A |
| 11. E | 31. B | 51. C | 71. E | 91. E |
| 12. D | 32. D | 52. A | 72. B | 92. C |
| 13. A | 33. A | 53. C | 73. B | 93. E |
| 14. C | 34. B | 54. A | 74. C | 94. A |
| 15. C | 35. A | 55. E | 75. C | 95. A |
| 16. D | 36. D | 56. C | 76. E | 96. B |
| 17. A | 37. B | 57. D | 77. D | 97. C |
| 18. C | 38. C | 58. A | 78. B | 98. A |
| 19. E | 39. B | 59. D | 79. C | 99. D |
| 20. B | 40. A | 60. A | 80. C | 100. B |

## TEST 3-D

| | | | | |
|---|---|---|---|---|
| 1. E | 21. D | 41. D | 61. D | 81. A |
| 2. B | 22. A | 42. C | 62. E | 82. B |
| 3. C | 23. B | 43. A | 63. C | 83. E |
| 4. A | 24. B | 44. D | 64. D | 84. D |
| 5. C | 25. B | 45. B | 65. B | 85. C |
| 6. C | 26. D | 46. C | 66. B | 86. C |
| 7. E | 27. E | 47. A | 67. C | 87. A |
| 8. D | 28. D | 48. E | 68. B | 88. B |
| 9. E | 29. B | 49. E | 69. D | 89. A |
| 10. C | 30. B | 50. E | 70. C | 90. B |
| 11. C | 31. E | 51. A | 71. A | 91. E |
| 12. A | 32. D | 52. D | 72. E | 92. D |
| 13. A | 33. C | 53. E | 73. C | 93. D |
| 14. B | 34. C | 54. D | 74. B | 94. B |
| 15. C | 35. C | 55. B | 75. E | 95. A |
| 16. A | 36. D | 56. B | 76. C | 96. E |
| 17. B | 37. C | 57. C | 77. C | 97. B |
| 18. E | 38. A | 58. C | 78. D | 98. D |
| 19. B | 39. E | 59. C | 79. B | 99. A |
| 20. C | 40. B | 60. C | 80. B | 100. C |

## TEST 3-E

| No. | Ans. | No. | Ans. | No. | Ans. | No. | Ans. | No. | Ans. |
|---|---|---|---|---|---|---|---|---|---|
| 1. | E | 21. | C | 41. | A | 61. | B | 81. | D |
| 2. | B | 22. | A | 42. | A | 62. | A | 82. | B |
| 3. | C | 23. | D | 43. | E | 63. | B | 83. | D |
| 4. | D | 24. | B | 44. | E | 64. | E | 84. | D |
| 5. | C | 25. | C | 45. | A | 65. | B | 85. | E |
| 6. | A | 26. | E | 46. | D | 66. | A | 86. | A |
| 7. | A | 27. | A | 47. | B | 67. | D | 87. | C |
| 8. | A | 28. | C | 48. | C | 68. | A | 88. | C |
| 9. | B | 29. | C | 49. | E | 69. | C | 89. | A |
| 10. | A | 30. | A | 50. | C | 70. | A | 90. | D |
| 11. | C | 31. | E | 51. | E | 71. | C | 91. | A |
| 12. | C | 32. | A | 52. | B | 72. | E | 92. | E |
| 13. | E | 33. | E | 53. | D | 73. | C | 93. | A |
| 14. | E | 34. | E | 54. | B | 74. | E | 94. | C |
| 15. | D | 35. | B | 55. | D | 75. | D | 95. | B |
| 16. | E | 36. | A | 56. | A | 76. | C | 96. | C |
| 17. | C | 37. | D | 57. | B | 77. | A | 97. | D |
| 18. | D | 38. | E | 58. | D | 78. | A | 98. | A |
| 19. | C | 39. | C | 59. | C | 79. | B | 99. | E |
| 20. | E | 40. | D | 60. | E | 80. | C | 100. | E |

## TEST 3-F

| No. | Ans. | No. | Ans. | No. | Ans. | No. | Ans. | No. | Ans. |
|---|---|---|---|---|---|---|---|---|---|
| 1. | A | 21. | C | 41. | C | 61. | D | 81. | E |
| 2. | E | 22. | A | 42. | C | 62. | A | 82. | E |
| 3. | A | 23. | D | 43. | E | 63. | A | 83. | A |
| 4. | C | 24. | C | 44. | A | 64. | D | 84. | B |
| 5. | B | 25. | D | 45. | C | 65. | B | 85. | D |
| 6. | C | 26. | A | 46. | D | 66. | E | 86. | B |
| 7. | A | 27. | D | 47. | E | 67. | C | 87. | C |
| 8. | D | 28. | A | 48. | C | 68. | D | 88. | D |
| 9. | C | 29. | B | 49. | A | 69. | D | 89. | B |
| 10. | D | 30. | B | 50. | B | 70. | B | 90. | B |
| 11. | B | 31. | A | 51. | E | 71. | B | 91. | A |
| 12. | D | 32. | E | 52. | D | 72. | D | 92. | D |
| 13. | E | 33. | E | 53. | C | 73. | C | 93. | B |
| 14. | E | 34. | D | 54. | D | 74. | C | 94. | E |
| 15. | E | 35. | C | 55. | A | 75. | B | 95. | E |
| 16. | B | 36. | A | 56. | A | 76. | B | 96. | C |
| 17. | C | 37. | A | 57. | C | 77. | C | 97. | E |
| 18. | C | 38. | C | 58. | C | 78. | A | 98. | A |
| 19. | C | 39. | D | 59. | B | 79. | D | 99. | E |
| 20. | D | 40. | A | 60. | A | 80. | C | 100. | E |

## TEST 3-G

| 1. D | 21. A | 41. C | 61. C | 81. B |
|---|---|---|---|---|
| 2. E | 22. A | 42. D | 62. A | 82. C |
| 3. E | 23. B | 43. D | 63. A | 83. A |
| 4. E | 24. C | 44. E | 64. C | 84. A |
| 5. A | 25. D | 45. D | 65. A | 85. A |
| 6. B | 26. C | 46. D | 66. E | 86. B |
| 7. A | 27. D | 47. D | 67. D | 87. D |
| 8. E | 28. B | 48. D | 68. C | 88. C |
| 9. B | 29. A | 49. E | 69. A | 89. B |
| 10. E | 30. D | 50. A | 70. B | 90. C |
| 11. B | 31. D | 51. E | 71. E | 91. E |
| 12. D | 32. B | 52. D | 72. C | 92. C |
| 13. A | 33. C | 53. D | 73. C | 93. E |
| 14. A | 34. D | 54. A | 74. C | 94. D |
| 15. C | 35. B | 55. D | 75. A | 95. A |
| 16. E | 36. C | 56. A | 76. E | 96. C |
| 17. E | 37. C | 57. A | 77. B | 97. D |
| 18. E | 38. C | 58. A | 78. A | 98. A |
| 19. E | 39. D | 59. C | 79. D | 99. E |
| 20. E | 40. E | 60. A | 80. D | 100. E |

## TEST 3-H

| 1. B | 21. C | 41. C | 61. A | 81. E |
|---|---|---|---|---|
| 2. B | 22. E | 42. A | 62. E | 82. C |
| 3. C | 23. E | 43. C | 63. A | 83. A |
| 4. D | 24. D | 44. A | 64. D | 84. A |
| 5. D | 25. B | 45. C | 65. B | 85. C |
| 6. E | 26. A | 46. D | 66. D | 86. E |
| 7. E | 27. B | 47. E | 67. E | 87. B |
| 8. B | 28. B | 48. E | 68. C | 88. C |
| 9. E | 29. C | 49. A | 69. A | 89. A |
| 10. D | 30. C | 50. D | 70. D | 90. C |
| 11. D | 31. D | 51. D | 71. B | 91. D |
| 12. D | 32. C | 52. C | 72. A | 92. D |
| 13. A | 33. C | 53. C | 73. D | 93. A |
| 14. C | 34. B | 54. E | 74. D | 94. B |
| 15. A | 35. D | 55. C | 75. B | 95. C |
| 16. E | 36. D | 56. B | 76. C | 96. D |
| 17. D | 37. B | 57. C | 77. B | 97. B |
| 18. E | 38. A | 58. E | 78. E | 98. C |
| 19. B | 39. C | 59. A | 79. A | 99. A |
| 20. A | 40. E | 60. B | 80. B | 100. B |

## TEST 3-I

| | | | | |
|---|---|---|---|---|
| 1. E | 21. A | 41. C | 61. B | 81. B |
| 2. C | 22. A | 42. B | 62. D | 82. D |
| 3. B | 23. C | 43. A | 63. A | 83. D |
| 4. C | 24. B | 44. C | 64. D | 84. C |
| 5. D | 25. B | 45. C | 65. A | 85. C |
| 6. B | 26. C | 46. B | 66. D | 86. B |
| 7. A | 27. D | 47. A | 67. C | 87. B |
| 8. D | 28. E | 48. B | 68. D | 88. E |
| 9. E | 29. B | 49. B | 69. A | 89. A |
| 10. A | 30. A | 50. E | 70. A | 90. B |
| 11. A | 31. B | 51. E | 71. A | 91. E |
| 12. B | 32. D | 52. D | 72. E | 92. A |
| 13. A | 33. B | 53. B | 73. C | 93. A |
| 14. B | 34. C | 54. E | 74. A | 94. E |
| 15. E | 35. A | 55. B | 75. E | 95. B |
| 16. B | 36. C | 56. E | 76. C | 96. A |
| 17. D | 37. B | 57. B | 77. E | 97. E |
| 18. C | 38. A | 58. D | 78. C | 98. D |
| 19. A | 39. E | 59. E | 79. E | 99. E |
| 20. A | 40. C | 60. B | 80. B | 100. D |

## TEST 3-J

| | | | | |
|---|---|---|---|---|
| 1. C | 21. E | 41. E | 61. E | 81. E |
| 2. B | 22. C | 42. E | 62. C | 82. E |
| 3. C | 23. B | 43. A | 63. A | 83. B |
| 4. A | 24. B | 44. D | 64. C | 84. C |
| 5. B | 25. E | 45. C | 65. D | 85. E |
| 6. E | 26. A | 46. B | 66. B | 86. C |
| 7. B | 27. D | 47. A | 67. E | 87. A |
| 8. A | 28. C | 48. D | 68. A | 88. A |
| 9. C | 29. E | 49. A | 69. B | 89. C |
| 10. A | 30. C | 50. C | 70. B | 90. A |
| 11. D | 31. B | 51. D | 71. B | 91. E |
| 12. D | 32. C | 52. C | 72. A | 92. D |
| 13. A | 33. E | 53. E | 73. C | 93. E |
| 14. D | 34. C | 54. D | 74. D | 94. E |
| 15. B | 35. A | 55. C | 75. C | 95. E |
| 16. C | 36. C | 56. A | 76. A | 96. D |
| 17. E | 37. C | 57. B | 77. D | 97. A |
| 18. A | 38. A | 58. C | 78. E | 98. A |
| 19. D | 39. C | 59. E | 79. B | 99. B |
| 20. E | 40. D | 60. B | 80. C | 100. E |

TEST 3-K

| | | | | | |
|---|---|---|---|---|---|
| 1. | D | 21. | C | 41. | B |
| 2. | E | 22. | E | 42. | B |
| 3. | D | 23. | E | 43. | C |
| 4. | A | 24. | E | 44. | C |
| 5. | B | 25. | C | 45. | B |
| 6. | E | 26. | A | 46. | A |
| 7. | B | 27. | C | 47. | E |
| 8. | B | 28. | C | 48. | A |
| 9. | C | 29. | B | 49. | D |
| 10. | B | 30. | C | 50. | D |
| 11. | B | 31. | C | 51. | B |
| 12. | C | 32. | A | 52. | D |
| 13. | C | 33. | E | 53. | A |
| 14. | B | 34. | B | 54. | B |
| 15. | D | 35. | B | 55. | B |
| 16. | C | 36. | B | 56. | C |
| 17. | E | 37. | C | 57. | D |
| 18. | D | 38. | A | 58. | A |
| 19. | A | 39. | E | 59. | B |
| 20. | E | 40. | D | 60. | A |

## TEST 8-A

| | | | | |
|---|---|---|---|---|
| 1. A | 11. A | 21. D | 31. B | 41. C |
| 2. D | 12. D | 22. E | 32. E | 42. C |
| 3. B | 13. E | 23. D | 33. E | 43. D |
| 4. B | 14. C | 24. B | 34. B | 44. D |
| 5. B | 15. E | 25. C | 35. B | 45. C |
| 6. C | 16. A | 26. D | 36. D | 46. E |
| 7. A | 17. A | 27. C | 37. A | 47. D |
| 8. C | 18. E | 28. C | 38. B | 48. A |
| 9. D | 19. C | 29. E | 39. B | 49. C |
| 10. B | 20. C | 30. E | 40. E | 50. C |

## TEST 8-B

| | | | | |
|---|---|---|---|---|
| 1. D | 11. E | 21. B | 31. D | 41. E |
| 2. A | 12. D | 22. B | 32. E | 42. D |
| 3. B | 13. C | 23. A | 33. B | 43. C |
| 4. C | 14. C | 24. D | 34. E | 44. B |
| 5. C | 15. A | 25. A | 35. C | 45. B |
| 6. B | 16. B | 26. E | 36. E | 46. A |
| 7. A | 17. B | 27. D | 37. B | 47. D |
| 8. A | 18. E | 28. E | 38. C | 48. E |
| 9. B | 19. E | 29. E | 39. C | 49. C |
| 10. C | 20. D | 30. E | 40. E | 50. E |

# APPENDIX

# FCC Field Offices

ALASKA, Anchorage Office
Federal Communications Commission
6721 West Raspberry Road
Anchorage, Alaska 99502
Phone: (907) 243-2153

*ARIZONA, Douglas Office
Federal Communications Commission
P. O. Box 6
Douglas, Arizona 85608
Phone: (602) 364-8414

CALIFORNIA, San Diego Office
Federal Communications Commission
4542 Ruffner Street
Room 370
San Diego, California 92111-2216
Phone: (619) 557-5478

*CALIFORNIA, Livermore Office
Federal Communications Commission
P. O. Box 311
Livermore, California 94551-0311
Phone: (415) 447-3614

CALIFORNIA, Los Angeles Office
Federal Communications Commission
Cerritos Corporate Tower
18000 Studebaker Road, Room 660
Cerritos, California 90701
Phone: (213) 809-2096

CALIFORNIA, San Francisco Office
Federal Communications Commission
424 Customhouse
555 Battery Street
San Francisco, California 94111
Phone: (415) 705-1101

COLORADO, Denver Office
Federal Communications Commission
165 South Union Blvd., Suite 860
Lakewood, Colorado 80228
Phone: (303) 969-6497

*FLORIDA, Vero Beach Office
Federal Communications Commission
P. O. Box 1730
Vero Beach, Florida 32961-1730
Phone: (407) 778-3755

FLORIDA, Miami Office
Federal Communications Commission
Rochester Building, Room 310
8390 N.W. 53rd Street
Miami, Florida 33166
Phone: (305) 526-7420

FLORIDA, Tampa Office
Federal Communications Commission
Room 1215
2203 N. Lois Avenue
Tampa, Florida 33607-2356
Phone: (813) 228-2872

GEORGIA, Atlanta Office
Federal Communications Comission
Massell Building, Room 440
1365 Peachtree Street, N.E.
Atlanta, Georgia 30309
Phone: (404) 347-2631

HAWAII, Honolulu Office
Federal Communications Commission
P.O. Box 1030
Waipahu, Hawaii 96797
Phone: (808) 677-3318

ILLINOIS, Chicago Office
Federal Communications Commission
Park Ridge Office Center, Rm 306
1550 Northwest Highway
Park Ridge, Illinois 60068
Phone: (312) 353-0195

LOUISIANA, New Orleans Office
Federal Communications Commission
800 West Commerce Rd., Room 505
New Orleans, Louisiana 70123
Phone: (504) 589-2095

*MAINE, Belfast Office
Federal Communications Commission
P. O. Box 470
Belfast, Maine 04915
Phone: (207) 338-4088

MARYLAND, Baltimore Office
Federal Communications Commission
1017 Federal Building
31 Hopkins Plaza
Baltimore, Maryland 21201
Phone: (301) 962-2729

*MARYLAND, Laurel Office
Federal Communications Commission
P. O. Box 250
Columbia, Maryland 21045
Phone: (301) 725-3474

MASSACHUSETTS, Boston Office
Federal Communications Commission
NFPA Building
1 Batterymarch Park
Quincy, Massachusetts 02169
Phone: (617) 770-4023

*MICHIGAN, Allegan Office
Federal Communications Commission
P. O. Box 89
Allegan, Michigan 49010
Phone: (616) 673-2063

MICHIGAN, Detroit Office
Federal Communications Commission
24897 Hathaway Street
Farmington Hills, Michigan 48335-1552
Phone: (313) 226-6078

MINNESOTA, St. Paul Office
Federal Communications Commission
693 Federal Bldg. & U.S. Courthouse
316 North Robert Street
St. Paul, Minnesota 55101
Phone: (612) 290-3819

MISSOURI, Kansas City Office
Federal Communications Commission
Brywood Office Tower, Room 320
8800 East 63rd Street
Kansas City, Missouri 64133
Phone: (816) 926-5111

*Licenses not available at * locations.

NEW YORK, Buffalo Office
Federal Communications Commission
1307 Federal Building
111 W. Huron Street
Buffalo, New York 14202
Phone: (716) 846-4511

NEW YORK, New York Office
Federal Communications Commission
201 Varick Street
New York, New York 10014-4870
Phone: (212) 620-3437

OREGON, Portland Office
Federal Communications Commission
1782 Federal Office Building
1220 S. W. 3rd Avenue
Portland, Oregon 97204
Phone: (503) 326-4114

PENNSYLVANIA, Philadelphia Office
Federal Communications Commission
One Oxford Valley Office Bldg.
2300 East Lincoln Highway
Room 404
Langhorne, Pennsylvania 19047
Phone: (215) 752-1324

PUERTO RICO, San Juan Office
Federal Communications Commission
747 Federal Building
Hato Rey, Puerto Rico 00918-2251
Phone: (809) 766-5567

TEXAS, Dallas Office
Federal Communications Commission
9330 LBJ Expressway, Room 1170
Dallas, Texas 75243
Phone: (214) 767-4827

TEXAS, Houston Office
Federal Communications Commission
1225 North Loop West, Room 900
Houston, Texas 77008
Phone: (713) 229-2748

*TEXAS, Kingsville Office
Federal Communications Commission
P. O. Box 632
Kingsville, Texas 78363-0632
Phone: (512) 592-2531

VIRGINIA, Norfolk Office
Federal Communications Commission
1200 Communications Circle
Virginia Beach, Virginia 23455-3725
Phone: (804) 441-6472

*WASHINGTON, Ferndale Office
Federal Communications Commission
1330 Loomis Trail Rd.
Custer, Washington 98240
Phone: (206) 354-4892

WASHINGTON, Seattle Office
Federal Communications Commission
One Newport, Room 414
3605 132nd Avenue, S.E.
Bellevue, Washington 98006
Phone: (206) 764-3324

# FCC Form #756

The following page contains an example of FCC Operator License application form #756. Thus form is used to apply for General Radiotelephone Operator License. To obtain a full size form - along with the special application form #155 you should write to:

FEDERAL COMMUNICATIONS COMMISSION
P. O. Box 358105
Pittsburgh, PA. 15251-5105

Most people have discovered that contacting their local FCC Field Office only causes delays in obtaining the desired forms #756 and new #155. So, when in doubt write to the address above - or telephone (202) 632-3337 for information on filling out the forms.

## APPLICATION FOR COMMERCIAL RADIO OPERATOR LICENSE

(Other than Restricted Radiotelephone Operator Permit)

RADIOTELEPHONE APPLICANTS — INSTRUCTIONS

- Answer all items completely. Type or print legibly all information and sign your name.
- Attach to this application any license listed in Item 9. If it is not attached, explain why.
- Mail this application as follows:

New license - Your nearest FCC Field Office.

Renewed, duplicate or replacement General Radiotelephone License - the FCC Field Office which issued the original license.

Renewed, duplicate or replacement Marine Radio Operator Permit - the Washington DC address shown below for radiotelegraph applicants.

The addresses of the field offices are listed on the back of this form. Do not mail radiotelephone applications (other than for renewed Marine Radio Operator Permits) to the Washington DC office.

| **APPLICATION FOR COMMERCIAL RADIO OPERATOR LICENSE** | 4. Legal Name | First | | Middle | Last |
|---|---|---|---|---|---|
| | 5. Mailing Address | Number and Street | | | |
| | | City | County | State | ZIP Code |

6.

| Sex | Height | | Weight | Color Eyes | Color Hair | Date of Birth (In numerals) | | |
|---|---|---|---|---|---|---|---|---|
| ☐ Male ☐ Female | Feet | Inches | | | | Month | Day | Year |

Check "YES" or "NO" to the following questions and provide the information requested. Yes No

7. Are you legally eligible for employment in the United States? .............................. ☐ ☐
(All U.S. citizens are considered, for the purpose of this application, to be legally eligible for employment in the U.S.)
8. Do you have a speech impediment, blindness, acute deafness or any other disability which will impair or handicap you in properly using the license you are applying for?
If "YES" attach details .................................................................... ☐ ☐
9. Have you held an FCC commercial radio operator license during the past 12 months?
If "YES" list the license held below .......................................................... ☐ ☐

| Class | Endorsement | Serial No., if any | Date Issued | Place Issued |
|---|---|---|---|---|
| | | | | |

10. Within the past two months have you taken an examination for a commercial operator license or endorsement?
If "YES" provide the following ........................................................ ☐ ☐

| Place of Exam | Date of Exam | Exam Element(s) Taken |
|---|---|---|
| | | |

11. I hereby apply for: (Check appropriate boxes.)

| | | |
|---|---|---|
| ☐ New | ☐ General Radiotelephone Operator License | ☐ Ship Radar Endorsement |
| ☐ Renewal | ☐ Marine Radio Operator Permit | ☐ Six Month Radiotelegraph Endorsement |
| ☐ Duplicate/ Replacement | ☐ Radiotelegraph 1st Class | |
| | ☐ Radiotelegraph 2nd Class | |
| | ☐ Radiotelegraph 3rd Class | |

12. If any examination is necessary, where do you wish to take it? (See examination schedule)
City and State for examination ____________________

I CERTIFY that I am the above-named applicant and that all statements made on this application and any attachment hereto are true and complete to the best of my knowledge.

Please sign here ➡ Signature of Applicant | Date Signed

A WILLFULLY FALSE STATEMENT IS A CRIMINAL OFFENSE. U.S. CODE, TITLE 18, SECTION 1001

# References

THE COMPLETE FCC HOME-STUDY COURSE
By Warren Weagant
Command Producstions, Custom House POB 2223, San Francisco, CA 94126

A complete set of training manual and cassette tape recordings and lessons for FCC General Radiotelephone Operator License. This self-study course provides beginners with fundamental concepts and comprehensive preperation for passing the federal government examination.

The 40 lesson course includes:

- Matter and Energy
- Magnetism
- Direct Current
- Alternating Current
- Inductance
- Capacitance
- Impedance
- Transformers
- Number Systems
- Test Equipment
- Circuit Problem Solving
- Solid State Theory
- PN Junction Transistors
- Power Supplies
- Transistor Theory
- Electron Tubes
- Voltage Regulators
- Communications Theory
- Tuned Circuits
- Receivers
- Detectors
- Audio Amplifiers
- RF Amplifiers
- Oscillators
- Mixers and Converters
- IF Amplifiers
- Control Circuits
- Receiver Alignment
- Transmitters
- Amplitude Modulation
- Frequency Modulation
- Troubleshooting
- Single-Sideband
- CW and FM Reception
- Transmission Lines
- Wave Propagation
- Antennas
- UHF Communications

Many students have discovered that both reading training manuals and listening to special cassette recorded material makes learning faster, easier and more permanent.

Cassette tapes permit you to hear and absorb FCC materials at anytime and at any place you choose. Listen in office, home or car to turn unproductive time into FCC license training sessions!

There is no substitute for the effective impact of this unique self-study training course. Each lesson is carefully prepared and edited to provide maximum focus on FCC exam answers.

You will find step-by-step solutions and answers for FCC math problems too. Created specifically for those people who need a better understanding of vital basics - and builds question by question in such a way that all solutions are understood - even by students with little or no electronics background.

Brochure and details about this course available directly from Command Productions. Our "Inforamtion Request Form" is the last page in the manual.

# Reader Comments and Feedback

Your comments are always appreciated and help us to continue to publish the most up to date and relevant study materials.

Please let us know how this testing manual works for you. The response you send to us will help form the content of future editions of this study guide.

1. Where:_______________ and when:__________ did you take the FCC examination. Your score:______________.

2. Did you find any material on the FCC exam that you were not prepared for? If so, what questions did you find difficult to answer? (if not enough room below, attach additional paper)

_______________________________________________

_______________________________________________

_______________________________________________

_______________________________________________

_______________________________________________

_______________________________________________

_______________________________________________

3. Do you have any suggestions for making these study materials easier for others to learn FCC material?

_______________________________________________

_______________________________________________

Your name:_______________________________________

Address:_________________________________________

City/State/Zip:____________________________________

MAIL TO: Warren Weagant, Command Productions, Custom House 2223, San Francisco, CA. 94126

# Free Information Request Form

Mail to:

COMMAND PRODUCTIONS
Radio Engineering Division
Custom House POB 2223
San Francisco, CA 94126

Please rush me free ordering information for the FCC license course materials checked below:

( ) "The Complete FCC License Home-Study Course"

( ) "Tests-Answers for FCC General Radiotelephone Operator License" (this training manual)

Please send information to:

NAME:________________________________________

________________________________________

ADDRESS:______________________________________

CITY:____________________ STATE:________ ZIP:__________

Check here ( ) if you also want information and quantity prices for schools and other educational institutions.

Check here ( ) if you would like us to send brochures about this FCC testing manual to your friends or associates. Please attach their names and addresses - or simply write on the reverse side of this form. Thank you.